Religion and Education Under the Constitution

A Da Capo Press Reprint Series

CIVIL LIBERTIES IN AMERICAN HISTORY

GENERAL EDITOR: LEONARD W. LEVY

Claremont Graduate School

Religion and Education Under the Constitution

By J. M. O'NEILL

DA CAPO PRESS • NEW YORK • 1972

Library of Congress Cataloging in Publication Data

O'Neill, James Milton, 1881-
   Religion and education under the Constitution.
   (Civil liberties in American history)
   Bibliography: p.
   1. Religious education—U.S. 2. Religion in the
public schools. I. Title.
   ɪLC405.05 1972ɪ   377'.0973   72-171389
   ISBN 0-306-70228-2

This Da Capo Press edition of *Religion and Education Under the
Constitution* is an unabridged republication of the first
edition published in New York in 1949. It is reprinted by
special arrangement with Harper & Row, Publishers, Inc.

Published by Da Capo Press, Inc.
A Subsidiary of Plenum Publishing Corporation
227 West 17th Street, New York, N.Y. 10011

Religion and Education
Under the Constitution

Religion and Education Under the Constitution

By J. M. O'NEILL
Chairman, Department of Speech
Brooklyn College

> "Congress shall make no law
> respecting an establishment
> of religion, or prohibiting
> the free exercise thereof."
> *The First Amendment*
> *to the Constitution*

HARPER & BROTHERS
NEW YORK

RELIGION AND EDUCATION UNDER THE CONSTITUTION
Copyright, 1949, by Harper & Brothers
Printed in the United States of America

FIRST EDITION

B-Y

Contents

Preface

*I*N OUR American democracy, all citizens who both understand and believe in the great founding documents of our history have to grant to all groups and varieties of their fellow citizens the political equality of the Declaration of Independence and the personal freedoms of the Bill of Rights. But too many otherwise intelligent and well informed men and women seem not to understand the great complexity of American society and the validity of the rights of all kinds of Americans to equality and freedom. We have over 250 Christian denominations, scores of Jewish and other non-Christian religious bodies, and representatives of all the races and racial splinters of the human family. They are Americans all. Regardless of race, creed, or color, they are all heirs and proprietors of the Declaration and the Constitution.

Most of us can read. We can read the words of the great documents that were exhibited on the Freedom Train, and spell out in them the legacy to all Americans, of every group, of every race, of every faith. But can we bring these words to life? Can we make equality and freedom real? Dare we read the will and give to every American the inheritance left him by the Founding Fathers? This is the central problem of civil liberties in these United States. If we can solve it, we can be proud, and hopeful of an ultimately free world; if we cannot, how can anyone have faith in freedom surviving on this planet?

This book is offered in the hope that it will contribute to the solution of this problem. I am convinced that a widespread failure to understand, rather than an informed but evil purpose, is the greatest obstacle encountered in the field of civil liberties today. I hope that this volume will do something to end the false assumptions, slogans, myths, and distortions of historical fact, which now confuse much of the discussion of civil liberties, particularly in the realm of the first

ix

clause of the First Amendment. I believe that clarity here will promote clarity elsewhere.

The recent propaganda against the religious clause in the Bill of Rights, and its sweeping success in the Supreme Court, constitute in immediate effect, and in threat as precedent, a real danger to our whole doctrine of civil liberties. Unless the American people stop the current trend, exemplified in the Supreme Court decision in the McCollum case, and force a return to the doctrines of democratic decision and of the Constitution as written and ratified by the American people, we shall drift inevitably into a regimented society under the unrestrained dictatorship of the men on the Supreme bench. The seeds of all of this are thick in the current propaganda under the slogan "the complete separation of church and state" and have in fact started some lusty sprouts in the language of the Justices of the Supreme Court.

In this book, I am not arguing for federal aid, or other public aid, to parochial schools; I am not trying to justify Mr. Taylor's appointment to the Vatican; I am not defending religious education or "released time." The wisdom or unwisdom of any of these is irrelevant to the question of whether a state or federal law providing for them violates the Constitution of the United States. My position is that these are all debatable questions on which Americans differ with complete propriety; that they should be debated, cordially, factually, and decided by our democratic procedures; and that all Americans should abide peaceably, without rancor, by the constitutional provision and statutes which result from the working of the democratic process.

This book is aimed specifically at a better understanding of civil liberties and against the widespread practice of attempting to *foreclose debate* and to *stop the democratic process* by distorting the Constitutional provisions in the Bill of Rights. Particularly is this done in regard to the First Amendment, in attempts to make it mean something that it does not say, and which Madison and the other members of the First Congress in 1789 did not believe and did not intend to put into the Constitution.

I believe that the preservation (and extension in understanding and observance) of the civil liberties as expressed in the First Amendment

and in the similar constitutional provisions and laws of the several
states, is the necessary foundation of, the legal prerequisite to, the
preservation of all our other freedoms. I am convinced that the greatest obstacles to the promotion of civil liberties in the United States
are (1) the extreme difficulty which intelligent and idealistic people
(who think they are completely devoted to civil liberties) have in
supporting civil liberties *except when such support aids some substantive cause in which they believe,* and (2) the almost absolute
inability of such people even to see the civil liberties problem in any
situation in which the observance of civil liberties seems to them to
favor the proponents of a substantive cause to which they are opposed.
The ability and the desire to separate the *constitutional rights of all
Americans* under the civil liberty provisions of our constitution from
the *merits of the case involved in any given dispute must become*
much more general if we are to remain a free people.

To my mind the greatest threat to our civil liberties in recent
times is to be found in Justice Rutledge's argument in the minority
opinion in the Everson case and in the Supreme Court decision in the
McCollum case. The acclaim which the opinions in these cases have
received on the part of people who should know better is, or should
be, a major danger signal. I refer to people who must know the most
important facts relevant to the First Amendment, the records of
Jefferson and Madison, of Congress, the Presidents, the Supreme
Court, and the forty-eight states (even if Justices of the Supreme
Court seem not to know them).

In my opinion the question of how children get to parochial schools
—or any other kind of schools, in New Jersey or elsewhere—or whether
"released time" for religious education continues in Illinois or elsewhere, is of trifling importance compared to the question of whether
the Justices of the Supreme Court shall pass on constitutional questions in the light of the language and meaning of the Constitution
or in the light of their private philosophies of religion and education.

I have just closed twelve years as member, and four as chairman,
of the Committee on Academic Freedom of the American Civil Liberties Union. This book is a direct outgrowth of my experience on
that committee. As that experience accumulated through the years

I became increasingly aware of the tremendous misunderstanding and confusion throughout the whole field of civil liberties, particularly in regard to the purpose and effect of the Bill of Rights. This volume was well started before the Supreme Court handed down the decisions in the Everson and McCollum cases. On reading the Supreme Court opinions in these cases I was shocked to find the extent to which the misunderstanding and confusion in regard to the Bill of Rights pervades even the Supreme Bench of the United States.

Any similarities between passages in this book and parts of the Appellee's brief in the *McCollum* case are neither merely coincidental nor instances of plagiarism. The following is a quotation from an unsolicited letter from Mr. John L. Franklin of Champaign, Ill., and Mr. Owen Rall of Chicago, Ill., the authors of that brief. This letter was sent to me to use as I might wish.

As attorneys appearing in the Supreme Court of the United States in behalf of the Champaign, Ill., Board of Education, and of the parents who intervened in support of religious education, in the McCollum case (333 U. S. 203), discussed in chapter 12 of Professor O'Neill's book, we publicly acknowledge our debt to the author of this volume.

Certain striking similarities between Professor O'Neill's work and our own printed arguments, in the Supreme Court, might be discovered by comparing the two. These striking similarities occurred because, by personal consultation with the author in the summer of 1947, by extended correspondence with him while we were preparing our argument, and by our examining a large section of his manuscript, we were enabled to draw freely upon the author's fertile ideas, careful historical research, and even his felicitous mode of expression. The author's generosity in these regards is unmatched in our experience.

In order to avoid any possible misapprehension, I wish to state explicitly that I am not here representing the Committee on Academic Freedom, the American Civil Liberties Union, nor any other organization or group with which I am in any way affiliated. The facts I present are the facts of history; the opinions and interpretations are mine alone.

J. M. O'NEILL

Lakeville, Connecticut, August, 1948

Religion and Education
Under the Constitution

Chapter 1

THE NATURE OF OUR PROBLEM

*J*N DISCUSSING the position of religion and education under the Constitution, I am not here concerned with any consideration of religion *per se*, or education *per se*, but only with education as education is related to religion, and only with religion in regard to its status under the United States Constitution. My subject is the constitutional restrictions concerning religion, religion in education, and education administered by religious organizations. This book is, therefore, in the first place a study of American history. The planning, writing, adoption, and ratification of the various parts of the federal Constitution are facts in American history.

If the phrases in the Constitution as facts in American history need to be interpreted from time to time, as they obviously do, they should be interpreted in the light of the facts of American history, and according to the proper canons of interpretation as a linguistic technique. It is obviously legitimate in this area, as in any other, to seek to find the proper meaning of an ambiguous phrase in the Constitution by determining what that phrase must have meant to the men who wrote it, adopted it, and ratified it. No one may properly deny that the relevant facts in American history can throw a legitimate light on the meaning of a passage in the Constitution or in any other historical document.

If one goes to the facts of American history for light on the meaning of any phrase in the Constitution, three conditions should be observed. *First,* the most meaningful and important facts of history connected with the phrase should be examined. *Second,* the facts of history which are cited in such an interpretation should be accurately cited. *Third*, the conditions surrounding the facts, the context of the times, should be examined for possible relevance, and if such relevance is discovered, all the conditions so relevant should be cited with the facts.

It makes no difference whether the examination of historical facts in the search for the accurate meaning of historical language is indulged in by professors of history, Justices of the Supreme Court, religious leaders, educational administrators, or interested laymen. All are equally under an obligation to know the history with which they deal and to cite it accurately. When a Justice of the Supreme Court undertakes scholarly investigation and scholarly writing, either argumentative or expository, he enjoys no immunity from the obligations of scholarship. How thoroughly certain Justices of our Supreme Court violated these obligations in the Everson case and the McCollum case is shown in detail in Chapters Sixteen and Seventeen.

The problem is, even more specifically than a problem in history, one in constitutional law. The facts of constitutional law that I shall deal with will be the facts about certain phrases in the Constitution, the language of the judicial decisions presumably interpreting those phrases, and passages relevant to the problems covered by those phrases from the recognized authorities in American constitutional law. For instance, the facts to be found in the official record of the First Congress, when the men of that Congress were discussing, perfecting, and adopting the Bill of Rights, constitute facts in American constitutional law. The reports of Congressional committees which deal with the First Amendment, and the disposition of those reports by Congress, are such facts. Clearly the decisions of the Supreme Court of the United States in cases which involved the First Amendment are facts of constitutional law. The debates regarding the Fourteenth Amendment, the circumstances surrounding its adoption, the history of the attitude of the Supreme Court toward it as shown in its decisions, are likewise all facts in the development of our constitutional law.

These may all be read by any person who is capable of reading the English language. The interpretations of them are of course limited by the knowledge and the semantic ability of the interpreter. As will be shown later in discussing some of the opinions of certain Supreme Court Justices my criticism is not that the Justices have interpreted historical facts or phrases in a way that seems to me unjustified from the standpoint of either semantics or history, but that these Justices of the Supreme Court apparently do not know the most important facts of our constitutional history which have a bearing on the questions they are deciding. The only other possibility is that they do know the facts but either callously ignore them, or willfully misrepresent them.

In the third place, the subject of this book is definitely a problem in civil liberties. Discussion of the meaning of civil liberties is to be found in Chapter Two. Here it is perhaps sufficient to say that the basic document in American civil liberties is the Bill of Rights adopted by the First Congress in 1789 and ratified as a part of the Constitution of the United States in 1791. Any discussion of the meaning and application of the First Amendment is inevitably and specifically a discussion in the field of civil liberties.

One does not have to go far in any investigation of civil liberties to realize that the whole field is confused by categorical slogans and historical myths. One of the most universal and, to my mind, currently the most harmful of these, is the use made of the current propaganda slogan "the complete separation of church and state." The substitution of the repetition of the slogan for rational discussion is the cause of most of today's confusion and conflict in regard to the relation of government to religion. The belief in this so-called great American principle is preventing understanding and cooperation where they are desperately needed today.

This spurious principle has recently been invoked by those opposing Mr. Taylor's appointment to the Vatican and by the opponents of "released time" in public schools for religious instruction, of school credit for such instruction, of public transportation for pupils of church schools, of Bible reading and prayers in the public schools, of N. Y. A. and G. I. Bill of Rights funds for students in church schools, of tax exemption of church property, and of federal aid to parochial schools.

Each and every one of these proposals is as debatable as, for instance, peacetime conscription. (None of them, however, is to be debated in this volume.) Each of them should be supported or opposed on its individual merits, the sole criterion being its value in terms of the public welfare. Above all, no one, by virtue of the side he is on in such a debate, should be held to be un-American, unconstitutional, or subversive of our traditions.

Today, appeals to this so-called principle are being used to deny opponents the opportunity of debate. Such appeals are attempts to gain debatable ends without the burdens and risks of debate. All opposition is sought to be ruled out by the assertion that it is opposition to the great constitutional American principle of complete separation of Church and State. There is no such great American principle and there never has been.

If there is such an American principle, it must have been formulated, adopted, or promulgated by some group or groups authorized to speak for America. The Supreme Court of the United States is not such a group. It has never been authorized to promulgate new doctrines or policies for the American people. The Court may interpret; they have no right to eliminate or amend any Constitutional provision ratified by the American people. Our Supreme Court is not yet in the position of the Russian Politburo.

If the American people have ever adopted the principle of complete separation of church and state, we should find the evidence of it in the federal Constitution, in the acts of Congress, or in the constitutions or laws of the several states. There is no such evidence in existence. In its absence, the mere opinion of private individuals or groups that *there should be absolute separation of church and state* (a condition that has not existed in recent centuries in any civilized nation on earth) does not create a "great American principle." To say that this principle is accepted by millions of Americans does not prove it to be an American principle to which all loyal Americans owe allegiance. The principles of Catholicism, Protestantism, and Judaism are all accepted by millions of Americans, but that does not make them *American* principles.

To me, American civil liberties constitute the most important part of American constitutional government. Our observance and enforce-

ment of civil liberties is the best index of the validity of our democracy. The protection and extension of civil liberties is the most
important function of government in peacetime. Ultimately, the defense of civil liberties is the best, if not the only, justification for war.

I am firmly of the opinion that civil liberties as expressed in our
constitutions, and in the laws passed in conformity to our constitutions, must be preserved inviolate, not only against the vagaries of
uninformed police officers, but also against the programs and pressures
of any group, religious or political, which would seek to subvert them
in order to promote its religious or political objectives. This must be
the principle of all who would preserve a free society in America,
and this principle must be applied entirely without regard to individual belief in the social desirability or philosophical validity of the
particular program involved.

Above all, we have a right to expect an informed and forthright
defense of our civil liberties as expressed in the Constitution by
Justices of the Supreme Court of the United States. As shown in
Chapters Eleven and Twelve we simply have not had this in the
Everson and McCollum cases. The recent and current attacks upon
the integrity of the First Amendment, almost all of which are carried
forward under the spurious slogan of "complete separation of church
and state," constitute the most serious threat to civil liberties in our
time in the United States. The Supreme Court in the McCollum
case in attempting to substitute this modern slogan for the language
of the Constitution has surrendered the First Amendment instead
of defending it.

Turning now to certain considerations of what our problem is not,
it seems appropriate to issue a number of warnings. In the first
place, the problem of the meaning of the First Amendment is not
a problem in religion.

The word "religion" in the title and text of this book means what
it meant to Jefferson and Madison and the writers and lawmakers
generally at the time of the writing of the Constitution and the Bill
of Rights. This is also obviously the most common and authentic
meaning in use at the present time. This meaning is essentially con-

RELIGION AND EDUCATION UNDER THE CONSTITUTION

stant, and has been throughout the whole period of American history in the writing of statesmen and theologians—Catholic, Protestant and Jewish.

Madison wrote in the *Memorial and Remonstrance* [1] of "Religion or the duty which we owe to our Creator and the Manner of discharging it."

Jefferson in his *Reply to the Danbury Baptists* [2] January 1, 1802, said:

Believing with you that religion is a matter which lies solely between man and his God, that he owes account to none other for his faith or his worship, that the legislative powers of government reach actions only, and not opinions . . .

In discussing *Freedom of Religion at the University of Virginia,* Oct. 7, 1822,[3] he wrote:

It was not, however, to be understood that instruction in religious opinion and duties was meant to be precluded by the public authorities, as indifferent to the interests of society. On the contrary, *the relations which exist between man and his Maker, and the duties resulting from these relations,* are the most interesting and most important to every human being, and the most incumbent on his study and investigation. (Italics mine.)

Jefferson clearly had the same concept of the meaning of religion when he wrote [4] "Religion is the alpha and omega of the moral law."

Webster's dictionary defines religion as

The service and adoration of God or a god as expressed in forms of worship, in obedience to divine commands, especially as found in accepted sacred writings or as declared by recognized teachers and in the pursuit of a way of life regarded as incumbent on true believers; as, ministers of religion.

Attwater's *A Catholic Dictionary (The Catholic Encyclopaedia Dictionary),*[5] quoting St. Thomas, defines religion

[1] See Appendix C, paragraph 2.
[2] Padover, Saul K. (Ed.), *The Complete Jefferson* (New York, Duell, Sloan & Pearce, 1943), p. 518. Appendix E.
[3] *Ibid.*, p. 957. Appendix D.
[4] Washington, H. A. (Ed), The Writings of Thomas Jefferson (New York, John C. Riker, 1857), Vol. I, p. 545.
[5] New York, The Macmillan Company, 1943, p. 449.

i. "Religion is a virtue by which men exhibit due worship and reverence to God . . ." *ii.* Also used as a system of beliefs and practices having reference to man's relation with God, e.g. the Catholic religion, the religion of Islam, the Bantu religion. . . .

Charles A. Beard [6] writes:

We are fortunate in having a definition of religion at law given to us by the Supreme Court of the United States. In passing upon a statute prohibiting polygamy [7] Justice Field speaking for the Court said, "The term religion has reference to one's views of his relation to his creator, and to the obligations they impose of reverence for his being and character, and of obedience to his will." In other words, he meant that religion has to do with views respecting the relations of the individual to a supreme and extramundane being.

The word "religion" may be used properly in different meanings in different contexts, provided the contexts make clear which meaning is intended in any given passage. However, the fact that a word may be used today by some people, sometimes, in a different sense from that in which Jefferson, Madison, the men of the first Congress, and others used it in a specific context in 1789, cannot possibly change the *purpose* which the men of 1789 expressed in the language which they used. Certainly it would be absurd to try to read into the First Amendment the meaning of "religion" as the word is used in the following modern passage:

The religion of the American majority is democracy. . . . Far from being "godless" the public schools are the principal instruments for the perpetuation of religious values among us. In fact the religion of public education is a more powerful factor in American life today than that of the churches. The only religion with which the great majority of American youth ever come into contact is the religion of public education where intolerance, bigotry, and race prejudice are not at home.[8]

The relations of our government to religion are necessarily whatever is expressed in our constitutions and laws dealing with these relations. In this country these have always been principally defined

[6] *The Republic* (New York, The Viking Press, 1943), p. 164.
[7] *Reynolds vs. United States*, 98 U. S. 145.
[8] Moehlman, C. H., *School and Church* (New York, Harper & Brothers, 1944), pp. ix-x.

by state constitutions and laws. Today, however, most of the argument about church and state concerns the national government and the United States Constitution.

Anyone who believes in our constitutional form of government, and especially in our system of civil liberties ought to be ready to defend the right of anyone to advocate any change in these constitutional and statutory provisions at any time. But, such provisions should be observed while they exist. Those who do not like them should try to change them through the democratic processes adopted by the American people for constitutional and statutory changes. If the Supreme Court is allowed to make the Constitution of the United States say whatever individual judges think it ought to say, instead of what it says, we have already lost our liberties. We are no longer living under the controllable provisions of constitutional government, but under the uncontrollable opinions of men.

If our current controversies are to be resolved in any orderly, peaceful, constitutional fashion, we must deal in proper order with three related questions:

1. What actually are the relations now expressed in our Constitution?

2. Should these relations be changed?

3. If so, how should we change them?

Obviously the first question has to be settled first. This book is an attempt to contribute to such a settlement. It is confusing and fruitless to discuss what changes should be made in the relations of church and state in America unless we know from what base we start. That base should be the First Amendment to the Constitution of the United States, particularly the first clause: "Congress shall make no law respecting an establishment of religion or prohibiting the free exercise thereof."

The First Amendment, as all other sections of the Constitution, applies to all religions equally. All individuals, groups, churches, and courts, loyal to the Constitution, loyal even to the idea of constitutional government, should support the First Amendment as it stands in the Constitution until such time as this amendment is altered *by the constitutional method* which has been written into the Constitution by the American people. If the members of any religious group find the First Amendment unsuited to their purposes, inconsistent with what they believe *should be* the Constitutional provisions for religion, they have a right to seek to have the Constitution changed. However, if they believe in democracy and constitutional government they will not seek to have it changed by the technique of "judicial legislation," to be brought about by a majority vote of the nine men who constitute the Supreme Court of the United States, and by so doing to circumvent the millions of voters who constitute the sovereign power of American democracy.

The First Amendment, particularly so far as its first phrase is concerned—"Congress shall make no law respecting an establishment of religion"—does not express any attitude whatever toward religion. It expresses no principle whatever of Catholicism, Protestantism, Judaism, Shintoism, or Atheism. It was meant to express and does express the wishes of the people who wrote it, adopted it, and ratified it, in regard to a specific problem in the delegation of powers by the people of the country to the federal government. The federal government is a government of delegated powers. It has no power except that which the people have given it through legally adopted constitutional provisions.

The phrase "Congress shall make no law respecting an establishment of religion" is a simple, specific prohibition of action by Congress in regard to a specific subject. It is a "keep out" sign. It seeks to make *explicit* what Hamilton in the *Federalist* (p. 92), and Madison in his letter to Thomas Jefferson of Oct. 17, 1788 (pp. 93-95), and Jefferson in his reply to Madison's letter of Mar. 5, 1789 (p. 209), all substantially agreed was *implicit* in the constitutional relationship between the individual states and the federal government when the original Constitution was ratified. This phrase was not put into the Constitution *to make any new arrangement.* It was simply to make what was the essential situation at the time so clearly and specifically stated that no one in the future could question what the situation was; namely, that the question of "an establishment of religion" for the whole United States by the Congress of the United States was a subject which Congress should not touch. It neither approved nor disapproved of the established religions then existing in the states. It made explicit the fact that Congress was powerless to act in favor of an establishment of religion for the nation. At the time there was no national establishment of religion. Obviously, therefore, there could never be one if Congress could never legislate on the subject. The phraseology finally adopted after long discussion (see Chapter Seven) accomplished the exact purpose of preventing a national church from taking the place of the dying state churches, and at the same time made possible the support of the Bill of Rights by those who still believed in *state*-established churches.

Various religious writers, both Catholic and Protestant, have within the last decade sought to find in the First Amendment some expression of religious, theological, or ecclesiastical doctrine. I submit that these are all futile searches. There is no such doctrine in the First Amendment. It is a purely political provision dealing with the allocation of legislative authority in regard to a specific topic. It is impossible to find any other meaning ascribed to it in the writings or official record of Jefferson (Chapter Five) or Madison (Chapter Six). The Justices of the Supreme Court in their "interpretation" of the First Amendment in the two cases above mentioned have not accurately quoted a single such passage or cited a single such fact. Neither have the two press releases, nor the manifestoes issued to date (June, 1948) by "Protestants and Other Americans United." There is no such passage or fact to be found in the many letters to the press, speeches to various organizations, etc., issued in recent years by others who have been trying to get the First Amendment out of their way.

Likewise, the First Amendment expresses no educational theory of any kind, good or bad, ancient or modern. The First Amendment has no application of any kind, was not designed to have any application of any kind, to any educational project, wise or unwise. Nothing was approved, nothing was disapproved in education any more than in religion.

Finally, and perhaps more important in the light of present controversies than any of the above considerations, is the fact that the First Amendment had nothing whatever to do with any theory of public financing or the propriety or impropriety of using public funds for any purpose whatever. Telling Congress that it could not deal with a certain subject was neither denunciation of, nor approval of, any type of public expenditure. Perhaps the most fantastic remark ever made in regard to the First Amendment by a responsible person speaking in a responsible setting is the remark of Justice Rutledge in the Everson bus case that the First Amendment prohibited any use of public funds in support of "religion in any guise, form or degree." When one has said that such a statement is complete nonsense, it has been given the most charitable characterization that could possibly be applied to it with any degree of accuracy. The Federal government has used public funds in support of religion in various guises, forms, and degrees from Washington's administration to Truman's, inclusive. Both Jefferson and Madison so used public funds throughout their administrations as President of the United States. Every state in the union has done likewise almost from the first day of its existence.

The detailed proof of the positions taken in this chapter will be found in the remainder of the book. Two things should be kept in mind constantly, though they cannot be discussed anew in each chapter. *First,* the Fourteenth Amendment (1868) added absolutely nothing to Constitutional *doctrine* in regard to religion and government, or "Church and State." The Fourteenth Amendment can be *only a channel* through which a restriction on Congress *may be* (not *must be*) passed on as a restriction on the legislatures of the various states. Any doctrine in regard to "the separation of church and state" which is in the Constitution must be found in the First Amendment.

Second, the Justices of the Supreme Court did not proclaim their new doctrine frankly and courageously as the expression of their private beliefs as to what is good for the American people. They based their case on the claim that their new doctrine is what the First Amendment *means and was designed to mean by Jefferson, Madison, and the other Founding Fathers.* The validity of the Supreme Court position in the McCollum case rests *in toto* on the validity of this claim. My position is that this claim is given all the respect to which it is entitled when it is labeled semantic and historical nonsense.

Chapter 2

CIVIL LIBERTIES IN THE UNITED STATES

*C*IVIL liberties are the freedoms *from government compulsion* to which a person is *entitled by law* because they are expressed in the constitutions, or the laws based on the constitutions, of the civil governments under which he lives. In a free society such as ours, they are the liberties which the people have reserved to themselves in setting up and defining the powers of their government. In America this means basically the constitutions and laws of the United States and of the individual state in which a person lives, or in which an action under consideration took place. To a minor extent civil liberties may be expressed in the charter or ordinances of a city, or in the similar documents of any civic unit as a township or county.

There are to be sure other concepts of the meaning of civil liberties, the more important of which are sometimes unfortunately confused with the fundamental meaning given above. If clarity is to be achieved whenever the term "civil liberties" is used in a sense other than the basic one given above, the special meaning should be made evident in the context. When a writer or speaker uses the label "civil liberties" for ideas which he thinks *should be included* in our constitution or laws but which have not yet been so included, he is not using language accurately. The private aspirations of Mr. Jones are not binding civic obligations on Mr. Smith. When one speaks of the civil liberties to which Americans are *entitled*, which all who believe in our constitutional system should *uphold*, and which our courts and other agencies of government *are bound by oath to pro-*

tect, we mean (or should mean) those which the American people have adopted and expressed formally in their constitutions and laws.

Civil liberties are identical for members of majorities and of minorities; they are identical for all persons to whom the constitutions and laws apply. Each person has a right, a legal right, to these liberties. Civil liberties and civil rights are therefore substantially synonymous. When the civil rights of one person are invaded or violated, the constitutions and laws of all are affronted. Such violations are offenses "against the state"; society itself is challenged. It follows that every officer of the government of any sort or rank who has sworn to uphold the constitutions and the laws and who neglects to do his part to protect the civil liberties of *anyone,* violates his oath of office and proves himself to be a faithless public servant.

Anyone, from the humblest citizen to the Justices of the United States Supreme Court, has necessarily, under our civil liberties, a right to work for amendments to the Constitution of the United States or that of any of the states. But no man, or party, or church, or court (again including the Supreme Court of the United States), has a right to amend the United States Constitution, or the state constitutions. The people have provided methods for amendments, and so long as we have constitutional governments and civil liberties these methods will be followed.

All citizens should be deeply concerned by violations of civil liberties. All citizens who understand and respect the framework of our democracy *are* deeply concerned. In a democracy (majority rule with minority rights) civil liberties necessarily have to be written into the constitutions and laws by the majority. But that does not make them the exclusive property and privilege of the majority. In civil liberties the smallest minority is on an equal footing with the largest majority.

The clearest and most authoritative statements from competent persons and organizations leave no doubt concerning the basic meaning of civil liberties.

The American Civil Liberties Union is a nonprofit, nonpartisan organization having a nationwide membership of persons of all religions views and sects. . . . It is devoted to the preservation and protection of the fundamental liberties guaranteed citizens of this country by Federal and State Constitutions.[1]

Obviously no one can rationally demand that the courts protect, and that all law-abiding citizens defend, any concept of civil liberties which is not to be found in the constitutions or the laws.

The principles of civil liberty are those inherent in a political democracy in which ultimate power rests in the people, and in which minority rights are as essential as majority rule. Our civil liberties are expressed mainly in the guarantees of the "Bills of Rights" of federal and state constitutions. Their practical application is subject to constant interpretation by the courts of new laws, problems and circumstances and of conflicts between one right and another.

Civil liberties are guarantees to citizens primarily in relation to their government and also in relation to one another. Basic to all the many aspects of civil liberties are freedom of speech, press and assembly as essentials of democratic procedures.

The ACLU stands on the general principles of freedom from governmental interference with citizens' liberties, of protection of those liberties where necessary by government itself, and of the equality of all citizens in the exercise of rights. It follows its own interpretations of the Bill of Rights [2] without any necessary reference to those of courts and legislatures.[3]

Professor George H. Sabine in the opening sentence of the preface to *Safeguarding Civil Liberty Today* [4] speaks of "our civil liberties— the basic freedoms protected by the bills of rights in our federal and state constitutions." In the same book [5] Professor Carl Becker gives a summary of the civil liberties guaranteed by the state and federal constitutions.

The fundamental constitutional safeguard against the unrestrained will of the people is defined in what are called the "bills of rights." Jefferson and his contemporaries believed that governments exist to secure the nat-

[1] Brief of American Civil Liberties Union as amicus curiae, in *Everson* vs. *Board of Education*, in the Supreme Court of the United States, October Term, 1946, p. 1.

[2] Necessarily "its own interpretations of the Bill of Rights" is chiefly useful in its activities outside of courtrooms. There the laws and the court decisions must (or should) control.

[3] Civil Liberty. A statement defining the position of the Civil Liberties Union. (New York, American Civil Liberties Union, 1945), p. 2.

[4] Ithaca, Cornell University Press, 1945, p. v.   [5] *Ibid.*, pp. 15-17.

ural rights of men, but some of these rights they regarded as sacred and imprescriptible. They endeavored, therefore, to place them above and beyond the reach of legislative action by enumerating them in the constitutions and declaring them to be rights which no government could ever impair or deny. They were enumerated in the first state constitutions, and afterwards, without change in the content and with very little change in the phraseology, copied in all subsequent constitutions. All Americans are supposed to know them as they know the multiplication table, and do know them just about that well. They are (just in case some of them may have slipped from your memory) freedom of religion, freedom of speech and the press, freedom of assembly and the right to petition the government, freedom to bear arms in defense of the country, freedom of one's house and person from unwarranted search and seizure, freedom from the billeting of soldiers, freedom of private property from confiscation except for a public purpose and with adequate compensation, freedom from arbitrary arrest and imprisonment, the privilege of the writ of habeas corpus, the right to a speedy and public trial by a jury of one's peers, to subpoena witnesses, and to have legal assistance in one's defense, and freedom from bills of attainder, ex post facto laws, excessive fines, and cruel and unusual punishments.

In setting forth these civil liberties of the citizen, the constitutions define a sphere of action which is entirely withdrawn from governmental control.

Professor Robert E. Cushman uses essentially the same definition.

We no longer speak about the "rights of man" or "natural rights"; we use the term civil liberty, but we mean by it these same rights and freedoms which our forefathers won for us and embodied in our bills of rights, and which are, therefore, under the protection of our courts of law.[6]

While our civil liberties are written in our constitutions and laws, and are therefore supposed to be the common freedoms of all Americans, *they are not self-enforcing.*

If the civil liberties are in form and spirit denied every day to someone, and no one bothers about it unless he is that someone, less than nothing is gained by pointing out that they are specifically enumerated and properly defined in forty-nine constitutions and may be defended in the courts.[7]

---

[6] *Ibid.*, p. 81.   [7] Becker, *ibid.*, p. 26.

Genuine enjoyment of one's civil liberties in the face of ignorant or hostile public opinion is impossible, and defending them in the courts is expensive. Furthermore, in courts in which ignorance or deep prejudice overrides any knowledge of the law, or sense of obligation to his oath, which the judge might otherwise exercise, defending civil liberties in the courts may be worse than futile.

"Civil" as an adjective in law is defined by Webster's dictionary as "Relating to the private rights of individuals in a community and to legal proceedings in connection with them." "Civil liberty" is defined as "exemption from arbitrary governmental interference with person, opinion, or property."

A significant event in our history, definitely related to the subject of this chapter, is the report of the President's Committee on Civil Rights, entitled *To Secure These Rights*.[8] While this report goes beyond the specific limits of civil liberties already expressed in the constitutions and laws of this country, and uses the somewhat more elastic term "civil rights," its preliminary analysis of its field is helpful both in understanding our present civil liberties (present in law even when not in fact) and in setting forth needed extensions of civil liberties in our constitutions and laws. In other words this report deals not only with our present legal civil liberties, but also with plans, programs, aspirations for improvement in this area.

The men who founded our Republic, as those who have built any constitutional democracy, faced the task of reconciling personal liberty and group authority, or of establishing an equilibrium between them. In a democratic state we recognize that the common interests of the people must be managed by laws and procedures established by majority rule. But a democratic majority, left unrestrained, may be as ruthless and tyrannical as were the earlier absolute monarchs. Seeing this clearly, and fearing it greatly, our forefathers built a constitutional system in which valued personal liberties, carefully enumerated in a Bill of Rights, were placed beyond the reach of popular majorities. Thus the people permanently denied the federal government power to interfere with certain personal rights and freedoms.

Freedom, however, as we now use the term, means even more than the traditional "freedoms" listed in our Bill of Rights—important as they are. Freedom has come to mean the right of a man to manage his own affairs

8 Reprinted in full by the newspaper *PM*, Nov. 2, 1947.

as he sees fit up to the point where what he does interferes with the equal rights of others in the community to manage their affairs—or up to the point where he begins to injure the welfare of the whole group. It is clear that in modern democratic society a man's freedom in this broader sense is not and cannot be absolute—nor does it exist in a vacuum—but instead is hedged about by the competing rights of others and the demands of the social welfare. In this context it is government which must referee the clashes which arise among the freedoms of citizens, and protect each citizen in the enjoyment of the maximum freedom to which he is entitled.

There is no essential conflict between freedom and government. Bills of rights restrain government from abridging individual civil liberties, while government itself by sound legislative policies protects citizens against the aggressions of others seeking to push their freedoms too far. Thus in the words of the Declaration of Independence: "Man is endowed by his Creator with certain inalienable rights. Among these are life, liberty, and the pursuit of happiness. To secure these rights, *governments are instituted among men.*"

The rights essential to the citizen in a free society can be described in different words and in varying orders. The three great rights of the Declaration of Independence have just been mentioned. Another noble statement is made in the Bill of Rights of our Constitution. A more recent formulation is found in the Four Freedoms.

Four basic rights have seemed important to this Committee and have influenced its labors. We believe that each of these rights is essential to the well-being of the individual and to the progress of society. 1. The right to safety and the security of the person. . . . 2. The right to citizenship and its privileges. . . . 3. The right to freedom of conscience and expression. . . . 4. The right to equality of opportunity.

An outstanding contribution to the related field of civil rights is *The Constitution and Civil Rights*, by Professor Milton R. Konvitz, of the School of Industrial and Labor Relations, Cornell University.[9] Serious scholars who are interested in civil rights will find this book a much needed, clear, factual, scholarly, well-documented supplement to the committee report, *To Secure These Rights*, referred to above. The distinction between civil liberties and civil rights which Dr. Konvitz makes in his Preface should be particularly helpful to all readers in this field.

This book does not treat of political rights, such as the right to vote. Nor does it treat of civil liberties, such as those mentioned in the Bill of

[9] New York, Columbia University Press, 1947.

Rights (freedom of speech, freedom of the press, freedom of assembly, religious freedom, the right to bear arms, the right to security against unreasonable searches and seizures, security against double jeopardy, and excessive bail, the right to trial by jury, security against self-incrimination, and so on). The scope of this book is defined by its title: *The Constitution and Civil Rights*. In its more technical, limited sense, the term civil rights, as distinguished from political rights and civil liberties, refers to the rights of persons to employment, and to accommodations in hotels, restaurants, common carriers, and other places of public accommodation and resort. The term contemplates the rights enumerated in the federal Civil Rights Act of 1875 and the various acts against discrimination found on the statute books of eighteen states.

For the reason that some of the federal civil rights acts speak of privileges and immunities, as well as rights, it is necessary to consider the constitutional meaning of the term "privileges and immunities." The book, therefore, deals with both civil rights and the privileges and immunities of citizens.

If we are ever to approach the realization of the ideal free society, we must achieve greater (a) understanding, (b) belief, (c) observance, (d) enforcement, and (e) constitutional and statutory amplification, in the whole field of civil liberty, civil rights, human freedom. To achieve and enjoy a full program of civil liberties, we need to look to all five of the steps just mentioned.

Understanding is not enough. But it would help a lot. Today, the bleak ignorance of mature, cultivated men and women who think they are devoted to, and well-informed in regard to, the form and content of our doctrine of civil liberties, is appalling. As we shall see later, even some judges in distinguished positions in American courts are apparently almost wholly ignorant of the most important facts in American history which have a bearing on civil liberties. This is clearly shown by their appeals to "the testimony of history" to bolster up fantastic interpretations of laws and constitutions. When such appeals to the testimony of history omit most of the vital and relevant facts of history and either misquote or distort the authentic records, ignorance is the mildest possible explanation.[10] The only

10 See Chapters Eleven and Twelve on the Supreme Court in the Everson case and the McCollum case.

explanation other than gross ignorance is even less complimentary to the judiciary.

Beyond understanding we must have belief in the civil liberties of those with whom we disagree. He who believes only in civil liberties for his side does not believe in civil liberties at all. The most powerful opponents of civil liberties ever known, such as Hitler, Stalin, Mussolini, did not get their top rating in this matter by preventing the freedom of opinion, speech, press, and religion of their followers and henchmen, but by imprisoning, enslaving, banishing, or executing those who disagreed with them. The American citizen who says, "I believe in civil liberties but I object to allowing Mr. A to preach his false doctrine in regard to x . . . y . . . z . . ." is philosophically, so far as this subject is concerned, at one with all the great and little dictators and tyrants of history and of today. *The essence of civil liberty is the right to be wrong.* That is, the civil right to be wrong, not necessarily the moral right, or the intellectual right. Civil liberties deny to *the government* the authority to determine what is right or true in theology, economics, biology, diet, or political theory. Unless you believe in your opponents' *civil right* to be wrong, you cannot really believe in your *civil right* to be right, but only in your *power* to be right.

When Arthur Garfield Hays, a distinguished lawyer and a Jew, went into court to defend the civil liberties of the German-American Bund, he was not endorsing or advocating the doctrines of the Bund or the vicious anti-Jewish preaching and practice of Hitler. He was defending the constitutions and laws of his country. He was defending the civil liberties of all Americans.

When Martin Conboy, another distinguished lawyer and a Catholic, who was at the time the official attorney of the Catholic Archdiocese of New York, went to the United States Supreme Court to defend the civil liberties of Jehovah's Witnesses, he was not subscribing to the anti-Catholic activities of Jehovah's Witnesses. He likewise was defending the Constitution of the United States and the civil liberties of all Americans.

When Wendell Willkie argued before the Supreme Court to prevent the cancellation of the citizenship of an American citizen because he was a Communist, Willkie was not supporting Communism. He was supporting the Constitution. He was defending the right to freedom of opinion of every American, regardless of his philosophy. He was defending American civil liberties.

Leon Whipple in his book, *The Story of Civil Liberty in the United States*,[11] is forced to the conclusion that "Whoever has power has civil liberty." This book is a case record of events in the field of American civil liberty from 1776 to 1917. Again and again the study of the record compels Professor Whipple to conclude that in our history, in spite of constitutions and laws, and the oaths of office of American executives, judges, and police officers, whoever had power had civil liberty. The civil liberties of the weak minorities have been pretty thoroughly disregarded. Lawlessness in the persecution of minorities which at times became unchecked savagery reached its peak in the decades just before the Civil War. The record between 1830 and 1860, which Whipple calls "The Mob Era" is one of intense intolerance and brutal treatment (reaching at times climaxes of burning, beating, and killing) of racial or religious minorities—Mormons, Catholics, Jews, Unitarians. The persecutions were usually carried on under high-sounding religious and political slogans, but were clearly in many, if not most, cases motivated by the fear of economic rather than philosophical competition.[12]

The modern motto of the American Heritage Foundation, "Freedom is Everybody's Job," and the admonition "Eternal vigilance is the price of liberty" are necessary guides to action today and tomor-

[11] New York, The Vanguard Press, 1927, pp.1-3.

[12] Probably the two best books on this period in the history of American civil liberties are *The Protestant Crusade* by Ray Allen Billington, Professor of History in Northwestern University (New York, The Macmillan Company, 1938), and *A History of Freedom of Teaching in American Schools*: Report of the Commission on Social Studies of the American Historical Association, by Howard K. Beale, Professor of History in the University of North Carolina (New York, Charles Scribner's Sons, 1941). These two books should be carefully read by anyone interested in a full discussion of the religious or educational implications of our doctrine of civil liberty in the United States. A third book, not so well written as these two, but valuable as a storehouse of well documented cases bearing directly on civil liberties in many instances, is the *History of Bigotry in the United States*, by Gustavus Myers (New York, Random House, 1943).

row. Everyone will lose his freedom if he leaves the job of protecting it to congressmen and Supreme Court judges. The vigilance that needs to be exercised every day, everywhere, is not that of the policeman, the county sheriff, or the soldier on sentry duty; it is the vigilance of all who believe in and wish to perpetuate a free society, governed by laws, not men.

Chapter 3

PROTESTANTISM, CATHOLICISM, AND ESTABLISHMENT

*J*N ALL of the discussion leading up to the adoption of the First Amendment by the Congress of 1789, it was "a condition and not a theory" which confronted the leaders in their fight to end or to prohibit religious establishments. Establishment was the rule not only in England and in Scotland, but in all of Europe, both Protestant and Catholic, and in most of America itself. At the beginning of the Revolution the Anglican Church or the Congregational Church held the position of full or partial establishment in all but four of the thirteen colonies.

The handful of Catholics in this country at the time played no important part in the disestablishment discussion. They numbered about 24,000 at the end of the Revolution, about two-thirds of them being in Maryland. As a small minority, even in Maryland (where the Episcopal Church had long since become the established church), they were naturally in favor of disestablishment. Early in the eighteenth century, when the dissenters and Quakers in Maryland were brought under the English Act of Toleration of 1689, the Catholics were excluded.

Professor William Warren Sweet[1] writes of this situation, "This has been termed one of the sarcasms of history. Maryland, which had been founded for the sake of religious freedom by the toil and treasure of Roman Catholics, was now open to all who call themselves Christians save Roman Catholics."

[1] *The Story of Religions in America* (New York, Harper & Brothers, 1930, 5th Ed.), p. 64.

Contrary to the frequent assertions of eminent men, both Catholic and Protestant, neither the genuine, specific American principle of "no established church," nor the vague spurious principle of "complete separation of church and state" is a Protestant, as distinct from a Catholic, principle. As late as August 3, 1947, a spokesman for the Protestant World Council of Churches, in discussing the proposed joint action on world problems by the World Council and the Catholic Church, said that collaboration "must be preceded by conversations between the highest courts on both sides, and must include a discussion of *the alternative theories of the relationship between church and state*" (italics mine). There are no such alternative theories that can be identified and defined. Both the principles mentioned above are purely political principles expressing no religious doctrine of any kind. The complete and absolute separation of church and state, such as the justices of the Supreme Court talk about in the Everson and McCollum cases (see Chapters Eleven and Twelve), is an unreal political abstraction. No civilized country in the world, no state in the United States, has ever recognized such a principle either in practice or in its laws or constitution. So far as the realities of government are concerned, there is no such thing.

Established or state religions, on the contrary, have been substantially universal throughout all history regardless of the predominant religion in the various countries. Established churches have been the almost unbroken rule ever since the Reformation in the Protestant countries of England, Scotland, Germany, Denmark, Sweden, and Norway, and in the countries of Eastern Europe which have broken away from the Roman Catholic Church. In Holland, Switzerland, England, and Canada the state has contributed to both Protestant and Catholic church schools.

The total record of history in all Christian countries, both Catholic and Protestant, as known to Americans of the late eighteenth century, was an unbroken record of established churches. In a world of universal *union* between *one* church and the government, a provision which prevented the Congress from creating such a union for the United States of America could be legitimately spoken of as a separation of church and state—so far as the United States as a nation was concerned. It was a type of separation. It was not complete and absolute separation, and it clearly had no reference of any kind to *state arrangements* concerning religion.

If the almost universal existence of state churches is good evidence, it is apparent, therefore, that outside the United States most Protestants and most Catholics agree on the principle of an established church. In this country, on the other hand, practically everyone agrees on the principle of *no* established church. So far as I know, not a single responsible spokesman or leader of any party, any religious denomination, or any other group of Americans, has advocated an establishment of religion in this country since the disappearance of the established Protestant churches in the first half of the nineteenth century. It is substantially true to say that today all Americans believe in no established religion in America. *This is a genuine American principle.*

When America, in the nation as a whole, prevented an establishment, and the individual states, eventually, got rid of established Protestant churches and provided for *no established church* in the various states, a brand new political principle (political not religious) came into being. This great American principle, now almost unanimously endorsed by Americans of every creed and party, has remained substantially unobserved throughout the rest of the world, Protestant and Catholic alike, ever since. In spite of the fact that there is probably no other public principle upon which greater unity could be obtained today, one might think, on the basis of some of the arguments now current concerning specific measures, that there is a fundamental disagreement in America on this issue between Catholics and Protestants.

The historical record in regard to special favors of government to religion should be considered under the two general headings of *Protestantism* and *Catholicism*.

I. Protestantism

Reference has already been made to the fact that all countries in the political and cultural background of the Americans in the latter part of the eighteenth century, whether the countries were Catholic or Protestant, had established churches. Many of the colonists who came to this country came to escape from the exactions of an established church (see p. 291). Further (since almost all of them came from the British Isles) they were escaping from established Protestant churches. They were not trying to escape from the Anglican or the Presbyterian churches but from the establishment of these churches.

In the fight that developed in America against American established churches, starting in the colonies and continuing after the revolution in the states, the fight was exclusively against established Protestant churches—six Anglican (or Episcopal) and three Congregational. The elimination of these established Protestant churches, finally accomplished in full with the disestablishment of the Congregational church in Massachusetts in 1833, did not end a variety of favored provisions for Protestantism in a number of states in the United States. According to Cornelison [1a] only Protestants could be elected to the United States House of Representatives or Senate from the state of New Hampshire until 1877. In New Jersey only Protestants could hold any public office of profit or trust until 1844.

Special governmental favor to Protestantism continued in a number of states long after the ratification of the First Amendment.

Many of the early constitutions of the original states set up Christianity as the state religion. Civil rights were guaranteed, but under some constitutions only to Protestants. The states were legally able, and many did for a short time continue, to support their particular denominations, and the requirement of religious tests for office-holding was continued even after the state-adopted churches were abandoned.

. . . .

There are, however, even to this date, remnants of provisions which show a bias toward particular religious beliefs. For example, New Hampshire adopted a provision in 1784 which is still in the current constitution, and which authorizes the public support of Protestant teachers of piety, religion, and morality.[2]

[1a] Cornelison I. A., *The Relation of Religion to Civil Government.* (New York: G. P. Putnam's Sons, 1895.) Pp. 96-111.
[2] "The State and Sectarian Education," *Research Bulletin of the National Educational Association*, XXIV, No. 1, 1946, p. 8.

Dr. Erwin L. Shaver of the International Council of Religious Education in addressing the 1948 Wisconsin Pastors' conference in Madison, Wisconsin,

urged that Protestants guard against becoming themselves involved in alliances between church and state. He remarked that whereas many Protestants are quick to criticize Catholics because nuns garbed in the habits of their orders teach in the public schools, their own clergymen are teaching in many public schools. In Missouri alone, he said, Protestant teachers are being paid by the state to teach religion in 282 rural schools.[3]

Practically every public school system in America used public money and property for the promotion of Protestantism until the period of the Civil War, and many of them long after that time. Professor Howard K. Beale of the University of North Carolina, in discussing this period writes:

While sectarianism was increasingly discouraged, practically all schools still included religion in their curricula. School opened with prayer. The Bible was read and portions of it memorized. Hymns were sung. The principles of Protestant Christianity, so far as they were accepted by all Trinitarian sects, were instilled into the children.[4]

Concerning the attitude of Catholics in this period Beale writes:

they contributed in taxes to the support of schools in which their teachers were not allowed to teach and could not have taught the required subjects anyway without violating their own consciences. Furthermore, the Catholics were not satisfied to have religion excluded from the schools. Like the Protestants, they wanted to teach religion to children, but again like the Protestants, they wanted to teach their own religion.[5]

The detailed story of anti-Catholic prejudice in America is fully told in *The Protestant Crusade* by Ray A. Billington, Professor of History in Northwestern University. Catholic children were flogged in a number of states for refusing to take part in the compulsory Protestant religious services in the public schools. In Philadelphia in 1842 when the Catholic Bishop Kenrick "respectfully asked that the Catholic

---

[3] *Christian Century* (May 12, 1948), p. 451.
[4] Beale, Howard K., *History of Freedom of Teaching* (New York, Charles Scribner's Sons, 1941), p. 95.
[5] *Ibid.*, p. 98.

children be allowed to use their own version of the Bible and that they be excused from other religious instruction in the public schools" [6] there ensued two years of bitterness and mob violence, the burning of two Catholic churches and a seminary, and finally three days of rioting in which thirteen people were killed and fifty wounded—in the City of Brotherly Love!

Between 1830 and 1870 most states legally removed the Protestant religion from the public schools, though the practice remained unchanged much longer in many places in spite of the law. At the same time the states prohibited the use of public funds for religious schools. Both of these purposes were accomplished usually by a single new state constitutional provision outlawing specifically the use of public money in schools in which religious doctrine was taught. A significant point about these measures is that not a single state relied on the state constitutional provisions which prohibited the union of church and state or laws "respecting an establishment of religion." The charging of this respectable old phrase with such a brood of illegitimate offspring as Justice Rutledge lays on its doorstep in the Everson case is a strictly modern invention. It will, let us hope in the name of historical truth, logic, and good English prose, soon pass away.

The ending of the use of the public schools as substantially Trinitarian Protestant schools at public expense, and the stopping of the growth of all other types of religious schools at public expense, leaving secularism as the only religious point of view in our educational system which is supported by public money, is a story in which there are doubtless many chapters yet to be written.

The records of the Congress of the United States for substantially a century after the adoption of the First Amendment contained innumerable items showing payment by Congress to Protestant missionaries and Protestant missions for spreading education and religion among the Indian wards of the United States government (see p. 117). In the 160 years since the United States began paying chaplains in the two houses of Congress, in the Army and Navy, in hospitals and

[6] Billington, Ray A., *The Protestant Crusade* (New York, The Macmillan Company, 1938), p. 221.

penal institutions, and in West Point and Annapolis, a great many, probably a majority, of chaplains have properly and inevitably been Protestants.

It is interesting to note here that Madison's second thought in reference to the payment of Congressional chaplains by the United States government (see p. 106) was based upon the idea that the election of such chaplains by a majority in the houses of Congress violated the principle of *equality* among the religions of America, not that the payment from public funds was unconstitutional.

He wrote in his *Detatched Memoranda:*

The tenets of the chaplains elected [by the majority] shut the door of worship agst the members whose creeds & consciences forbid a participation in that of the majority. To say nothing of other sects, this is the case with that of Roman Catholics & Quakers who have always had members in one or both of the Legislative branches. Could a Catholic clergyman ever hope to be appointed a chaplain? [7]

For a detailed, well-documented, and readable account of the struggle among Protestant denominations for positions of influence in public education, and for public funds for denominational education, see Gobbel, *Church-State Relationships in Education in North Carolina.*[8] This contest went on for about a century after the adoption of the First Amendment. The constitution of North Carolina adopted in 1776, provided that "There shall be no establishment of any one religious church or denomination in this State in preference to any other. . . ."[9] North Carolina was an overwhelmingly Protestant state. The denominations concerned were the Episcopalian, Presbyterian, Methodist, and Baptist. The controversy centered about the state university and the private colleges as one phase, and the public school system as the other. One or two examples must suffice. These are offered not to show that either the United States Constitution or the Constitution of North Carolina was violated or even "attacked" in this century-long campaign. These examples demonstrate that in the almost wholly Protestant state of North Carolina

[7] *William and Mary Quarterly*, 3rd Ser., III (October, 1946), p. 558.
[8] Gobbel, Luther L. (Durham, Duke University Press, 1938).
[9] Article 34, Constitution of 1776, North Carolina, *ibid.*, p. 30.

for the first century after the date of the First Amendment the leading Protestant clergymen and educators of that state were unfamiliar with the doctrine of "complete separation of church and state" as a great Protestant American, constitutional principle. From the evidence available (less well organized for most states) it seems clear that this situation in North Carolina was typical rather than unique. The following quotations show the nature of the contest.

The Presbyterian Synod, by resolution adopted in 1847, requested "such members of the Synod as may be Professors in the University" to report to the Synod "whatever most concerns morals and true religion, with such suggestions as they may deem most appropriate to their office." [10]

Neither the Baptists nor the Methodists felt that they had a fair representation either on the board of trustees or faculty of the reopened University. Dr. Birkhead (President of the Board of Trustees of Trinity College, Methodist) alleged, furthermore, that those in control had little or no use for Methodism.[11]

Dr. Birkhead questioned the fairness of "Episcopal control" of the University when there were only 45,000 Episcopalians as compared with 100,000 Methodists in the state.[12]

They (the Methodists and Baptists) are taxed, not simply to build up a rival institution where Episcopalians have undue influence and control; but indirectly at least to destroy their own institution.[13]

The following figures are given:

150,000 Methodists—One Faculty member
204,000 Baptists—One Faculty member
6,000 "religiously unpopular and unprogressive
    Episcopalians"—3 Faculty members [14]

Superintendent Wiley, Head of Public School system, 1852-1865 ("one of the foremost educational leaders in the United States"—"a Presbyterian of the Presbyterians") "emphasized religion in education and sought to establish a deep religious purpose in the public schools of the state." [15]

[10] Ibid., p. 57.
[11] Ibid., p. 81.
[12] Ibid.
[13] Ibid., p. 82.
[14] Ibid., p. 84.
[15] Ibid., p. 181.

The state constitution made it impossible for those "who deny the Being of God, or the divine authority of the Old or New Testament". to hold any civil trust. Wiley wanted this "strictly enforced" in hiring teachers.[16]

II. CATHOLICISM

In discussing Catholics and any aspect of democracy (particularly when the words and deeds of ancient times and other countries are used against American Catholics of today) the following salutary warnings of Professor Garrison of the University of Chicago, should be heeded.

A true picture cannot be wholly consistent, for the facts are not. No vast, complex, and long-enduring institution can be uniformly as good as the best, or as bad as the worst, that can be said about it and proved from its record. This is equally true of Protestant attitudes toward individual human rights and democratic principles. In saying that the Catholic tradition in relation to democratic rights is not wholly consistent within itself, it is not necessarily implied that there is inconsistency in Catholic dogma or official theory.[17]

Data about "democracy" or "democratic rights" in any tradition of long continuance cannot be found by looking under "D" in any alphabetical index of historical materials covering the whole sweep of the Christian centuries. Democracy is a modern word; Greek, of course, in its origin, but it had a longer and deeper sleep than other classical concepts; and it awoke later, and presently began to have a changed content, with less exclusive reference to form of government and a wider connotation of respect for the universal rights of man as a person.[18]

The conclusion I wish to draw from these notes on the history of the "democracy" is that we must not expect to find it attached to affirmations of the rights of man before the eighteenth century. The medieval Christian tradition contained some democratic values, but they did not bear that label. For a period of fifteen centuries or more, covering the greater part of history of the Roman Catholic Church and the first two centuries of Protestantism, nobody believed in political democracy—except a few prophetic and adventurous souls.[19]

[16] *Ibid.*, pp. 180-184.
[17] W. E. Garrison, *Religion and Civil Liberty in the Roman Catholic Tradition* (Chicago, Willett, Clark & Company, 1946), pp. 4-5.
[18] *Ibid.*, p. 5.   [19] *Ibid.*, pp. 5-6.

Throughout the current campaign to subvert the First Amendment there seems to be a widespread attempt to make this a Catholic vs. a Protestant fight. The decision in the Everson case, upholding a New Jersey law which permitted the payment of bus fares for pupils attending Catholic schools, was characterized by one journal as a situation in which "Protestantism Takes a Licking," and was frequently referred to in much the same terms by many speakers and writers. In that decision the Constitution missed "taking a licking" by one vote. But the licking was administered with interest a year later in the McCollum case. Following the decision in the latter case when a group of twenty-four distinguished Protestant clergymen and educators issued a press release to restate and affirm the Constitutional "interpretation of the American doctrine of separation of church and state, and to protest against the interpretation that has been formulated by the Supreme Court," *The Christian Century* [20] referred to the release editorially under the heading "Protestants Take the Catholic Line."

There is still potent propaganda force in some of the ancient bugaboos about the Catholic Church. The wholly false assumption that "complete, absolute separation of church and state" is a Protestant, American constitutional principle, is furthered by the equally false assumption that Catholics are opposed to a fundamental American constitutional principle.

There are two outstanding characteristics of the modern propaganda that are relevant here. The first is that it seeks to discuss the constitutional provision of the First Amendment, never in the language of the First Amendment but always in terms of the modern slogan—the separation of church and state. The other is that any remark or decision of a Catholic public official or educational administrator which the propagandists do not like is ascribed without documentation to "the Roman Catholic hierarchy" or to "Catholic pressure." It is a common thing to assign to the Roman Catholic hierarchy the responsibility for all sorts of activity on the part of individual Catholic citizens in circumstances under which at least one or more of the following is usually true:

[20] June 30, 1948.

1. The statement of the individual Catholic deals with a matter concerning which there is no "Catholic position."

2. The matter is one concerning which the thinking of clerical and lay Catholics differs as widely as does that of the members of other groups.

3. The matter is one concerning which it is improbable that any member of the Catholic hierarchy had anything whatever to do.

For instance, Dr. C. C. Morrison [21] in discussing the sending of Mr. Myron Taylor to the Vatican as the representative of the President, and Mr. Truman's statement that this assignment would end when the peace treaties are signed, says: "But the President is under tremendous pressure from the Catholic hierarchy which has long sought and lobbied for the recognition of the Holy See by our government." Of course Dr. Morrison offered no proof of any kind for this statement. However, Mr. Cordell Hull's memoirs, as published in the *New York Times* of May 11, 1948, proved conclusively that no member of the Catholic hierarchy had anything whatever to do with this matter. If, as Dr. Morrison claimed, this decision was due to pressure from the Catholic hierarchy, then it follows inevitably that President Roosevelt and Secretary Hull are guilty of falsification in regard to this important item of United States history. The Rev. Willard Johnson (a Protestant minister) discusses this situation in an excellent article [22] in which he specifically mentioned the fact that "there is no evidence that Catholics sought" the sending of Mr. Taylor to the Vatican.

It is frequently asserted, but never proved, that American Catholics seek a special, privileged, exclusively favored position among the religions of our country in the relation of the Catholic Church to the government, and in so doing are disloyal to the Constitution or are "attacking" the First Amendment. I recently encountered the strange argument that in seeking public aid or services *to all religious schools on an equal basis* Catholics are seeking a special or privileged position because there are more children in Catholic religious schools than in

---

[21] Pamphlet, *The Separation of Church and State in America* (Indianapolis International Convention of Disciples of Christ, 1947), pp. 5-6.
[22] "Whose Country is This?," *Christendom*, XII, No. 4, 1947.

the religious schools of any other church or denomination. I do not recall hearing this particular argument of special privilege to Catholics because there were more Catholic youth in the armed services in the recent war than young men from any other church in America. When I had five sons in uniform in World War II, no one accused me of seeking any special privilege over fathers who had one or two sons, or none, in the armed forces. Equality before the law for the individual American of all denominations was the objective of Jefferson and Madison and the other Founding Fathers, not equality only for groups or organizations of equal size. If we are to cut down the privileges of American citizenship to be enjoyed by Catholics or any other groups because there are so many (or so few) of them, then we should likewise cut down their right to vote and their duty to pay taxes and to fight for their country. As Chief Justice Hughes said in rejecting the position of the Interstate Commerce Commission that railroads could deny Pullman accommodations to Negroes on the plea of "comparatively little colored traffic": "It is the individual who is entitled to equal protection of the laws—not merely a group of individuals or a body of persons according to their numbers." [23]

I have referred above to the position of the Catholics in Maryland (most of the Catholics in the United States at the time of the Revolution) and the remarks of Professor Sweet in regard to that situation. The activity of the Catholics Daniel Carroll in the House of Representatives and Charles Carroll in the Senate, in the working out of the Bill of Rights, is given in Chapter Seven.

Professor Billington [24] sets forth in considerable detail the unvarying support of the American constitutional provisions regarding an establishment of religion by American Catholics throughout our history. I quote:

"When I signed the Declaration of Independence," wrote one of the several Catholics affixing his signature to that document, "I had in view not only our independence from England, but the toleration of all sects professing the Christian religion, and communicating to them all equal

[23] *Mitchell* v. *Interstate Commerce Commission*, 313 U. S. 80 (1941).
[24] Billington, Ray Allen, Professor of History, Northwestern University, "American Catholicism and the Church-State Issue," *Christendom*, V, No. 3, 1940, pp. 355-365.

rights." Later, in the drafting of the Constitution Catholics played a leading part in the debates on religious freedom and helped write those basic clauses which prohibited religious tests for officeholding and which denied Congress the right to make any law "respecting an establishment of religion, or prohibiting the free exercise thereof." These guarantees were enthusiastically acclaimed by all American Catholics. "Thanks to genuine spirit and Christianity," the Reverend John Carroll wrote in the *Columbian Magazine* for December, 1787, "the United States have banished intolerance from their system of government. . . . Freedom and independence, acquired by the united efforts, and cemented with the mingled blood of Protestant and Catholic fellow citizens, should be equally enjoyed by all." [25]

Professor Billington sums up the long struggle for disestablishment in the following passage:

Between 1786, when Virginia severed the political bond between religion and government, and 1833, when lagging Massachusetts finally fell into line, the battle for disestablishment went on in state after state. In each struggle a popular leader emerged to absorb most of the glory; but the real heroes were the rank and file of the Presbyterians, Baptists, Quakers and Catholics.[26]

Madison in his "Detatched Memoranda" in referring to his famous "Memorial and Remonstrance" uses this statement:

It met with the approbation of the Baptists, the Presbyterians, the Quakers, and the few Roman Catholics, universally; of the Methodists in part; and even of not a few of the Sect [Anglican] formerly established by law.[27]

From the day of the ending of the struggle for disestablishment in the United States down to the present, outstanding American Catholics, both laymen and clergy, have constantly reiterated American Catholic support of the only doctrine of separation of state and church which the American people have ever sanctioned, namely, the prohibition of the establishment of any religion.

From the clear and emphatic statement of Bishop John Carroll in 1787 down to the following quotation from Professor John A. O'Brien of Notre Dame University writing in the *Christian Century* of May

[25] *Ibid.*, p. 358.   [26] *Ibid.*, p. 359.
[27] *The William and Mary Quarterly*, 3rd. Ser. III (Oct., 1946), pp. 555-556.

19, 1948, the record of American Catholicism is one of vigorous and consistent support of the American constitutional principle.

First, the assumption that Catholics do not really believe in the separation of church and state, nor in religious liberty, nor in equality of treatment for all.[28]

Contrary to the impression of many of our Protestant friends, Catholics believe as strongly as any group in the separation of church and state in America. Whatever may have been the historical conditions that prompted union of the two in the countries of Europe, such conditions certainly do not prevail in the United States. Long ago Cardinal Gibbons expressed the conviction of American Catholics:

"The separation of church and state in this country seems to Catholics the natural, the inevitable, the best conceivable plan, the one that would work best among us, both for the good of religion and of the state. . . . American Catholics rejoice in our separation of church and state; and I can conceive of no combination of circumstances likely to arise which should make a union desirable either to church or to state. . . . For my part, I should be sorry to see the relations of church and state any closer than they are at present. . . . I thank God we have religious liberty."

The conviction so well expressed by the primate of the Catholic Church in America has been deepened, broadened and strengthened by the passing years. Never have I heard a Catholic question it.

Furthermore, Catholics believe in the equality of all churches before the law. Far from seeking to maneuver their church into a position of special privilege, they would resent any effort to do so. Like that of other Americans, their policy is simply: No discrimination, no favoritism; equal treatment and equal rights for all.[29]

In passing, it might be noted here that both Cardinal Gibbons and Professor O'Brien, in common with such other writers as Jefferson, Eckenrode, Billington and others, use the expression "separation of church and state" in its accurate constitutional sense.

Other outstanding members of the Catholic hierarchy whose emphatic statements to the same effect are well known (or can be easily found in any good library in a few minutes) are those of Bishop John England of Charlestown in 1824, characterized by Billington as the "most prominent leader of Catholicism in the generation suc-

[28] "Equal Rights for All Children," *The Christian Century* (May 19, 1948), p. 473.   [29] *Loc. cit.*

ceeding Carroll," [30] Archbishop Spaulding, Archbishop Ireland, and innumerable priests not members of the Hierarchy, such as Father Isaac T. Hecker, the founder of the Paulist Fathers, and laymen, such as Governor Alfred E. Smith in his campaign for the Presidency of 1928. In the absence of any accurate statement to the contrary, space should not be taken for further substantiation on this point.

The one statement used almost without exception by those who attack American Catholicism on the charge that it refuses to accept the American doctrine is to be found in Ryan and Boland's *Catholic Principles of Politics*.[31] This is a book of genuine worth, in most ways and on most pages an altogether admirable text book. It has, however, been the occasion of a great deal of misunderstanding. Passages from this book have been widely misused under the silly assumption that all Catholics believe (or are expected to believe) every statement in it because it is printed with the *Imprimatur* of Cardinal Spellman.

The book itself, since it deals with the subject of politics, on which the Catholic Church never makes *ex cathedra* pronouncements, of necessity discusses many topics on which there is disagreement among Catholic writers. Certain controversies among Catholic philosophers and theologians, such as Thomas Aquinas, Duns Scotus, Bellarmine, Suarez, Cathrein, Meyer, Haller, Taparelli, Cronin, and Costa-Rosetti, are carefully though briefly presented. These differences of opinion, some of them lasting over centuries, ought to demonstrate to any thoughtful reader (who doesn't already know it) that Catholics, both lay and clerical, differ in regard to political philosophy and specific political programs.

Granting that this book has been improperly used by men anxious to make a case against the Catholic Church, the fault has not been theirs alone. Drs. Ryan and Boland have been guilty of some inaccurate and inept statements that should not occur in any volume of such distinguished authorship. For instance, on pages 312-313, this passage occurs:

[30] *Op. cit.*, p. 359.
[31] Ryan, John A., and Boland, Francis J., *Catholic Principles of Politics* (New York, The Macmillan Company, 1943). The earlier edition of this book was called *The State and the Church*. My page references are all to the later book.

The policy of the United States is the most conspicuous and significant. Our Federal and State constitutions forbid the legal establishment of any form of religion, thereby ensuring the separation of Church and State, and apparently making inevitable a policy of neutrality or indifference. Nevertheless, our Federal and State governments have never adopted such a policy. Their attitude has been one of positive friendliness toward religion. Some of the manifestations and expressions of this policy are: The appointment of an annual day of public thanksgiving by the President of the United States and the Governors of the several States; the employment of chaplains to open with prayer the sessions of the National and State legislatures; the provision of chaplains for the Army and Navy; the exemption of church property from taxation; the general policy of promoting the interests of religion, and many other acts and practices, for example, the recent action of the school board of New York City in placing the school buildings at the disposal of the various denominations for the purpose of giving religious instruction.

The confusion here is rather extreme. It is not clear what is meant by "legal establishment of any form of religion." If the authors mean other than a single "national religion" for the United States, they are in error in discussing it as a policy expressed in the federal Constitution. If they do mean the setting up of a single religion in a position of exclusive privilege under the federal government (which is clearly what the First Amendment means) (see p. 96), then their statement that the Federal government has never adopted such a policy is quite untrue. We have certainly never had any other policy.

The authors do not (and obviously cannot) explain how prohibiting Congress from setting up a national church insures "the separation of church and state" in a way that is inconsistent with Thanksgiving Day proclamations, chaplains in Congress, the Army, Navy, tax exemption, and the numerous ways in which the federal government and the government of every state has aided religion in various ways. None of these matters constitutes setting up "an establishment of religion."

Probably one of the most harmful passages in all the writings by American Catholics (harmful to American understanding in general and to Catholics and Catholicism in America in particular, by promoting dissension between Catholics and non-Catholics), quoted or referred to in almost every attack against the Catholic Church in America, is the following:

Suppose that the constitutional obstacle to proscription of non-Catholics has been legitimately removed and they themselves have become numerically insignificant: what then would be the proper course of action for a Catholic State? Apparently, the latter State could logically tolerate only such religious activities as were confined to the members of the dissenting group. It could not permit them to carry on general propaganda nor accord their organization certain privileges that had formerly been extended to all religious corporations, for example, exemption from taxation. While all this is very true in logic and in theory, the event of its practical realization in any State or country is so remote in time and in probability that no practical man will let it disturb his equanimity or affect his attitude toward those who differ from him in religious faith. It is true, indeed, that some zealots and bigots will continue to attack the Church because they fear that some five thousand years hence the United States may become overwhelmingly Catholic and may then restrict the freedom of non-Catholic denominations. Nevertheless, we cannot yield up the principles of eternal and unchangeable truth in order to avoid the enmity of such unreasonable persons. Moreover, it would be a futile policy; for they would not think us sincere.

Therefore, we shall continue to profess the true principles of the relations between Church and State, confident that the great majority of our fellow citizens will be sufficiently honorable to respect our devotion to truth, and sufficiently realistic to see that the danger of religious intolerance toward non-Catholics in the United States is so improbable and so far in the future that it should not occupy their time or attention.[32]

If Fathers Ryan and Boland, in this supposition, with the qualifications of "apparently," "could logically," "in logic and in theory," are only *guessing* as to *what might happen* in an overwhelmingly Catholic United States "some five thousand years hence," they should say so explicitly—and let those who accept their guess place their bets accordingly! If, however, what they are trying to say is that according to the teaching of the Catholic Church which is accepted by all learned Catholic theologians and other scholars, this is what the Catholic Church teaches today, or what informed American Catholics believe today, or what American Catholics must be-

[32] *Ibid.*, pp. 320-321.

lieve five thousand years from now, then Fathers Ryan and Boland are clearly in error. This passage has been repudiated for years by informed Catholic laymen and clergy on the grounds of ambiguity and inaccuracy. In fact it is (in some of its legitimate interpretations) vitally inconsistent with many other passages in the Ryan and Boland book.

Probably the core of the position of Drs. Ryan and Boland that is not accepted by most informed American Catholics, is most sharply expressed in this passage:

> Error has not the same rights as truth. Since the profession and practice of error are contrary to human welfare, how can error have rights? How can the voluntary toleration of error be justified? As we have already pointed out, the men who defend the principle of toleration for all varieties of religious opinion, assume either that all religions are equally true or that the true cannot be distinguished from the false.[33]

The authors of this passage are guilty of an imperfect disjunction. The opposing position is not "that the true cannot be distinguished from the false" by any one under any circumstances, but that making such a distinction in the field of theology is *not the business of civil government*. This is sound Catholic and sound American doctrine.

The Rev. John Courtney Murray, S. J., Editor of *Theological Studies*, discussed the relationship of Church and State at a meeting of the American Catholic Theological Society in Chicago on June 28, 1948. The following is quoted from an editorial comment entitled "Governments and Heresy," [34] which should go far toward correcting the bad impression created by the passages quoted above from Ryan and Boland.

> "The question," said Father Murray "obviously raises the whole problem of the rights and power of government in the field of religion. And as this problem is analogous to the problem of the right and power of the Church in the field of temporal affairs, its solution must depend on, and be made harmonious with, the solution adopted for the latter problem."
>
> It was Father Murray's suggestion that "the asserted right of a 'Catholic government' to repress heresy rests on, and derives from a concept of the power of the Church in temporal matters that is indefensible today."

---

[33] *Ibid.*, p. 318.   [34] *America* (July 10, 1948), p. 323.

Hence a Catholic may correctly assert such a supposed "right," in Father Murray's conclusion, "only if he is speaking relatively," that is to say, in relation to certain specific regimes which have occurred in the past. This hypothesis no longer exists:

"It will not return, and should not return to the world even if, by the grace of God, religious unity should return to the world. Consequently, the right and duty of the Christian prince to suppress heresy, correctly asserted in this hypothesis, but relatively to it, enjoys no absolute and permanent status in virtue of Catholic principle as such."

Jacques Maritain, the distinguished Catholic philosopher, is clear and emphatic in stating a position that is at once the basic American constitutional theory and sound Catholic teaching. He writes: Governments "must cooperate with religion, not by any kind of theocracy or clericalism nor by exercising any sort of pressure in religious matters, but by respecting and facilitating, on the basis of the rights and liberties of each of us, the spiritual activity of the Church and of the diverse religious families which are grouped within the temporal community." [35] Also: "To inject into political society a special or partial common good, the temporal common good of the faithful of one religion, even though it were the true religion, and which would claim for them a privileged position in the state, would be to inject into political society a divisive principle and, to that extent, to jeopardize the temporal common good." [36]

Established churches, Catholic and Protestant, are and always have been *political* creations set up by governments. They put the power of the government, the policeman's gun and club, behind the theology, the doctrine, of the church, which is established by the government. That the government is an incompetent and improper arbiter or teacher in the field of religion is consistent Catholic and American doctrine. The American constitutional position which Catholic statesmen helped to formulate, is that the government must keep hands off religious doctrine, must treat all religions alike, and must allow

[35] Maritain, Jacques, *The Rights of Man and Natural Law* (New York, Charles Scribner's Sons, 1943), p. 22. This whole volume, as well as Maritain's *Christianity and Democracy* (New York, Charles Scribner's Sons, 1945), are illuminating reading for anyone interested in the relation of democracy to Catholic teaching.
[36] *Ibid.*, p. 27.

to all freedom of worship and religious practice. The only accepted limitations on this last is that of preventing practices injurious to others
or repugnant to our constitutional and statutory regulations concerning
immoral or criminal conduct.

This is the doctrine of Jefferson and Madison which has had the
endorsement of Catholics without a significant dissenting voice from
colonial times down to date.

The most accurate and detailed answer to the Ryan and Boland
book on this point which I know of is an article entitled "On Modern
Intolerance." [37] The author is a Catholic attorney in New York City,
active in the National Conference of Christians and Jews, former
teacher of philosophy in Fordham University, and of law in New
York Law School. The article is reproduced in full as Appendix H.

The reader who will turn to that Appendix and read the discussion
of the case of *Minersville School Dist.* v. *Gobitis,* and note carefully
Mr. Justice Frankfurter's language in giving the decision of the Supreme Court in that case, may be interested in putting alongside the
Frankfurter doctrine, and the Ryan-Boland doctrine, the following
statement from F. Ernest Johnson, Director of the Department of Research and Education of the Federal Council of Churches.

One of the expressions most frequently heard in current religious discussions is the "separation of church and state." Those words are commonly taken as defining a principle that is at once basic in the federal
Constitution and central in Protestant doctrine. It should be clear that
a phrase which is taken to define both a secular political principle and
a religious principle is less than truly definitive. I suggest that the basic
principle is freedom, and that the separation of church and state is a
political *policy* designed to effectuate religious freedom on the one hand
and political freedom on the other. As a policy it grows out of practical
necessity due to the fact that our population is religiously heterogeneous.
*If we were all of one faith the distinction between church and state
would be only a functional one: "separation," in its present context,
would be unknown.* (Italics in this sentence mine.)

Thus, espousal of the separation of church and state by a religious
group is not the affirmation of a religious principle, but is rather acceptance of a public policy designed to protect religious freedom and

[37] Vaughan, James N., *The Commonweal* (May 9, 1941), pp. 53-56.

to prevent the domination of the state, at any level, by any one church or combination of churches.[38]

Drs. Ryan, Boland, and Johnson seem to be in close agreement as to what *might* happen in the distant future in a religiously homogeneous America. Justice Frankfurter states the political philosophy which would justify such a program.

The only relevant *American* principle we have in this country (or did have until the Supreme Court issued its ukase on March 8, 1948) is expressed in constitutional provisions in the nation and in all of the states which prohibit the setting up of "an establishment of religion"—an established church—of any kind. We have never had any other sort of "separation of church and state" that anyone can legitimately call either an American or a constitutional principle. This doctrine is not only accepted by all men of all creeds and all parties in America, but would unquestionably be defended vigorously by all Americans. Our modern controversies in this area are all the result of propaganda by private groups and individuals who seek to further their special programs in religion and education by subverting the First Amendment and putting in its place the modern slogan of superlative ambiguity, "the separation of church and state."

[38] Johnson, F. Ernest, "Some Crucial Contemporary Issues," *Social Action*, XIII, No. 9 (November 15, 1947), p. 14.

Chapter 4

THE CURRENT ATTACK ON THE
FIRST AMENDMENT

*T*HE First Amendment is under attack. It has been under attack before, notably in the last half of the last century. From the close of the Civil War until about 1900 there were many revivals of the religious antagonisms that had characterized the "mob era" (see pp. 20-21), 1830 to 1860. These attacks were easily handled by the responsible representatives of the American people in Congress. They were frank, open attempts to amend the Constitution by the only method the American people have ever approved for changing our fundamental national law.

Between 1870 and 1888 no less than eleven different formulations of proposed amendments to put into the Constitution of the United States restrictions on the freedom of the states in such domestic concerns as religion and education, were introduced into Congress.[1] Congress repudiated every one of the proposals. In fact, only one of the eleven passed either house of Congress. That was the Blaine amendment. Like the other ten, this would have prohibited public support by the states, of religion in education. The wording of the different proposals naturally differed somewhat, but each was essentially an attempt to make the Constitution forbid public funds to support religion either in public schools or in private or church schools. While none of them went so far as the demands for the

---

[1] Ames, Herman V., *Proposed Amendments to the Constitution, 1789-1889*, (Washington, D. C., Government Printing Office, 1897), pp. 277-278.

absolute "untouchableness" of religion in the uninhibited phrases of the Supreme Court Justices in the Everson and McCollum cases, they were serious attacks on the work of Jefferson, Madison, and the men of the First Congress.

However, all of these attempts to break down the freedom of the several states to support or cooperate with the forces of religion in the training of American children (or to refuse such support or cooperation if they wish) were *denied* admission to the Constitution by the authorized spokesmen of the American people. These denials all came *after* the Fourteenth Amendment. In spite of this fact, the present Justices of the Supreme Court conclude, without bothering to explain how, that this much repudiated doctrine is now "a basic Constitutional principle!" By this "Alice in Wonderland" type of "interpretation" of Constitutional history, any doctrine that actually passed Congress and was ratified as an amendment to the Constitution by the people of the country, should be incontinently banned by the Supreme Court as clearly unconstitutional!

The recent attacks on the First Amendment are much more dangerous than those of the nineteenth century. Today, atheists and other Americans united for the banishment of religion from American education, if not from American life, have adopted a more subtle strategy. There is now no open attack by way of an attempt to amend the Constitution by the democratic process prescribed by the Founding Fathers and adopted by the American people. The current plan is to destroy the First Amendment by wholly circumventing the will of the American people. The scheme has been to get the Supreme Court *to assume* that the Constitution has all along meant what the people have consistently refused to allow it to mean. This plan narrowly missed success in the decision of the Everson case (Chapter Eleven), but was successful in the dissenting opinions and in the *dicta* in the majority opinion. It succeeded a year later when in the McCollum case (Chapter Twelve) the Court surrendered completely. They gave up the first clause of the First Amendment "without firing a shot" in defense of the work of Jefferson and Madison, as expounded for a century and a half by the great scholars in constitutional law,

Story,[2] Cooley,[3] Corwin,[4] and as defended by the Supreme Court (see Chapter Eight) from the beginning down to the fumbling in the Everson case and the surrender in the McCollum case.

On May 2, 1947, Congressman Joseph K. Bryson of South Carolina, following in the footsteps of many others, as referred to earlier, introduced into the House of Representatives a bill (H.J.Res. 187) proposing "an amendment to the Constitution of the United States providing that neither Congress nor any of the several States shall aid any educational institution wholly or in part under sectarian control." When the Eightieth Congress adjourned in 1948, this bill died in committee.

Recently a new organization, "Protestants and Other Americans United for Separation of Church and State," has appeared, essentially offering its services as the spearhead of the current campaign. Its purpose is expressed as follows: " 'Protestants and Other Americans United' is determined to assert its full strength to the end that there shall be no more breaches in this wall [separating Church and State]; that the breaches already made shall be repaired, and that the complete separation of church and state in an undivided state-supported educational system shall be maintained." [5]

When the January 12, 1948, *Manifesto* of this organization appeared (following two preliminary press releases in both of which those Americans who differed with the new group were referred to as subversive of the Constitution), I wrote to the six signers of the *Manifesto* to ask if they would personally support the Bryson Bill and advocate its support by "Protestants and Other Americans United." Four of the six signers answered "no" to both questions; one, Dr. Edwin McNeil Poteat, answered "yes" to both, and the sixth, Dr. John A. Mackay, did not answer at all.

---

[2] Story, Joseph, *Commentaries on the Constitution* (Boston, Hilliard, Gray & Co., 1891), 5th ed., Vol. 11, sec. 1873.

[3] Cooley, Thomas M., *Constitutional Limitations* (Boston, Little, Brown & Company, 1878), 4th ed., pp. 584 ff.

[4] Corwin, Edward S., *The Constitution—What it Means Today* (Princeton, Princeton University Press, 1947), 9th ed., pp. 154-156.

[5] *A Manifesto* (Washington, D. C. Protestants and Other Americans United, 1948), p. 6.

There was in these letters no dissent from the objectives of the Bryson Bill. These leaders, however, working (so they say) for the protection of the great constitutional principle of complete separation of church and state (which is not in the Constitution), explicitly decline to work for their objectives *by the democratic process prescribed by the Constitution for its amendment.* They may have learned that throughout our history the American people have refused to allow any amendment embodying the core of their doctrine to be put into the Constitution. If our history is good evidence, the people of the country will have none of it. The plan is, therefore, to get it by Supreme Court edict without consulting the will of the people.

The questions I asked, with the comments and answers, follow:

1. Do you personally wish this bill adopted and submitted to the States for ratification?

2. Do you approve of support of this bill by "Protestants and Other Americans United for Separation of Church and State"?

	Question 1	Question 2
Bishop G. Bromley Oxnam of New York, in a letter dated January 28, 1948, used the following phrases: ". . . a conference was held in Washington, attended by a number of religious leaders all interested in the objective. They reached the conclusion that an attempt to amend the Constitution was not the way to get the results. Any amendment would be interpreted by the Supreme Court. The Supreme Court can at the present time give such interpretation to the amendments to the Constitution that involve the separation of church and state as to reach the same end. It was their judgment, therefore, that it would be much wiser to follow through the matter of cases that look to Supreme Court decision upon this	No	No

issue than to attempt a Constitutional amendment."

"Whether it [Protestants and Other Americans United] would support a movement to amend the Constitution to achieve this result I do not know. I think not."

Dr. *Charles Clayton Morrison*, Editor Emeritus, *The Christian Century* (Feb. 24, 1948):	No	No

". . . a confession that the Constitution does not already take care of these matters."

Dr. *Louis D. Newton*, President Southern Baptist Convention (Jan. 30, 1948):	No	No

". . . frankly doubtful whether it could be put through at this time and to press for its enactment without success would hurt the cause of religious freedom."

Dr. *Joseph Martin Dawson*, Executive Secretary Joint Conference, Committee on Public Relations, Baptists of the United States (Jan. 31, 1948):	No	No

"I had lunch with Mr. Bryson today and we discussed the situation. The new organization, *Protestants and Other Americans United for Separation of Church and State,* through its legal committee's advice, decided for strategic reasons not to push the amendment plan for the present. Mr. Bryson has surrendered none of his convictions as to the claims of his bill, but is disposed to abide by the judgment of the new organization."

It is evident from the above phrases that the open deliberation and decision prescribed by the Constitution, and followed in the last great period of attack on the First Amendment before the current one, is being avoided here. This circumventing of the democratic process is explained as "for strategic reasons," because it is "frankly doubtful whether it [a Constitutional Amendment] could be put through at this time," because it is "not the way to get the results," and is held to be "much wiser" to "look to Supreme Court decisions upon this issue than to attempt a Constitutional Amendment." In the light of a century and a half of American history, which this program seeks to overrule, it can probably be defended simply as strategy, but I submit that it constitutes a clear threat to the integrity of the Bill of Rights, to the democratic method of deciding public questions, and even to constitutional government itself.

Incidentally it is interesting to compare this strategy with the following quotation from Mr. Dawson's recent book.[6] He writes that non-Catholics "possess stupendous and abundant means for safeguarding the Constitution. Protestants and Other Americans United may solve the problem [of furnishing a central organization to promote and defend the principle of separation of church and state]. Protestants alone, if they but worked at the job together, have enough churches, enough publications, and enough schools [7] to keep America true to its best traditions."

Recently a lawyer of position and influence answered me as follows:

I am not concerned with what either Jefferson or Madison thought. I am concerned with the purpose of this provision as that exists here and now. I am interested in what has happened in the years since 1791 to give clear purpose to this particular amendment, and the one authoritative body whom we have entrusted with the matter of saying what the purpose of the Constitution is, is the Supreme Court.

My lawyer friend said "purpose," not "effect," in both clauses of this sentence. The *purpose* or *intent* of any passage in the Constitution could come only from the thought of the men responsible for the passage when it was written, and could not be altered by the thinking of men a century and a half later.

Shortly after this encounter with the lawyer, I received a letter

[6] Dawson, Joseph Martin, *Separate Church and State Now* (New York, Richard R. Smith, 1948), p. 85.
[7] Does he mean the public schools? These, if the various state constitutions are being observed, ceased to be Protestant schools something over 50 or 75 years ago.

from another person of position and influence. The closing statement of this letter is: "The naïve attempts now being made by Catholics to tell us what the Founding Fathers meant when they wrote the First Amendment are beside the point." I am not certain whether my correspondent intended to imply that it would be all right for non-Catholics to discuss the meaning of the Founding Fathers, or simply that the work of the Fathers on the Constitution is irrelevant *per se.*

If the attitude expressed in these statements is accepted and allowed to control, we have already lost our liberties. In such circumstances the Supreme Court is free to make the Constitution mean whatever the Justices wish it to mean. The intent, the purpose, of the American people, as expressed in the constitutional provisions they have adopted and ratified, are irrelevant. They have no force or effect. We are essentially in the position of the Russian peasants under the Politburo. We shall then have, from now on, only the liberties which are granted us from week to week by the majority of the Supreme Court. We shall no longer have constitutional government. We shall no longer be able to use the democratic process to achieve the purposes of the American people. The carefully expressed will of the people will be no longer binding on the Supreme Court.

When one considers that "what Madison and Jefferson thought" was expressed in the First Amendment, that its *purpose* was to express that thought, that its wording was in large part Madison's work, this situation is rather frightening. If we are to depart so far from our history, from our theory of constitutional government, from the very meaning and purpose of a written constitution, as to say that the "purpose" of any passage in the Constitution becomes whatever the majority of the Supreme Court think it *ought to be,* the days of constitutional government are over.

If what the American people have deliberately put into the Constitution is to be disregarded by the Supreme Court, and its exact opposite (which the American people have specifically and repeatedly refused to allow to go into the Constitution) is to be enforced simply because the new doctrine fits the "zeal" and the "prepossessions" of the men who happen to be on the Court at any given time, then the Constitution ceases to be living law and becomes only an outmoded historical curiosity. So long as the American people accept the perversion of history, constitutional provisions, and the English language, which pervade the opinions in the Everson and McCollum cases, they are consenting to live under the dictatorship of the Supreme Court. Our country will have effectively dropped the control of a written constitution.

Most of the current controversies are concerned with the first phrase of the religious clause; namely, "Congress shall make no law respecting an establishment of religion." The people who in recent years have gone about the country proclaiming that this language creates a complete and absolute separation of church and state have in few instances made any attempt to justify that interpretation. They simply assume it and proclaim it. Probably the most important defense of that position is in the dissenting opinion in the Everson bus case written by Justice Rutledge. This opinion is important only on account of its source and the acclaim given it by those with whose emotions it is in harmony. It is a thoroughly specious argument.

The basic position of Justice Rutledge is stated in these words: The Amendment's purpose was . . .

Necessarily to uproot all such relationships (as those of the establishment of a single sect, creed, or religion)
to create a complete and permanent separation of the spheres of religious activity and civil authority by comprehensively forbidding every form of public aid or support for religion.

He speaks of the

threat to maintaining that complete and permanent separation of religion and civil power which the First Amendment commands is through use of the taxing power to support religion, religious establishments, or establishments having a religious foundation whatever their form or special religious function.

The Amendment, according to Justice Rutledge,

torbids state support, financial or other, of religion in any guise, form or degree

outlaws all use of public funds for religious purposes.[8]

The Everson bus case is covered in detail in Chapter Eleven. This case is referred to here in order to give the essence of the doctrine in the Rutledge opinion. This is the doctrine of *The Christian Century*, and the new organization, "Protestants and Other Americans United." It is, so far as I am able to find out, the aim of the promoters of the modern slogan "the complete separation of church and state." The Rutledge opinion is the most elaborate and the most famous attempt to justify that slogan that I have found. It has been hailed as a marvelous argument, sound, logical, and scholarly. It is (as shown in Chapter Eleven) an almost perfect example of the opposite of all these. It has all of the externals and none of the realities of scholarship.

The most serious danger in the Rutledge opinion is that it will be widely accepted by the uncritical and the uninformed. This exact effect has been promoted by certain publicists and religious and educational spokesmen who should know better. These propagandists have apparently allowed their ardent devotion to certain religious and educational theories to black out a large part of any relevant knowledge of history and constitutional law which they may have possessed. An extreme instance is Max Lerner's signed editorials in *PM* of February 20 and May 18, 1947. In the first he says: "At once the deepest and most brilliant treatment of the whole issue is in Justice Rutledge's long thirty-five page dissenting opinion. In the decade since Justice Brandeis' resignation from the Court, I do not recall an opinion which more satisfyingly combined historical thoroughness [sic], legal acumen and logic, and moral passion."

In the second editorial Mr. Lerner (in criticizing the Aiken Bill and its predecessor, the Murray-Morse-Pepper Bill, both of which included federal aid to parochial schools), protests against a "compromise" . . . "on the question of what the Constitution calls 'an establishment of religion.'" He would rule out all parochial schools because "they are part of a religious establishment." Such swallowing

[8] 330 U. S. 1 at 31, 32, 33, 44.

whole of the Rutledge doctrine which is denied by some 160 years of recorded American history to the contrary, is certainly no subject for compromise. But relief ought to be obtained by an hour or two spent in reading in any good library.

The refutation of the Rutledge doctrine can be found in the following sections of our history: in the records of Jefferson (Chapter Five), of Madison (Chapter Six), of Congress (Chapter Seven), the Supreme Court (Chapter Eight), of the several states (Chapter Nine). It can also be found in the official acts of all Presidents of the United States and in the writing of the leading American scholars in the field of Constitutional law (see pp. 62-65).

The controversies of today in regard to relations of government to religion are primarily the result of the attempt to substitute the slogan "Complete separation of church and state" for the specific language of the First Amendment. The slogan is in direct conflict with the Amendment. The attempted substitution violates the integrity of the Bill of Rights by amending the Constitution by "judicial legislation" rather than by the constitutional method contained in the Constitution itself. This attempt plans to circumvent the democratic process adopted by the people of the United States, and to accomplish its purpose by getting the majority of the Justices of the Supreme Court to reverse the clear expression of the American people in every record which our history affords. It plans to make the Constitution mean something which defies not only the language and the purpose of the Founding Fathers but the record of the chosen representatives of the American people in Congress from 1791 to 1948, and of the Supreme Court down to the decision in the McCollum case on March 8, 1948.

In addition to this main attack on the First Amendment, there has recently been tried a minor attempt to capture or destroy the first clause of the First Amendment. Let us dispose of this skirmish first before going on to consider the main attack.

The skirmish is an attempt to give the word "respecting" a new and unwarranted meaning. The result would be to develop a new species of ambiguity, and so add to the widespread confusion that has already resulted from the recent attempts to substitute the words "complete separation of church and state" for the language of the Constitution. This new attempt to mangle the First Amendment in a way that would leave it so vague that no one could possibly tell what it meant, was given formal expression in an address delivered by Dr. Charles Clayton Morrison, formerly editor of *The Christian Century*, at the International Convention of Disciples of Christ, Buffalo, New York, July 30, 1947.[9]

Dr. Morrison brings out his new tactic for amending the Constitution of the United States in the following passage:

> The Constitution does not merely forbid an *establishment* of religion; it forbids the making of "any law *respecting* the establishment of religion"—that is, pointing in the direction of such establishment, or carrying implications that might develop into such establishment. Any law, or any official act in the administration of law, which tends toward the establishment of religion, or recognizes a particular religious organization as having a claim to a special relationship to the state, is a violation of the constitutional prohibition *respecting* the establishment of religion, and a violation of the constitutional guarantee of full religious liberty.[10]

Imagine a group of constitution makers led by James Madison writing a provision for the United States Constitution in language which meant: "Congress shall make no law pointing in the direction of, or carrying implications that might develop into, an establishment of religion"!

All Congress was trying to do (according to Madison, his contemporaries and the legal scholars and historians) was to comply with the state resolutions and petitions asking them to keep Congress off the subject of an established religion for the nation as a whole, and leave the relations of government and religion to the individual states. (See page 112.) So the First Amendment was written to forbid Congress to touch the subject. This left the states wholly free to do as they pleased. Dr. Morrison and "Protestants and Other Americans United" do not like this arrangement. They therefore try to change the First Amendment to admit the old "This is the first step" argument, under which anyone can always oppose anything

---

[9] *The Separation of Church and State in America*, a pamphlet (Indianapolis, 1947).   [10] *Ibid.*, p. 4.

which he does not like but which he is unable to attack openly and directly.

The idea that the word *respecting* means "pointing in the direction of" or "tending toward" or "carrying implications that might develop into," is not supported by the dictionaries. According to Webster's International Dictionary *respecting* means "considering; in view of, with regard or relation to; regarding; concerning." In other words, the first clause of the First Amendment forbade Congress to make a law regarding or concerning "an establishment of religion."

I find no suggestion either in Webster's or other dictionaries, or in Webster's *Dictionary of Synonyms*, or in other authorities on synonyms, which indicates any authority whatever for Dr. Morrison's adventure in semantics. Webster's *Dictionary of Synonyms* gives as synonyms for the word *respecting*: "concerning, regarding, about, anent."

I think those who are acquainted with James Madison's power in the use of words and his facility particularly in expressing exact meanings in constitutions and laws, will agree that he would not use the word "respecting" when he meant "pointing in the direction of." Such a prohibition would be as vague and ambiguous as a provision that we should have separation of church and state in the United States. This strange new theory concerning the word "respecting" received endorsement in a long editorial in *The Christian Century*,[11] and also in the *Manifesto* of "Protestants and Other Americans United[12] for the Separation of Church and State" (which was signed by Dr. Morrison among others).

In the *Manifesto* the word *respecting* is interpreted as meaning "leading toward," which is of course a perfectly good synonym for "pointing in the direction of or tending toward," but for the word *respecting* it is not a synonym at all. The editorial of November 26 has a number of very accurate sentences which clash directly with this particular thesis. It says, for instance, that "the first clause (respecting an establishment of religion) is sharply specific." It is indeed. Why destroy its admirable specificity by dropping Madison's good old word *respecting*, concerning the meaning of which there need be no possible doubt by anyone who has access to a dictionary,

[11] November 26, 1947.   [12] January 12, 1948.

and substitute therefor a thoroughly vague and ambiguous phrase such as "tending toward," or "leading toward"?

The editorial of November 26 says further:

At first glance it seems that the fathers chose a rather awkward way of phrasing the prohibition of a religious establishment. Why did they not say merely, and more forthrightly, "Congress shall not establish any religion by law"? The key to the answer is in the word *respecting* an establishment of religion. This word means something. It meant something to the drafters of the first amendment. It means "pertaining to," or "tending toward," an establishment of religion.

The fathers did not prohibit an establishment of religion. They prohibited any law about an establishment of religion in the United States, *either for it or against it*. If anyone wants an elaborate discussion of how Congress came to adopt the words finally used, they should read the *Annals* of the First Congress. We can all agree that the word *respecting* means something. In fact most words that James Madison ever used meant something. If one is in any doubt about what it means why not refer to Madison's statement of his purpose or consult a dictionary? Such recourse will discover that it means "concerning" or "about." That it does not mean "tending toward." *Respecting* is a specific, easily understood word. "Tending toward" simply means anything at all that is "looking in the direction of."

The main attack on the First Amendment advanced in all proclamations that we have a great constitutional principle of complete separation of church and state, is an attempt to make the phrase "an establishment of religion" in the Constitution mean, in Justice Rutledge's words, "religion, religious establishments or establishments having a religious purpose whatever their form or special religious function." The basis of this position, quite literally the only justification for it in any Supreme Court opinion, proclamation, article or letter to the press, which I have been able to find, is that this was *the intention* or *the purpose* of Jefferson, Madison, and others who were responsible for the First Amendment of the Constitution.

If "an establishment of religion" can be made to mean this in the Constitution, and If the Fourteenth Amendment can be made to prohibit the states from having a law or constitutional provision concerning religion, or religious organizations, or institutions, then the secularists, atheists, and others united, will have succeeded in wiping out *in toto* the first clause of the First Amendment as planned, adopted, and ratified by the Founders of this Republic, and as observed and interpreted by the individual states, the Congress of the United States, the Presidents of the United States, and the Supreme Court of the United States from 1791 to March 8, 1948.

The essential question, therefore, in all the current controversies in this area is simply the meaning of the phrase "an establishment of religion" in the First Amendment. This was the vital question before the Supreme Court in both the Everson and the McCollum cases. How the Supreme Court dodged and mishandled this question is covered in Chapters Eleven and Twelve.

My thesis is that the words "establishment of religion" meant to Madison, Jefferson, the members of the First Congress, the historians, the legal scholars, and substantially all Americans who were at all familiar with the Constitution until very recent years, *a formal, legal union of a single church or religion with government, giving the one church or religion an exclusive position of power and favor over all other churches or denominations.*

The proof of this thesis runs through a large part of this volume. It is summarized here under twelve headings:

1. *Petitions.* The First Amendment was written in compliance with resolutions and petitions from individual states asking for an amendment to the Constitution which would prevent one sect or denomination from having a position of preference or privilege over all other sects or denominations (see p. 112). It seems a fair inference, which is completely supported by Madison's specific statement in the First Congress, that the First Amendment was designed to accomplish exactly what was asked for by the petitions which occasioned it.

2. *Language.* The language of the First Amendment, to anyone familiar with the vocabulary of the eighteenth century and earlier, indicates the carrying out of the same purpose. That this is the meaning of the language of the first clause of the First Amendment is

backed up by the dictionaries and encyclopedias. *The Encyclopedia Britannica* [13] has this to say about "establishment."

In a special sense the word is applied, . . . to certain religious bodies in their relation to the state.

Perhaps the best definition that can be given, and which will cover all cases, is that establishment implies the existence of some definite and distinctive relation between the state and a religious society (or conceivably more than one) other than that which is shared in by other societies of the same general character. . . . It is not concerned with what pertains to the religious society *qua* society, or with what is common to all religious societies, but with what is exceptional. It denotes any special connection with the state, or privileges and responsibilities before the law, possessed by one religious society to the exclusion of others; in a word establishment is of the nature of a monopoly.

3. *The Context of the Times.*   The context of the times indicates the same meaning of this phrase. Jefferson and Madison and a great many others were opposed to established churches. Of the nine established Protestant churches in the colonies at the beginning of the Revolution four had been eliminated by 1789. Five were still in existence. These established churches had been either Episcopalian or Congregationalist. There was a widespread fear, quite natural under the circumstances, among the members of other churches that if we had a single church established by the United States government it would probably be one of these two. In addition to those members of these two churches who were opposed on principle to the establishment of any church, their own or any other, the establishment of a national church was generally opposed by the members of other churches of the country. The Catholics (most of whom lived in Maryland) under the leadership of Bishop John Carroll and his cousins, Daniel and Charles, who were both active in the First Congress in procuring the First Amendment were for the prohibition of a national establishment. The Presbyterians under the leadership of John Witherspoon (who came to this country after fighting the established Presbyterian church of Scotland), and the Baptists under the leadership of Isaac Bacchus, were quite naturally opposed to a national establishment of religion.

[13] Ed. 14, Vol. VIII.

However, in Virginia when the separation of the Anglican church from the government of Virginia was being debated, the Methodists and the Presbyterians seem not to have been as unanimously and consistently for the abolition of establishment as the Baptists and the Catholics. According to Eckenrode,[14] "The establishment was not without its defenders (in the first Virginia State Assembly, October 1776). The Methodists who seldom interfered as a religious organization in political affairs, asked, on October 28, for the retention of the state church: 'We therefore pray that as the Church of England ever hath been, so it may still continue to be established'." Madison in a letter to Monroe, dated April 12, 1785 (quoted by Eckenrode) [15] wrote: "The Episcopal people are generally for it (assessment) though I think the zeal of some of them has cooled. The laity of the other sects are generally unanimous on the other side. So are all the clergy, except the Presbyterians who seem as ready to set up an establishment which is to take them in as they were to pull down that which shut them out."

The context of the times further indicates that the promoters of the First Amendment had no idea of making it a provision for the removal of religion from education, or for the prohibition of public financial support of religious educational institutions. None of the men of that time knew anything about education that was not associated with religion. Certainly if James Madison had intended to write into the Constitution such an unheard of and revolutionary doctrine as the absolute prohibition of any contact between government and religious education, he would have said so in clear constitutional language. It seems obvious that if such a thought ever occurred to the authors of the First Amendment they rejected it, and it follows that if the idea did not occur to them, or, if having thought of it they rejected it, it is impossible intelligently to conclude that they intended to express it when they said something else.

4. *Madison's Words.* The purpose or intention of the First Amendment insofar as it refers to an establishment of religion was positively and clearly stated by Madison in the First Congress as re-

14 *Separation of Church and State in Virginia.* p. 47.
15 *Ibid.*, pp. 90-91.

ported in the *Annals* of Congress (see p. 96). This alone should be conclusive.

5. *Jefferson's Words.* The written words of Thomas Jefferson support this interpretation and only this interpretation. No Supreme Court Justice, nor any propagandist off the bench, has ever, so far as I could find out, cited a single instance in which Thomas Jefferson ever used the words "established church," "establishment of religion," or simply the common contraction, "establishment" or "disestablishment" to mean other than an exclusive arrangement such as I have stated above. For instance: In his *Notes on Virginia, Query XVII,*[16] Jefferson wrote:

But every State, says an inquisitor, has established some religion. No two, say I, have established the same. Is this a proof of the infallibility of establishments? Our sister States of Pennsylvania and New York, however, have long subsisted without any establishment at all. The experiment was new and doubtful when they made it. It has answered beyond conception. They flourish infinitely. Religion is well supported; of various kinds, indeed, but all good enough; all sufficient to preserve peace and order.

New York and Pennsylvania had no "establishment," but they had religion, religious organizations and institutions. They had religious education, and, as throughout the whole country at that time, substantially no education not under religious auspices.

6. *The Virginia Legislation.* The implications of the Virginia legislation and remarks about it, particularly by Madison and Jefferson, bear out the meaning of "an establishment of religion" which I have used above. As before stated, small fragments of Jefferson's *Bill for Religious Freedom* have been wrenched from context and improperly used to bolster up the Rutledge doctrine (see pp. 75 ff.). Also Madison's *Memorial & Remonstrance* has been misreported and misinterpreted for the same purpose as shown on page 198. Madison's *Memorial & Remonstrance*, as clearly stated in the document itself, was in opposition to the establishment of the Christian religion as the state religion of Virginia. He was remonstrating against an ex-

[16] Padover, Saul K., *The Complete Jefferson* (New York, Duell, Sloan & Pearce, Inc., 1943), p. 676.

clusive position of favor for the Christian religion, as against all other religions. Not only did Madison say this plainly in the *Memorial* itself, but Jefferson said the same in the following passage: [17]

The bill for establishing religious freedom, the principles of which had, to a certain degree, been enacted before, I had drawn in all the latitude of reason and right. It still met with opposition; but, with some mutilations in the preamble, it was finally passed; and a singular proposition proved that its protection of opinion was meant to be universal. Where the preamble declares, that coercion is a departure from the plan of the holy author of our religion, an amendment was proposed, by inserting the word "Jesus Christ," so that it should read, "a departure from the plan of Jesus Christ, the holy author of our religion"; the insertion was rejected by a great majority, in proof that they meant *to comprehend, within the mantle of its protection, the Jew and the Gentile, the Christian and Mahometan, the Hindoo, and Infidel of every denomination.*

Conclusive evidence to the same effect is found elaborately stated by Eckenrode.[18] Justice Rutledge apparently knew of Eckenrode's brochure. He quoted a *part of a sentence as a whole, independent sentence* from Eckenrode interpreting Madison on Virginia legislation in order to show what Madison meant, not in Virginia legislation, but in the First Amendment. But Justice Rutledge *did not* quote what Madison himself said he meant in the First Amendment (see p. 96). The whole sentence in Eckenrode from which Judge Rutledge quoted the last part only, beginning with the second "if", indicates, as Eckenrode does throughout, that Madison's *Memorial & Remonstrance* was an attack upon "an establishment of religion" in the exact sense in which I am using the phrase. The sentence reads as follows:

The principle of assessment is wrong: if it were lawful to establish Christianity as the state religion, it would be lawful to establish a single sect, and if it were lawful to impose a small tax for religion, the admission would pave the way for oppressive levies.[19]

---

[17] *Ibid.*, p. 1147.
[18] Eckenrode, Hamilton J., *Separation of Church and State in Virginia* in Virginia State Library report (Richmond, Davis Bottom, Supt. of Public Printing, 1910). See particularly p. 85.   [19] *Ibid.*, p. 105.

Again Eckenrode said "an objection to assessment was found in the fact that the bill provided for no religion but Christianity, excluding Jews and Mohammedans." [20]

Throughout his work Eckenrode uses the word "establishment" alone to mean clearly the exclusive position of privilege which the Anglican church held in Virginia until that church was "separated" from the State of Virginia. In fact Eckenrode's title *The Separation of Church and State in Virginia* is a perfect example of the accurate use of the expression, "separation of church and state." There had been a formal, legal bond or union ·between the Anglican church and the government of Virginia which gave the members of the Anglican church a special status of privilege enjoyed by the members of no other church. By state legislation this union was broken and the church and the state were separated. But as Eckenrode remarks [21] and as is proved beyond question in discussing current relations between government and religion in Virginia (see pp. 146 ff.) "the question of the existing relation of church and state had not been entirely settled" by the separation of the Anglican church from the government of Virginia.

7. *The Record of Congress.* The record of the Congress of the United States, which has been subject to the restrictions of the First Amendment since 1791, demonstrates that the Congress of the United States has never interpreted the First Amendment in terms of the Rutledge doctrine in a single instance from 1791 down to its adjournment on June 20, 1948 (see Chapter Seven).

8. *The Record of the Presidents.* The official records of Jefferson and Madison as President of the United States constitute positive proof that neither Jefferson nor Madison believed the First Amendment meant what the Justices of the Supreme Court in 1947-8 say was the intention of Madison and Jefferson that it should mean (see Chapters Five and Six). Every President in our history has used public funds in aid of religion (see pp. 115 ff.).

9. *The Record of the States.* The record of the individual states (as shown in Chapter Nine) is proof that the First Amendment has never been interpreted by any state in the Union to mean what the

[20] *Ibid.*, p. 107.   [21] *Ibid.*, p. 116.

Justices of the Supreme Court have recently said it has meant from the beginning.

10. *Historians.* Historians, secular and religious, have for centuries used the expression "establishment of religion," "established church" or just "establishment" or "disestablishment" as defined on page 56. I have not been able to discover a single instance to the contrary. Since the subject is mentioned in substantially all the works on American history, the history of England, and of all European countries, it seems unnecessary to take the space to cite the literally innumerable examples of such use of this term in the total absence of any instance to the contrary.[21a]

It is true that many writers have used the phrase "separation of church and state" accurately as Eckenrode used it above. Quite a few have used the expression "complete separation of church and state" when they were obviously referring to the ending of, or the prevention of, a formal exclusively favored position of a single religion. This use of the phrase with the modifier "complete" has caused some readers to assume that such writers have intended by the phrase "complete separation of church and state" the whole of the Rutledge doctrine. Doubtless had these writers used instead of the word "complete" the word "clear" or "positive," "definite" or "clean-cut," they could have avoided the misinterpretation. However, I have found no instance of this use in the writings of a responsible scholar in which it is not clear from the context that he was intending to say that the ending or prevention of a favored status for one church or religion was a *completely* accomplished job. These writers were not saying that cooperative contacts between government and religion were prohibited over the total, *complete* field of possible contacts.

11. *The Legal Scholars.* The outstanding scholars in the field of constitutional law in the United States are in agreement in regard to the meaning that I have indicated above: exclusive preference and privilege granted to one church or one religion by the government.

This places all of America's most distinguished authorities on con-

[21a] For typical, clear, modern usage by eminent historians see Nevins and Commager, A Short History of the United States, pp. 21-27, 78, 112-114.

stitutional law in direct opposition to the position taken by Supreme Court Justices in the McCollum and Everson cases. In discussing the religious clauses of the First Amendment, Mr. Justice Story writing in 1833 in his *Commentaries on the Constitution of the United States,* made it clear that the First Amendment was not designed to be unfriendly to religion, but rather to preserve an equality between sects, and most important, to leave the matter of religion entirely to the states. Story stated, in part:

every American colony, from its foundation down to the revolution, with the exception of Rhode Island, if, indeed, that State be an exception, did openly, by the whole course of its laws and institutions, support and sustain in some form the Christian religion; and almost invariably gave a peculiar sanction to some of its fundamental doctrines. And this has continued to be the case in some of the States down to the present period [1833] without the slightest suspicion that it was against the principles of public law or republican liberty.[22]

Story then sets out in the same section enough of the Massachusetts Bill of Rights to show "its pointed affirmation of the duty of government to support Christianity, and the reasons for it." This Bill of Rights provided in part that

the legislature shall from time to time authorize and require, the several towns, parishes, etc., to make suitable provision at their own expense for the institution of the public worship of God, and for the support and maintenance of public Protestant teachers of piety, religion, and morality, in all cases where such provision shall not be made voluntarily.[23]

The author continues:

Probably at the time of the adoption of the Constitution, and of the amendment to it now under consideration, the general if not the universal sentiment in America was, that Christianity ought to receive encouragement from the state so far as was not incompatible with the private rights of conscience and the freedom of religious worship. An attempt to level all religions, and to make it a matter of state policy to hold all in utter indifference, would have created universal disapprobation, if not universal indignation.[24]

[22] Ed. 5 (1891), Vol. II, sec. 1873.
[23] *Loc. cit.*   [24] *Ibid.*, sec. 1874.

Coming to the "real object of the amendment," Story says:

The real object of the amendment was not to countenance, much less to advance, Mahometanism, or Judaism, or infidelity, by prostrating Christianity; but to exclude all rivalry among Christian sects, and *to prevent any national ecclesiastical establishment which should give to a hierarchy the exclusive patronage of the national government.* It thus cuts off the means of religious persecution (the vice and pest of former ages), and of the subversion of the rights of conscience in matters of religion, which had been trampled upon almost from the days of the Apostles to the present age.[25] [Italics mine.]

Nowhere in Story's work is there even an intimation that the purpose or effect of the First Amendment was to prevent the use of public property for the equal benefit of all religions.

Judge Thomas M. Cooley in discussing the meaning of an establishment of religion in *state constitutions* wrote as follows:

The [State] legislatures have not been left at liberty to effect a union of Church and State, or to establish preferences by law in favor of any one religious persuasion or mode of worship. There is not complete religious liberty where any one sect is favored by the State and given an advantage by law over other sects. Whatever establishes a distinction against one class or sect is, to the extent to which the distinction operates unfavorably, a persecution. The extent of the discrimination is not material to the principle; it is enough that it creates an inequality of right or privilege.[26]

The subsequent paragraphs in which Cooley summarizes the explicit provisions in state constitutions against state aid to sectarian religion and sectarian education are no part of the author's discussion of a law respecting "an establishment of religion," thus plainly indicating his view that such subjects were not included under a prohibition of an establishment of religion.

Edward S. Corwin states:

Congress may make *no law at all* "respecting an establishment of religion," nor yet "prohibiting the free exercise" of religious belief; and it may not

25 *Ibid.*, sec. 1877.
26 Cooley, Thomas M., *Constitutional Limitations* (Boston, Little, Brown & Company, 1878), 4th ed., p. 584.

make laws which *abridge* "the freedom of speech or of the press" or the rights of assembly and petition.[27]

Also:

> An establishment of religion means a state church, such as for instance existed in Massachusetts for more than forty years after the adoption of the Constitution.[28]

12. *The Supreme Court.* The record of the Supreme Court in regard to the first clause of the First Amendment is given in some detail in Chapter Eight. The record is clear and consistent whenever the Court had occasion to touch upon the meaning of "an establishment of religion" down to the Everson bus case. In that case the *dicta* of the majority opinion, and the whole of the dissenting opinion of Justice Rutledge, are based on misreporting and misinterpretation of Madison and Jefferson, and erroneous references to previous Supreme Court cases. Additional light on the record of the Supreme Court will be found in Chapters Ten, Eleven and Twelve, on the Fourteenth Amendment, and the Everson and McCollum cases. I believe that it is thoroughly proved in those chapters that the position taken in the McCollum decision in regard to the meaning of "an establishment of religion" in the First Amendment rests only on the misreporting and misrepresentation of the records of Madison and Jefferson, and on what Mr. Justice Jackson referred to in his strangely concurring opinion as the "prepossessions" of the Justices and their "zeal" for their own "ideas of what is good in public instruction."

[27] Corwin, Edward S., *The Constitution—What It Means Today* (Princeton, Princeton University Press, 1947), 9th ed., p. 154.
[28] *Ibid.*, pp. 155-156.

Chapter 5

THOMAS JEFFERSON ON GOVERNMENT AND RELIGION

$\mathcal{T}$HOMAS JEFFERSON was a prodigious writer of letters on public questions and an uncommonly active citizen and public official. He held public office throughout most of his active life, and wrote voluminously on all sorts of topics. Outside of official documents his principal writings consisted of some twenty-five thousand letters.[1]

Consequently, there is no good excuse for anyone who can read to remain long in doubt about Thomas Jefferson's attitude on the important public questions of his time. Clearly the relation of government to religion was one such question. To Jefferson it was one of the most important. It was so much in his thoughts, and was dealt with so often in official documents, letters, and in official actions, that the almost unvarying misrepresentation of Jefferson on this subject by those who seek to get rid of the doctrine of the First Amendment is particularly shocking.

Three basic principles which Jefferson sought constantly to promote and to protect were democratic political decisions, freedom and equality in religion, and authority in the several states in such areas as religion and education ("domestic concerns") rather than in the federal government. The program of those enlisted today under the modern slogan "complete separation of church and state" is subversive of all three of these principles. Yet there is scarcely a manifesto writer, editor, or a Supreme Court Justice supporting this

[1] Padover, Saul K. (Ed.), *Democracy by Thomas Jefferson* (New York, D. Appleton-Century Co., 1939), p. 1.

propaganda today who does not seek to make Jefferson the father of his thought.

JEFFERSON ON STATE VS. FEDERAL AUTHORITY

Jefferson was a sincere believer in state authority in domestic affairs and a determined opponent of encroachment upon the state authority by the federal government. In his *Solemn Declaration and Protest of December 1825,* in which he was dealing with the alleged right of the federal government to build roads, canals, and other improvements within the territory of the states, particularly Virginia, he wrote as follows:

They (the states) entered into a compact (which is called the Constitution of the United States of America), by which.they agreed to unite in a single government as to their relations with each other, and with foreign nations, and as to certain other articles particularly specified. They retained at the same time, each to itself, the other rights of independent government, comprehending mainly their domestic interests.[2]

Farther in the same document he spoke of "the rights retained by the States, rights which they have never yielded, and which this state shall never voluntarily yield."

He writes in a letter to William Johnson, 1833,. "I believe the States can best govern our home concerns and the General Government our foreign ones." [3]

In the document known as the *Kentucky Resolutions of November 1798,* which Jefferson is believed by scholars to have written, we find the following:

Resolved, That it is true as a general principle, and is also expressly declared by one of the amendments to the Constitution, that "the powers not delegated to the United States by the Constitution, nor prohibited by it to the States, are reserved to the States respectively, or to the people"; and that *no power over the freedom of religion, freedom of speech, or freedom of the press being delegated to the United States by the Constitution, nor prohibited by it to the States, all lawful powers respecting the same did of right remain, and were reserved to the States or the people;* . . . that in addition to the general principle and express decla-

---

[2] Padover, Saul K. (Ed.), *The Complete Jefferson* (New York, Duell, Sloane & Pearce, Inc., 1943), p. 134. [3] *Ibid.,* p. 323.

ration, another and more special provision has been made by one of the amendments to the Constitution, which expressly declares, that "Congress shall make no law respecting an establishment of religion, or prohibiting the free exercise thereof, or abridging the freedom of speech or of the press": thereby guarding in the same sentence, and under the same words, the freedom of religion, of speech, and of the press: insomuch that whatever violated either, throws down the sanctuary which covers the others, and that libels, falsehood, and defamation, equally with heresy and false religion, *are withheld from the cognizance of federal tribunals*.[4] [Italics mine.]

In Jefferson's second inaugural address of March 4, 1805, he made the following comment in regard to his activity in his first administration concerning religion:

In matters of religion, I have considered that its free exercise is *placed by the Constitution independent of the powers of the General Government*. I have therefore undertaken, on no occasion, to prescribe the religious exercises suited to it; but have left them, as the Constitution found them, *under the direction and discipline of state or church authorities* acknowledged by the several religious societies.[5] [Italics mine.]

Further statements so clear that no one should be able to misinterpret them and which are directly contrary to the position of Justice Rutledge in the Everson dissent, to the Black *dicta* in that case, and to the decision of the Supreme Court in the McCollum case, are common in Jefferson's writings. As shown in the discussion of these two cases (Chapters Eleven and Twelve) the chief substantiation of the Justices' position (insofar as there is any justification attempted in the opinions) rests upon extreme misrepresentation of the positions of Jefferson and Madison.

Here are some additional statements of Jefferson which places him squarely opposed to the McCollum decision:

"I am for preserving to the states the powers not yielded by them to the Union." [6]

"The true theory of our Constitution is surely the wisest and best, that the states are independent as to everything within themselves, and united as to everything respecting foreign nations." [7]

4 *Ibid.*, pp. 129, 130.   5 *Ibid.*, p. 412.
6 "Letter to Elbridge Gerry, 1799," Padover, *Democracy*, p. 47.
7 "Letter to Gideon Granger, 1800," *Ibid.*, p. 47.

". . . the essential principles of our government . . . the support of the state governments in all their rights, as the most competent administrations for our domestic concerns." [8]

"The true barriers of our liberties in this country are our state governments." [9]

Throughout his life Jefferson feared and opposed federal encroachment on the states. In 1825 he wrote:

I see. . . . with the deepest affliction, the rapid strides with which the federal branch of our government is advancing towards the usurpation of all the rights reserved to the States, and the consolidation in itself of all powers, foreign and domestic; . . . .

. . . .

And what is our resource for the preservation of the constitution? Reason and argument? You might as well reason and argue with the marble columns encircling them. . . .

Are we then *to stand to our arms*. . . ? No. *That must be the last resource*, not to be thought of until much longer and greater sufferings. . . . We must have patience and longer endurance . . . and separate from our companions only when the sole alternatives left are the dissolution of our Union with them, or submission to a government without limitation of powers. Between these two evils, when we must make a choice, there can be no hesitation.

But in the meanwhile, *the States should be watchful to note every material usurpation on their rights*; to denounce them as they occur in the most peremptory terms; to protest against them as wrongs to which our present submission shall be considered, not as acknowledgments or precedents of right, but as a temporary yielding to the lesser evil, until their accumulation shall overweigh that of separation.[10] [Italics mine.]

Jefferson particularly feared usurpation by the Supreme Court (apparently with considerable warrant!) In 1820 he wrote:

The judiciary of the United States is the subtle corps of sappers and miners constantly working under ground to undermine the foundations of our confederated fabric. They are construing our constitution from a coordination of a general and special government to a general and supreme one alone. . . .

Having found, from experience that impeachment is an impracticable

[8] "First Inaugural, Mar. 4, 1801," *ibid.*, p. 50.
[9] "Letter to De Tracy, 1811," *ibid.*, p. 81.
[10] "Letter to W. B. Giles," Padover, *Democracy*, pp. 83-85.

thing, a mere scare-crow, they consider themselves secure for life; they sculk from responsibility to public opinion. . . .

A judiciary independent of a king or executive alone, is a good thing; but independence of the will of the nation is a solecism, at least in a republican government.[11]

Also in 1820 he wrote:

To consider the judges as the ultimate arbiters of all constitutional questions is a very dangerous doctrine indeed, and one which would place us under the despotism of an oligarchy. . . . The constitution has erected no such single tribunal, knowing that to whatever hands confided, with the corruptions of time and party, its members would become despots.[12]

In 1821 Jefferson wrote:

It has long, however, been my opinion, and I have never shrunk from its expression (although I do not choose to put it into a newspaper, nor, like a Priam in armor, offer myself its champion), that the *germ of dissolution of our federal government is in the constitution of the federal judiciary*; an irresponsible body (for impeachment is scarcely a scarecrow) working like gravity by night and by day, gaining a little to-day and a little to-morrow, and advancing its noiseless step like a thief, over the field of jurisdiction, *until all shall be usurped from the States*, and the government of all be consolidated into one. To this I am opposed; . . . .[13] [Italics mine.]

Jefferson's remedy for the usurpation by the Supreme Court is found in a letter written in 1821.

For the difficult task in curbing the Judiciary in their enterprises on the Constitution . . . the best remedy I can devise would be to give future commissions to judges for six years the Senatorial term with a re-appointmentability by the president with the approbation of *both* houses. If this would not be independence enough, I know not what would be. . . .

The Judiciary perversions of the Constitution will forever be protected under the pretext of errors of judgment, which by principle are exempt from punishment. Impeachment therefore is a bugbear which they fear not at all. But they would be under some awe of the canvas of their conduct which would be open to both houses regularly every sixth year.

[11] "Letter to T. Ritchie," *ibid.*, pp. 97-98.
[12] "Letter to Jarvis, 1820," *ibid.*, pp. 98-99.
[13] "Letter to C. Hammond, 1821," *ibid.*, pp. 99-100.

It is a misnomer to call a government republican, in which a branch of the supreme power is independent of the nation.[14]

Maybe a way can be found still to "rally and recall" the people to the terms of the First Amendment, as Jefferson suggested in 1802.

. . . It is certain that though written constitutions may be violated in moments of passion or delusion, yet they furnish a text to which those who are watchful may again rally and recall the people; they fix too for the people the principles of their political creed.[15]

Let us hope that the American people will themselves decide in the middle of the twentieth century what they want in the Constitution to guide their government in the solution of twentieth century problems. If they will, they can defeat the attempt to substitute for current democratic decision an *imaginary* dead hand from the eighteenth century. Jefferson hoped for this. He wrote in 1816:

. . . Each generation . . . has a right to choose for itself the form of government it believes the most promotive of its own happiness. . . . A solemn opportunity of doing this every nineteen or twenty years should be provided by the constitution. . . . This corporeal globe, and everything upon it, belong to its present corporeal inhabitants, during their generation. They alone have a right to direct what is the concern of themselves alone. . . . If this avenue be shut . . . , it will make itself heard through that of force, and we shall go on, as other nations are doing, in the endless circle of oppressions, rebellions, reformations; and oppression, rebellion, reformation, again; and so on forever.[16]

One should not need further to labor the point that Jefferson believed in democratic decisions instead of Supreme Court dictation. He believed emphatically that the doctrine written into the Constitution should be changed only by the decision of the whole people.

In his letter to William Johnson on the Usurpation of the Supreme Court, June 12, 1823, he spoke of the two "canons which will guide us safely," as follows:

1st. The capital and leading object of the constitution was to leave with the States all authorities which respected their own citizens only, and to transfer to the United States those which respected citizens of

14 "Letter to Pleasants, 1821," *ibid.*, pp. 100-101.
15 "Letter to Dr. Priestly, 1802," *ibid.*, p. 103.
16 "Letter to S. Kercheval, 1816," *ibid.*, p. 104.

foreign or other States: to make us several as to ourselves, but one as to all others. . . . Between citizens and citizens of the same State, and under their own laws, I know but a single case in which a jurisdiction is given to the General Government. That is, where anything but gold or silver is made a lawful tender, or the obligation of contracts is otherwise impaired. . . .

2nd. On every question of construction [of the Constitution], carry ourselves back to the time when the Constitution was adopted, recollect the spirit manifested in the debates, and instead of trying what meaning may be squeezed out of the text, or invented against it, conform to the probable one in which it was passed.[17]

In regard to Jefferson's theory of how the Supreme Court should interpret or construe the Constitution, he speaks further in the same letter of "The Constitution of the United States of America (constructed according to the plain and ordinary meaning of its language, to the common intendment of the time, and of those who framed it)" and protests against the position "that a power has been given, because it ought to have been given, *et alia talia*. The States supposed that by their tenth amendment, they had secured themselves against constructive powers."[18] He proposes that changes in the relations of the federal government to that of the states might be made: "provided it be done regularly by any amendment of the compact, in the way established by that instrument."[19] In other words, Jefferson believed that the relationship of the federal government to the states, particularly in regard to the rights not specifically delegated to the United States (or which the Bill of Rights prohibits Congress from exercising), should be altered only by properly adopted and ratified constitutional amendments.

The contemporary propagandists (on or off the Supreme Court bench) for the spurious slogan "the complete separation of church and state" regularly attempt to bolster their position by misusing three fragments of sentences taken out of verbal contexts, out of the context of the times, and violently out of the context of Jefferson's other writings, his whole political philosophy, and his official record as President of the United States.

[17] Padover, *Complete Jefferson*, p. 322.
[18] *Ibid.*, p. 322.   [19] *Ibid.*, p. 136.

These three fragments are from his Bill for Establishing Religious Freedom (Appendix B), and his Reply to the Baptists of Danbury, Connecticut (Appendix E).

JEFFERSON'S BILL FOR RELIGIOUS FREEDOM

Jefferson's Bill for Religious Freedom in Virginia, first submitted to the legislature of Virginia in 1779 and passed in 1786, is one of the significant milestones in the history of religious freedom. It has been held in such high esteem by so many for so long that propagandists are naturally tempted to use it in their appeals. To most Americans it is a persuasive document. Its legitimate use is above adverse criticism. However, the attempt to get from it any support for the thesis that the First Amendment means, or was designed to mean, a complete separation of church and state in America, or specifically a prohibition of the use of public funds in impartial support of religion, is an offense that can be most charitably explained as incompetence in reading eighteenth-century English prose, ignorance of American history and constitutional structure, and almost complete unfamiliarity with the life and works of Thomas Jefferson. Without analyzing any such attempt on the part of any propagandist to see which of these weaknesses the attempt exemplifies, we can at least be sure we are on safe ground when we characterize it as a violation of what John Erskine called the "moral obligation to be intelligent."

First: The inference that what any man advocated as *state law* he would necessarily believe in as a provision of the federal Constitution, or as a national law, is obviously bad. Any man, regardless of his personal theory of state-federal relationships, could believe a law good for Virginia and not want it as a constitutional provision binding on all of the several states. When the man in question happens to be Thomas Jefferson, who all his life drew the sharpest kind of a line between the federal government and the authority of the states, and who insisted that each state was sovereign in all matters of domestic concern, such an inference becomes wholly ridiculous.

Second: Even if one were to grant that the Virginia law could be properly taken as expressing the purpose and meaning of the first clause of the First Amendment, or as Jefferson's belief of what each and every state should be required by the federal Constitution to observe, there is not a syllable in that law that warrants the conclusions that have been drawn from it in regard to bus legislation, "released time," public support of religion, and the complete separation of church and state. The whole law is expressed in one sentence (Section II of Appendix B). It "enacts" four things: In Virginia no man shall (1) be compelled by the government to attend or support any religious worship, place, or ministry whatsoever, nor (2) be punished or interfered with by the government on account of his religious opinions or beliefs, but (on the contrary) all men shall be free (so far as the government is concerned) (3) to profess and argue for his religious opinions and beliefs, and (4) such activity shall in no way affect his civil capacities.

That is the whole of the Virginia law which Thomas Jefferson wrote in 1779 and which was finally passed (after Madison's *Memorial and Remonstrance* had defeated the attempt to make Christianity the established religion of Virginia) in 1786. Note that it is concerned primarily with prohibiting state laws in regard to opinion, belief, worship, as these matters were universally covered in laws setting up "establishments of religion." The Virginia statute has no clear reference of any kind to public money, sectarian schools, religion in education, or the complete separation of church and state. There are probably few if any literate Americans who do not endorse all four of the provisions of the Virginia law for religious freedom. I do not know of one. Nor can I recall having read any published statements by any American of any church or any party advocating any measure inconsistent with these principles.

Not only do these four provisions of the Virginia law deal with the almost invariable features of "an establishment," but the long preamble deals also with theories and practices of churches "established" by governments which make government officials the judges of the validity of religious opinions and make civil rights dependent upon religious belief. In this context the first clause of the law could certainly mean that no man shall be compelled to attend or support any religion whatsoever that is selected for his attendance and support by the government. This is also the burden of the preamble. This is the meaning that best harmonizes with the context of the bill itself and the context of the times.

Furthermore, neither New Jersey in the Everson case nor Illinois in the McCollum case had *a law* which *required* anyone to attend or support any religious *worship*, religious *place*, or religious *ministry*. Jefferson was throughout this Bill, as throughout his whole life, fighting government dictation that a citizen, in order to have full and equal rights of citizenship, must attend and support, and refrain from opposition to, or hostile criticism of, the particular church or religion favored by the government—regardless of which one. Jefferson wanted no government force or power for any one religion, any church whatsoever. *No other reading of this clause* in the Virginia bill is consistent with Jefferson's other writings (see pp. 76-78), with official actions as President of the United States, or with the record of the State of Virginia in using public funds in cooperative contacts between government and religion in education, from 1786 to 1948. (See p. 146). In fact there exists no evidence at all that the idea of prohibiting equal, impartial public support of religion or religious education ever so much as entered the mind of Thomas Jefferson. There is a great deal of evidence in both his words and his actions that had the idea been presented to him, he would have opposed it vigorously. He could have taken no other position and defended his own record.

The first Jeffersonian phrase often misused in the modern attack on the First Amendment is taken not from the Virginia statute itself, but from its preamble (Section I). The preamble is, of course, not part of the law. It is rather the argument for the law. It is a striking example of the rhetoric of eighteenth-century political documents. It is one sentence of some six hundred words, or more accurately still it is a six-hundred word introductory clause. "Well aware (here follow fourteen separate statements each beginning with the word 'that'), We the General Assembly of Virginia do enact that" (here follows the Virginia law). One of the fourteen items of which the Virginia Assembly declared itself to be well aware (the fifth "that" clause) is as follows:

"That to compel a man to furnish contributions of money for the propagation of opinions which he disbelieves and abhors, is sinful and tyrannical; . . . ." Anyone who will consider the whole sentence (or clause) of which this is a fragment, will see that the whole passage is a detailed protest against the "impious presumption of legislature and ruler" that opinions and beliefs can be influenced by "temporal punishments . . . or by civil incapacitations," against allowing "the civil magistrate to intrude his powers into the field of opinion." This is another expression of Jefferson's lifelong opposition to the government dictating the particular theology or type of worship preferred by the persons in control of the government. He objected to the government compelling contributions of money to support the religion of the government from men who disbelieved and abhorred that religion. This position is, so far as I know, accepted by substantially all Americans of today of every creed, party, and section of the country. I do not know of a single exception.

This clause is not repeated in the "law" which follows it, Section II, except as it may be covered by the word "support" in the first clause of the law. One or both of these fragments are frequently used by ethically or intellectually careless propagandists to show that Jefferson opposed the use of tax money to support religion "in any guise, form, or degree," or that he wrote into the Virginia law the provision that tax money could not be used to propagate opinions which any taxpayer disbelieved or abhorred. That these positions are wholly untenable is shown by the following:

1. He advocated the use of public funds in Virginia in 1814 for a school of theology for the training of clergymen—a department of "Theology and Ecclesiastical History." "To these professional schools will come . . . the lawyer to the school of law. The ecclesiastic to that of theology and ecclesiastical history." [20]

2. He advocated giving "to the sectarian schools of divinity the full benefit [of] the public provisions made for instruction in the other branches of science, . . . such regulated use also as may be

[20] "Plan for an Educational System," Padover, Complete Jefferson, p. 1067. See also Padover, Jefferson (New York, Harcourt, Brace, Cotet & Company, 1942), p. 397.

permitted to the other students, of the library which may hereafter be acquired either by public or private munificence. But always understanding that these schools shall be independent of the University and of each other. Such an arrangement would complete the circle of the useful sciences embraced by this institution, and would fill the chasm now existing, on principles which would leave inviolate the constitutional freedom of religion." [21]

In his Regulations for the University (1824) Jefferson wrote: [22]

"Should the religious sects of this State, or any of them, according to the invitation held out to them, establish within, or adjacent to, the precincts of the University, schools for instruction in the religion of their sect, the students of the University will be free, and expected to attend religious worship at the establishment of their respective sects, in the morning, and in time to meet their school in the University at its stated hour.

"The students of such religious school, if they attend any school of the University, shall be considered as students of the University, subject to the same regulations, and entitled to the same rights and privileges.

"One of its large elliptical rooms on its middle floor shall be used for annual examinations, for lectures to such schools as are too numerous for their ordinary school-room, and for religious worship, under the regulations to be prescribed by law."

3. Jefferson, as President, used tax money throughout his administration, for chaplains in the army, navy, and Congress, without contrary recommendation or countermanding order as Commander-in-Chief, and to support religious education and worship among the Indians (see pages 116, 206).

4. There is no record of Jefferson's protest against Virginia's continuing to use tax money in various ways to promote cooperation between government and religion or religious education. Even today Virginia is one of the states that has a large number of the common practices of such cooperation either required or permitted. In fact, Virginia had in 1946, sixteen of the eighteen (with tax exemption included) common types of cooperation between state governments

---

[21] *Ibid.*, p. 958. See Appendix D.
[22] Padover, *Complete Jefferson*, pp. 1110-1111.

and religion in education, all of which use government resources.[23] (See also p. 146.)

Various acts of any government of a people having any degree of heterogeneity, must necessarily use tax money to promote opinions and practices that are against the beliefs of part of the population. Unless tax money had been so used public education in this country could never have been started. In fact, it took some hard fought law suits [24] to compel some taxpayers to support public high schools. If the principle which the attackers of the First Amendment are currently trying to squeeze out of these fragments should become the law of this country, it would wipe out our entire system of public education. Surely some taxpayer could be found who would express a disbelief in some opinion that was being promoted by almost every subject included in the program of any public school or college.

Throughout our country pacifists pay taxes to support West Point and Annapolis, the Army and the Navy. Christian Scientists pay taxes to support medical schools, hospitals, departments of bacteriology, and other "disbelieved" sciences in colleges and universities. Fundamentalists and their opposites in religion, conservatives and liberals in economics, the right and the left in politics, are all taxed alike without any consideration of their individual beliefs or opinions. Many millions of taxpayers in the various religious denominations pay many millions of dollars every year to support a system of public education which they hold promotes secularism and atheism which they "disbelieve and abhor." Anyone who is working to get enacted into law the principle of not using tax money to promote any opinion which any taxpayer opposes either does not know what he is doing or else he is a dangerous enemy of all tax-supported education.

JEFFERSON'S WALL OF SEPARATION

Jefferson's figure of speech, "a wall of separation between church and state," is probably more often misused in the modern attack on the First Amendment than any other phrase in his writings. The

---

[23] N. E. A. *Research Bulletin*, Vol. XXIV, No. 1 (Washington, National Education Association, 1946), pp. 36, 42.

[24] See *Stewart v. School Dist. No. 1, Kalamazoo*, 30 Michigan, 69 (1878).

present Justices of the Supreme Court are strangely addicted to trying to substitute this phrase for the first clause of the First Amendment. They do this not only by wrenching Jefferson's metaphor out
of its verbal context but also by omitting consideration of the constitutional and historical situation at the time. Justice Black in the
majority opinion in the Everson case goes even beyond these limits.
He substantially misquotes Jefferson's little letter of courtesy by
employing the technique known to students of argument as "garbling." [25] Justice Black's reference to Jefferson's famous metaphor is
a perfect example of garbling. He said: "In the words of Jefferson,
the clause against establishment of religion by law was intended to
erect 'a wall of separation between Church and State.'" By comparing this statement with what Jefferson actually said, it will be observed that Justice Black garbled Jefferson in the following ways:

1. Jefferson said nothing whatever about "the clause against establishment of religion." There is no clause *against* establishment of
religion in the First Amendment or elsewhere in the Constitution.
The First Amendment prohibited Congressional legislation *either for
or against an establishment of religion.* Congress has to keep hands
off. They could make no law "respecting" the subject. This was a
bar to *a* nationally established religion because at the time of the
adoption of the Amendment there was no national religion. So obviously, if Congress could make no law of any kind in regard to an
establishment, they could never create one. But the Amendment
prohibited a law by Congress opposing a national religion as effectively as a law favoring one.

2. Jefferson said nothing about an "establishment of religion *by
law,*" which would have included state law—New Jersey law. He
was necessarily talking about an establishment *by law of Congress,*
United States law for the nation as a whole. This left the legislature
of New Jersey and every other state as free to have the laws it liked

[25] To garble a passage is to mutilate it so as to mislead. Strictly speaking, it
is not misquotation. It avoids misquoting by putting some of the words of a
passage *accurately* within quotation marks, and omitting other words which
qualify the meaning of the words quoted. The garbler then makes statements
concerning the quoted phrases, or including them, which misrepresent the original
passage. It is a common device of poor debaters. The use of it may be due to
ignorance of the subject under discussion or incompetence in rhetoric.

in religion and education, and everything else, as if the First Amendment had never been thought of. Jefferson, of course, knew this simple fact of constitutional history. He could not have said or meant what Justice Black reported without evincing ignorance of constitutional provisions he had himself promoted, and without being vitally inconsistent in the positions he took again and again in regard to the constitutional relation of the federal government to the several states.

3. Jefferson did not say that the First Amendment was *intended* to do anything. Jefferson was obviously talking about the first clause of the First Amendment. He referred to it as something done, not something expressing *an intention* still to be accomplished. This is important because of the attempts on the part of both the majority and the minority in the Everson case, and by many others, to argue that Madison and Jefferson *intended* the First Amendment to mean something that is in no way expressed in its language. This position is taken in spite of the fact that no one could possibly have had such an intention if he understood the constitutional situation in which he was acting in adopting the Amendment in the Congress or in ratifying it in the states. No one should assume that Jefferson was unaware of the difference in authority between Congress and the state legislatures. Anyone who knows Jefferson's history and writing *knows* that Jefferson was fully aware of the constitutional separation of powers between the federal and state governments. Jefferson, therefore, necessarily knew that the First Amendment was *not intended* to have any effect whatever on any regulations of any kind, anywhere, covering the relations of any governmental agency to religion or religious education except a nationally created exclusively favored position for *one* religion as against all other religions.

These are some things Jefferson did not say—the Supreme Court to the contrary notwithstanding. This luxuriant garbling of a simple and wholly appropriate figure of speech concurred in by a majority of the Supreme Court, is an almost pathetic example of judicial ineptitude.

Jefferson did use the phrase "a wall of separation between church and state." He used this figure of speech in a reply which he made as President of United States to an address of congratulation and good wishes by a committee representing the Danbury, Connecticut, Baptist Association on January 1, 1802. The whole sentence from which this figurative fragment has been taken is absolute proof that President Jefferson could not have been thinking of a wall of any kind, high or low, pregnable or impregnable, which had any relation whatever to most of the matters mentioned in the elaborate rewriting of the first clause of the First Amendment in Black's *dictum*.

Jefferson's long sentence which included the famous figure of speech, spoke of the First Amendment as "that act of the whole American people which declared that their legislature should 'make no law respecting an establishment of religion or prohibiting the free exercise thereof,' thus building a wall of separation between church and state." [26] His next sentence was: "Adhering to this expression of the supreme will of the nation in behalf of the rights of conscience, I shall see," etc. The rights of conscience are of course endangered by established churches, but are never endangered by treating all religions *equally* in regard to support, or nonsupport, by a government that allows religious freedom. Justice Black did not give any reference to Jefferson's text, but only to a law case in which a reference to it was made. Had the Justice been familiar with Jefferson's little letter of courtesy, he might have known that Jefferson could not possibly have meant (and clearly did not say) what the Supreme Court of the United States speaking through Justice Black said that Jefferson *said*—"in the words of Jefferson." Of course, the "act of the whole American people" was the ratification by the states, and "their legislature" was the Congress. So Jefferson could have been thinking of the wall separating church and state *only* in regard to matters which were under the authority of the Congress at that time or were mentioned in the Amendment itself. Such matters did not include authority over religious affairs, education, the relation of religion to education, public support of either, or safety and health provisions for children. Government authority over all such matters, except any laws about a *nationally established religion* and *national restrictions* on religious freedom, was, and remained, exclusively and unambiguously the responsibility of the individual states. It is inex-

[26] Padover, *Complete Jefferson*, p. 518. *See* Appendix E.

cusable for anyone who has knowledge of and respect for Jefferson to hold that Jefferson's metaphor had any reference at all to these matters.

The Supreme Court lifted this metaphor out of its context in one of the many brief, casual responses which President Jefferson made thirteen years after the First Amendment was originally drafted. The Court essentially substituted it for the literal language of the Constitution. This is like taking on a given subject, as the basis for Supreme Court decisions, figurative passages from Franklin Roosevelt's political speeches rather than the literal language of the laws and constitutional provisions on the same subject. In the Everson case this figure of speech was the essential text of the majority opinion, the peroration of which is cast exclusively in the figurative language of the Great Wall of Separation: "The First Amendment has erected a wall of separation between church and state. That wall must be kept high and impregnable. We could not approve the slightest breach. New Jersey has not breached it here." [27]

Lawyers, judges, and propagandists in specific controversies have been leaning on this wall for years. Attempts have been made to use it to achieve a division in American thought and practice as though it were as real as the Great Wall of China. This practice has been too general to be lightly dismissed. Jefferson's wall has bedevilled many important public questions. It has been transformed into the spurious "great American principle of complete (or absolute, or unequivocal)separation of church and state." It has even been exalted into a great "constitutional principle," and has been accepted as a controlling mandate from the Founding Fathers. Justice Frankfurter in the McCollum case actually considers how the Supreme Court can "illuminatingly apply the 'wall-of-separation' metaphor," instead of applying the First Amendment which was the problem before the Court. [28]

These errors are not Jefferson's. His imaginary figurative wall is a legitimate figure of speech to suggest a permanent boundary line, a

[27] 330 U. S. 1 at 18.
[28] 333 U. S. 203 as reported in *The United States Law Week* (Washington, D. C., March 9, 1948), p. 4229.

boundary that indicated that the federal government and a single religion could not be made one, that the power of the government and that of any one church could not be given organic unity and made the same power. He might have used the figure of the line fence, but the greater permanence of a boundary marker that was embedded in the Constitution (or perhaps because he was addressing men who lived among the stone walls of Connecticut) doubtless made a wall seem a more fitting figure. At any rate, we know conclusively, if we know Jefferson, that he could not possibly have been thinking of a wall so high, so impregnable, so absolute, so completely without gates, or stiles, or friendly openings, as forever to prohibit any intercourse, neighborly help, or cooperation of any kind between government and religion.

In interpreting this little address of courtesy by President Jefferson additional light may be obtained by remembering that he was addressing the representatives of the Danbury, Connecticut, Baptists who at that time, and for years afterwards, did not enjoy a status of full religious liberty and equality. The established Congregational Church of Connecticut had preferred status. No other religious group had equal rights with the Congregationalists in Connecticut until 1818 and for years after that only other *Christian* denominations! Certainly the Baptists of Connecticut knew this. Moreover, the fact that Jefferson knew it is attested by his rather bitter references to the New England Congregationalists in his discussions of civil and religious freedom. Even today the Constitution of Connecticut provides: "Each and every society or denomination of Christians in this state shall have and enjoy the same and equal powers, rights, and privileges. . . ." This situation was remedied in 1843 by an extreme example of judicial legislation when the Supreme Court of Connecticut in doing the right thing in the wrong way, decided (with magnificent disregard for the meaning of language and the intent of constitution makers) that "Christians" meant "any religious group or organization."

Suppose Jefferson had actually said in plain, literal language what these Supreme Court Justices assume he meant by his figure of speech. He would have said essentially this: that the First Amendment provided that public resources could not be used to aid or promote religion in any way, or to aid education under religious auspices; that there could be no cooperation between the spheres of government and religion; that there must be absolute and complete "separation" between religion and government.

Had Jefferson said that in 1802, he would have been talking complete nonsense. He would have been saying that the Constitution contained provisions in which he thoroughly believed but which his administration was violating in a number of ways without the slightest effort on his part to stop the violations. He would have been proclaiming that a situation existed which all observant citizens knew did not exist in the nation as a whole nor in any state in the union. He would have been insulting the intelligence of those he was addressing. So we have here two particularly wild assumptions by the United States Supreme Court. (1) Jefferson said something in an address of courtesy in 1802 which was complete nonsense. (2) That nonsense became 160 years later part of the Constitution of the United States to replace a section formally adopted by the American people and maintained by the responsible representatives of the American people against repeated attacks, all aimed at putting the above "nonsense" into the Constitution.

Thomas Jefferson is often referred to—and properly—as one of the great founders of religious freedom in this republic, one of the architects of our system of relations between government and religion. He wrote much about religion and government. Yet, no propagandist for the complete separation of church and state whom I have discovered in a wide search has been able to quote a single statement from the voluminous writings of Thomas Jefferson in this field which shows that he ever used the phrase "establishment of religion," or "established church," in any other sense than the one which I have given; namely, of a formal, legal union between *one religion* and the government. Nor did he ever use a phrase which indicated his opposition to the use of public money in support of religion or religious education except as an aspect of an established church or religion. He was opposed to "an establishment of religion" in all of its aspects (as all Americans are today). It had many aspects, among which public support of the favored religion was one, but only one, and, incidentally, the one least emphasized in Jefferson's writings. But Jefferson was not opposed to religion, or religious organizations, or to the use of public funds and resources to aid religious activities so long as no one religion was favored over the others. Further Jefferson was greatly concerned with the promotion of personal and political morality, and he said, "Religion is the Alpha and Omega of the moral law." [29]

Jefferson's fundamental position was in opposition to the idea that the government was a competent authority on what constituted true or false theology or form of worship. He objected to putting the force of the government behind the doctrines of any one religion. In his letter to Elbridge Gerry of 1799, eight years after the ratification of the First Amendment, twenty years after he wrote the Virginia law for Religious Freedom, he summed up his position in these words: "I am for freedom of religion, and against all maneuvers to bring about a legal ascendency of one sect over another." [30]

In Jefferson's own tabulation of his Services to His Country (1800?) he lists this point: "I proposed the demolition of the church establishment, and the freedom of religion." He makes no mention of the separation of church and state, public support of religion, or religion in education.[31]

Jefferson expressed many times this twofold objective of his long campaign for the proper relations between government and religion, and with never any substantial variation. In February, 1809, he phrased it this way: [32]

No provision in our constitution ought to be dearer to man than that which protects *the rights of conscience against the enterprizes of the civil authority*. It has not left the religion of its citizens under the power of its public functionaries, were it possible that any of these should consider a conquest over the consciences of men either attainable or applicable to any desirable purpose. . . . , and I trust that the whole course of my

[29] Washington, H. A. (Ed.), *The Writings of Thomas Jefferson* (New York, John C. Riker, 1857), Vol. I, p. 545.
[30] "Letter to Elbridge Gerry, 1799," summarizing Jefferson's political philosophy, Padover, *Complete Jefferson*, p. 48.
[31] *Ibid.*, p. 1288.   [32] *Ibid.*, p. 544.

life has proved me a sincere friend to *religious as well as civil liberty.*
[Italics mine.]

In 1822, in the opening sentence of his statement on "Freedom
of Religion at the University of Virginia" (Appendix D), he again
refers to "all sects of religion on an equal footing" and "freedom of
religion."

Jefferson throughout his life sought these two objectives in the
relations of government and religion. First, he wanted *religious freedom* for all religions and, second, he wanted *equality* for all religions.
To Thomas Jefferson, freedom and equality were not synonymous.
The equality of deprivation, denial, and suppression of all the people
under a dictatorship, such as exists in Russia, is not freedom. Equality is not enough. The program of the Founding Fathers was equality
and freedom, equality *in* freedom. So long as we preserve *equality*
and *freedom* for the people of all religions, we preserve the doctrine
of Jefferson and of the First Amendment.

Chapter 6

JAMES MADISON AND THE FIRST AMENDMENT

*J*AMES MADISON and Thomas Jefferson are the two most important of the Founding Fathers whose work gives us the twofold American political doctrine of no established religion and religious freedom. As in the case of Jefferson, these two doctrines to Madison were related but not identical.

Religious freedom meant freedom to *worship* as one pleased, according to the dictates of conscience, or not to worship at all. It meant "the free exercise" of religion, freedom to hold, express, teach, and argue for any religious beliefs—so long as these activities did not constitute a threat to public order or morality. It meant freedom to go to church (any church) or to stay away.

An established religion, or an establishment of religion, meant that some *one religion* was singled out by the government and given a position of exclusive favor. Such a position usually had a number of features. Exclusive support by public funds for the established religion was universal in the eighteenth century in the Catholic and Protestant establishments of Europe and in the nine established Protestant churches in the American colonies. This is not wholly true today, however, in the prevailing Protestant establishments of northern Europe, as in England and Sweden. In addition to tax support, religious establishments had commonly such additional features as exclusive privileges in the matter of holding public office, serving as jurymen and witnesses in the courts, and in education. These features were summed up by Jefferson as "civil incapacitations" in his Bill for Religious Freedom (see p. 76), and were covered by Madi-

son in his *Memorial and Remonstrance* in this statement (see p. 281):
"It [establishment] degrades from *the equal rank of Citizens* all those
whose opinions in Religion do not bend to those of the Legislative
authority."

Anyone familiar with the history of the time, anyone who has
read the *Annals* of the First Congress, must admit that the one
man who had most to do with the phraseology of the First Amendment was James Madison. Anyone who has read the comments of
scholars, biographers, and historians, on James Madison, and who has
read a half-dozen paragraphs of Madison's clear, meticulously worded,
and often brilliant prose, will doubtless agree that James Madison's
ability to express his thoughts in the English language was outstanding, and that his ability accurately to phrase political documents, constitutions, and laws was unusual and unquestioned. Therefore, it
seems pertinent to ask why, when anyone wants to know what James
Madison's purpose was in the First Amendment, he does not consider
and accept the language of James Madison in the Amendment itself,
and what Madison said about the purpose of the Amendment in the
Annals of the First Congress. Insofar as Justice Rutledge went to
these sources at all—and he did refer to them here and there—he
refused to accept the language of the Amendment and he omitted
in some strange way to quote Madison's most illuminating passages
in regard to the meaning of the First Amendment. He gave us Eckenrode's *interpretation* of something that Madison wrote about some
other subject, in trying to arrive at what Madison meant in the First
Amendment, but he did not quote Madison on the First Amendment.

Madison's position on the First Amendment can be found in any
good library—in his letter to Thomas Jefferson in October, 1788, in
his private notes on his speech on the First Amendment in the First
Congress, and in the *Annals* of the First Congress. All these statements are consistent and all of them negate the positions taken by
Justice Rutledge.

Madison's *Memorial and Remonstrance* (Appendix C), has frequently been misinterpreted and certain phrases in it have been taken
cut of context and used to support positions which James Madison

did not take. As anyone can see who will take the trouble to read the *Memorial*, it was an attack upon "A Bill Establishing a Provision for Teachers of the Christian Religion." Madison was remonstrating simply against making the Christian religion the established religion of the State of Virginia. He cited fifteen numbered reasons "against the said bill." Not one of the fifteen is phrased in terms of public support of religion as such or in opposition to religion in education.

Madison's familiar statement in opposition to "forcing the citizen to contribute three pence" is inaccurately used in various documents. Probably the most familiar of these is Justice Rutledge's dissenting opinion in the Everson case. There it is used to support the claim that James Madison was opposed to the use of any public money, regardless of how little, in support of religion. This is not at all what Madison said and is a violent distortion of Madison's clear position. It is taken out of what is probably the most widely quoted passage in Madison's *Memorial*, and strangely enough it is the passage in the *Memorial* which probably more clearly than any other shows precisely that Madison was arguing against "an establishment of religion" in the exact and literal sense in which he consistently used the phrase. This is the consistent use by Jefferson also and other writers on established religion or established churches for some centuries. This illuminating passage is as follows:

Who does not see that the same authority which can *establish Christianity, in exclusion of all other Religions,* may *establish with the same ease any particular sect of Christians, in exclusion of all other Sects?* That the same authority which can force a citizen to contribute three pence only of his property for the support of *any one establishment,* may force him to conform to *any other establishment* in all cases whatsoever? [Italics mine.] (See p. 279.)

It seems incredible that anyone could read this passage and still honestly believe that Madison was doing other than opposing an exclusive status of government favor for one religion. He was simply using the word "establishment" as applied to religion in its common, centuries-old meaning. Yet Justice Rutledge [1] says this bill "was nothing more nor less than a taxing measure for the support of

[1] 330 U. S. 1 at 36.

religion." This is not true. It was clearly a taxing measure for the *exclusive* support of the Christian religion, and so provided for "an establishment of religion" in the exact meaning of the term as used by scholars and statesmen of the time.

In the long campaign against established religion in Virginia the *Memorial and Remonstrance* played a most important part. It killed off the 'attempt to put an establishment of Christianity in place of the establishment of the Anglican Church, and so cleared the way for Jefferson's Bill for Establishing Religious Freedom. In writing of this Jefferson said that by it "a great majority" of the Virginia Assembly "meant to comprehend, within the mantle of its protection, the Jew and the Gentile, the Christian and Mohammedan, the Hindoo, and Infidel of every denomination." [2]

Justice Rutledge [3] wrote that the *Memorial* "is a broadside attack upon all forms of 'establishment,' both general and particular, non-discriminatory or selective." This shows thorough misunderstanding of Madison's document. The *Memorial* is in its plain language an attack on the *particular* and *selective* establishment of the Christian religion. Furthermore there cannot be, and never has been, a *general* and *nondiscriminatory* "establishment of religion." The statement contains a flat contradiction in terms. "Establishment" means, and meant to Madison, and always has meant to careful scholars and historians, a position of exclusive government favor granted to *one* religion.

The attempt to make the phrase "an establishment of religion" in the Constitution mean something that it did not mean to Jefferson, Madison, and their contemporaries, is the work of modern propagandists campaigning for the spread of certain doctrines in theology and education. They have discovered that capturing or destroying the First Amendment will simplify their task of forcing their ideas on the people of all the forty-eight states without consulting the wishes of the people in any of them. An edict from the Supreme Court circumvents the democratic process of amending the Constitution and gives them a wholesale victory. In so doing it completely destroys Madison's accomplishment in the First Amendment by depriving the

2 Padover, *Complete Jefferson*, p. 1147.   3 330 U. S. 1 at 37.

state of the specific freedom which that amendment was designed
to preserve to them, freedom from outside dictation.

Both Madison's attitude in regard to the *need for a clause* on religion in the Bill of Rights in the Constitution, and his *purpose and
meaning in the clause* of which he is the essential author, are widely
misrepresented by the current propagandists for the complete separation of church and state. This double misrepresentation is particularly
striking in Justice Rutledge's dissenting opinion in the Everson case.

In regard to Madison's attitude Justice Rutledge used the following statements: [4]

The Amendment . . . is the compact and exact summation of its author's views formed during his long struggle for religious freedom."
It [the First Amendment] is at once the refined product and the terse
summation of that history [which] includes not only Madison's authorship
and the proceedings of the First Congress, but also the long and intensive
struggle for religious freedom in America, more especially in Virginia."
In the documents of the times, particularly of Madison, . . . but also in
the writings of Jefferson and others . . . is to be found irrefutable confirmation of the Amendment's sweeping content.

Madison

epitomized the whole of that tradition [the struggle for religious liberty]
in the Amendment's compact, but nonetheless comprehensive, phrasing.

This is historical nonsense.

The idea that James Madison went into the First Congress in the
spirit of a crusader to fight for putting into the Constitution of the
United States a summation of the long struggle for religious freedom, "to establish freedom for the nation as he had done in Virginia," "to tear out the institution (of the establishment) not
partially but root and branch, and bar its return forever," [5] is quite
contrary to the atmosphere and function of the First Congress (see
pp. 110-116) and to Madison's own statements.

The omission of a Bill of Rights from the original Constitution is
concisely covered by the following passage from Cooley: [6]

---

[4] 330 U. S. 1 at 31, 33, 39.   [5] *Ibid.*, p. 40.
[6] Cooley, Thomas M., *Constitutional Limitations*, (Boston, Little, Brown,
& Company, 1883), 5th ed., pp. 313, 314.

As the government of the United States was to be one of enumerated powers, it was not deemed important by the framers of the Constitution that a Bill of Rights should be incorporated among its provisions. If, among the powers conferred, there was none which would authorize or empower the government to deprive the citizen of any of those fundamental rights which it is the object and the duty of government to protect and defend, and to insure which is the sole purpose of bills of rights, it was thought to be at least unimportant to insert negative clauses in that instrument, inhibiting the government from assuming any such powers since the mere failure to confer them would leave all such powers beyond the sphere of its constitutional authority. And, as Mr. Hamilton argued, it might seem even dangerous to do so. "For why declare that things shall not be done which there is no power to do? Why, for instance, should it be said that the liberty of the press shall not be restrained, when no power is given by which restrictions may be imposed? I will not contend that such a provision would confer a regulating power; but it is evident that it would furnish, to men disposed to usurp, a plausible pretense for claiming that power. They might urge, with a semblance of reason, that the Constitution ought not to be charged with the absurdity of providing against the abuse of an authority which was not given, and that the provision against restraining the liberty of the press afforded a clear implication that a right to prescribe proper regulations concerning it was intended to be vested in the national government. This may serve as a specimen of the numerous handles which would be given to the doctrine of constructive powers by the indulgence of an injudicious zeal for bills of rights."

Madison agreed in part with Hamilton, taking the position that a Bill of Rights was not necessary, but would do no harm and might be useful if carefully phrased. As he wrote to Jefferson, he was in favor of a Bill of Rights, as an amendment to the Constitution, chiefly because others were so anxious to have it included.[7] But Jefferson wanted a Bill of Rights included to guard against abuses of power and as a text by which to try the acts of the federal government.[8] Madison sponsored the First Amendment, exactly expressing Jefferson's fear of Congress, as a "Keep Out" order. Congress should make *no law*. His position was, as given succinctly in his notes for

[7] "Letter to Jefferson, Oct., 1788," in Hunt, Gaillard (Ed.), *The Writings of James Madison* (New York, G. P. Putnam's Sons, 1904), Vol. V, p. 269.
[8] "Letter to Madison, March, 1789," in Padover, *Complete Jefferson*, p. 123.

his speech on the Bill of Rights in the First Congress: "Useful not essential." [9]

Madison's attitude in regard to the need for a clause on religion in the Bill of Rights is shown by the following:

On October 17, 1788 Madison wrote to Jefferson, who was then in Paris, a long letter about his attitude toward a Bill of Rights.[10] In it he said:

My own opinion has always been in favor of a bill of rights; provided it be so framed as not to imply powers not meant to be included in the enumeration. At the same time I have never thought the omission a material defect, nor been anxious to supply it even by *subsequent* amendment, for any other reason than that it is anxiously desired by others. I have favored it because I supposed it might be of use, and if properly executed could not be of disservice. I have not viewed it in an important light— 1. because I conceive that in a certain degree, though not in the extent argued by Mr. Wilson, the rights, in question are reserved [to the states] by the manner in which the federal powers are granted; 2. because there is great reason to fear that a positive declaration of some of the most essential rights could not be obtained in the requisite latitude. I am sure that the rights of conscience in particular, if submitted to public definition would be narrowed much more than they are are likely ever to be by an assumed power. One of the objections in New England was that the Constitution by prohibiting religious tests, opened a door for Jews, Turks and infidels; 3. because the limited powers of the federal Government and the jealousy of the subordinate Governments, afford a security which has not existed in the case of the State Governments, and exists in no other; 4. because experience proves the inefficacy of a bill of rights on those occasions when its control is most needed. Repeated violations of these parchment barriers have been committed by overbearing majorities in every State. .'. . What use then it may be asked can a bill of rights serve in popular Governments? I answer the two following which, though less essential than in other Governments, sufficiently recommend the precaution: 1. The political truths declared in that solemn manner acquire by degrees the character of fundamental maxims of free Government, and as they become incorporated with the national sentiment, counteract the impulses of interest and passion. 2. Although it be generally true as above stated that the danger of oppression lies in the interested majorities of the people rather than in usurped acts of the

[9] Hunt, *op. cit.*, p. 389.   [10] *Ibid.*, p. 269.

Government, yet there may be occasions on which the evil may spring from the latter source; and on such, a bill of rights will be a good ground for an appeal to the sense of the community.

In advocating the ratification of the Constitution as originally adopted without a Bill of Rights, Madison again expressed his belief that the federal government did not have the right to legislate in matters of religion even without a Bill of Rights, because no such right had been delegated to the federal government by the people in the Constitution.

In the Virginia Convention, June 5, 1788, Madison said:

I confess to you, Sir, were uniformity of religion to be introduced by this system, it would, in my opinion, be ineligible; but I have no reason to conclude, that uniformity of government will produce that of religion. This subject is, for the honor of America, perfectly free and unshackled. The government has no jurisdiction over it—the least reflection will convince us, there is no danger to be feared on this ground.[11]

In saying that "the government has no jurisdiction" Madison obviously meant the federal government—or the "general government" as he usually called it. At another point in the same discussion he reminded the Virginia delegates that under the Constitution as it stood, "there is not a shadow of right in the general government to intermeddle with religion." [12] Justice Rutledge actually quoted this last passage and part of the one above,[13] evidently without realizing how they contradict his position.

Madison approached his task in the First Congress of getting what is now the First Amendment adopted for submission to the states for ratification as part of the Constitution in the same frame of mind. Such an amendment was "not necessary," the federal government has no power to produce "uniformity of religion" "throughout the nation" (by creating an established religion for the country as a whole); but making this implicit situation explicit in the Constitution would do no harm if it was carefully done. So we find Madison on June 8, 1789, speaking on the Bill of Rights, in the First Congress, saying this:

[11] *Ibid.*, V, p. 132.
[12] *Ibid.*, p. 176.

[13] 330 U. S. 1 at 38-39.

. . . that is to say, if all power is subject to abuse, that then it is possible the abuse of the powers of the General Government may be guarded against in a more secure manner than is now done, while no one advantage arising from the exercise of that power shall be damaged or endangered by it. We have in this way something to gain, and, if we proceed with caution, nothing to lose.[14]

Later in the same speech he said:

The first of these amendments relates to what may be called a bill of rights. I will own that I have never considered this provision so essential to the Federal Constitution as to make it improper to ratify it, until such an amendment was added; at the same time, I always conceived, that in a certain form, and to a certain extent, such a provision was neither improper nor altogether useless.[15]

Finally we have Madison's attitude toward the inclusion of the Bill of Rights in the Constitution completely expressed in six words. In his notes for the speech he delivered in Congress for the Bill of Rights, he had this item:

"Bill of Rights—useful not essential—" [16]

Madison's purpose in phrasing the First Amendment, the meaning which he considered the First Amendment carried, is no deeply hidden secret. The only mystery in regard to Madison's purpose is deliberately built up and fictitious. The real mystery is why Justice Rutledge should try to deduce it from fragments taken out of context, as in his use of the words "the principle of assessment was wrong" without revealing that Madison was writing about assessment for *the exclusive benefit of one religion* or by frequent reference to what Madison, Jefferson and others said about *something else.* True, Madison's objection was not to the size of taxes in support of an establishment of religion; it was to any tax for the support of *one* religion. Certainly Madison did not oppose taxes, large or small, in impartial support of religion in general, either in discussing the Virginia legislation or the First Amendment.

The attempt to discover what Madison meant by the language of the First Amendment by quoting what he and Jefferson said about state legislation in Virginia (even if accurately understood and ap-

[14] Hunt, *op. cit.*, p. 375.   [15] *Ibid.*, p. 380.   [16] *Ibid.*, p. 389.

plied) has to be based on the assumption that these men believed that the Virginia statutes and the Constitution of the United States should necessarily contain identical provisions, and that the First Amendment brought this about. This assumption is nonsense to anyone who knows Jefferson and Madison.

In addition to the statements quoted above, Madison clearly expressed his concept of the meaning of the First Amendment in the following remarks when the Amendment was under discussion in the first Congress. When his original wording "nor shall any national religion be established" had been tentatively changed to version Number Two, "no religion shall be established by law," Madison said

he apprehended the meaning of the words to be, that Congress should not establish a religion, and enforce the legal observation of it by law, nor compel men to worship God in any manner contrary to their conscience. Whether the words are necessary or not he did not mean to say, but they had been required by some of the State Conventions

who seemed to fear that Congress might

make laws of such a nature as might infringe the rights of conscience, and establish a national religion; to prevent these effects he presumed the amendment was intended, and he thought it as well expressed as the nature of the language would admit.[17]

Madison, like Jefferson, throughout his work in building the American system of the relation of government to religion, distinguished between religious freedom *per se* and an establishment of religion. Gay [18] in speaking of Madison's work in the Virginia Convention of 1776, wrote that Madison "meant not only that religious freedom should be assured, but that an established church, which, as we have already seen, he believed to be dangerous to liberty, should be prohibited." Years later Madison again indicated his conception of the meaning of the religious clause of the First Amendment, phrasing its twofold purpose in words strikingly parallel to Jefferson's frequent summary of his efforts in the field of the relation of religion to gov-

[17] Benton, T. H. (Ed.), *Annals of Congress*, Abridged by J. C. Rives (New York, D. Appleton-Century Company, 1858), Vol. I, pp. 729-731.
[18] Gay, Sidney Howard, *James Madison*, (New York, Houghton, Mifflin & Co., 1899), p. 17.

ernment. In his later years, evidently after he retired from the Presidency in 1817, Madison wrote: [19]

They [the people of the United States] have the noble merit of first unshackling the conscience from persecuting laws, and of establishing among religious sects a legal equality.

The question may be asked: Why, since Madison was admittedly as opposed to an establishment of religion as he was to restrictions on the free exercise of religion, should he have been content with only a prohibition of any law by Congress on the subject of an establishment (either for or against)? The First Amendment clearly "took sides" on the freedom of religion, speech, press, right of assembly and of petition. Why not on an establishment of religion? Probably the answer is to be found in the fact that many men in the first Congress still believed in established churches in the states, as did many people even in the states which had disestablished their churches.[20]

Clearly Madison and the other men of the Congress of 1789 wanted the Bill of Rights adopted and ratified. There were still established churches in five of the states whose ratification was much desired. (A few years earlier there had been in nine of the thirteen colonies.) Both Madison and Jefferson had expressed concern with the attitude of the New Englanders in tenaciously fighting disestablishment. Had Congress phrased the First Amendment into a *condemnation* of an establishment of religion as it condemned interference with freedom of religion, press, speech, assembly, and right of petition, it would have been inviting opposition to ratification. It would have been endangering ratification with no practical benefit whatever, since a prohibition and any law either for or against an establishment accomplished the whole purpose (i.e., to prevent a *national establishment*), because at the time there was no national establishment. If Congress could not touch the subject, there never could be one. Probably anyone who knows Madison will agree that James Madison was a good enough politician to realize this.

[19] *Detatched Memoranda, William and Mary Quarterly*, 3rd Ser. III (Oct. 1946), p. 554.
[20] See Parsons, Wilfrid S. J., *The First Freedom* (New York, Declan X. McMullen Company, 1948), chs. 2 and 3.

James Madison has long been recognized by historians, biographers and commentators as a man of distinct competence in the use of the English language. His writings like those of Jefferson are replete with references to established religion and established churches, and, as was the common practice of the day, with references to "establishment" without the use of the associated words church or religion. A careful search has not revealed a single instance in which it is not perfectly clear from Madison's contexts that he uses these phrases in every instance, as did Jefferson, to mean a formal, legal position of special favor granted to one church or one religion by the government.

An establishment of religion is everywhere an act of government, not an act of a church or a religious organization, and establishments of religion historically always and everywhere have been government favor to a single church or religion. The idea that James Madison uses this expression to mean anything other than this is unsupported by any valid evidence of any kind which is referred to in any document, Supreme Court opinion, or other argument supporting the theory that Madison ever *believed in* a complete and absolute separation of church and state, the prohibition of the use of public funds for religious purposes, or the prohibition of religion in public education either in state or nation.

If James Madison had wanted to phrase this Amendment in a way which would have prohibited Congress from legislating in favor of any of these matters, I am confident that he could have found the words to do just that. In the absence of any evidence that he ever believed in any of these ideas, it is obviously improper to believe that he meant to express them when he used language which said something else. No literate mind, certainly not any such superlatively literate mind as that of James Madison, could possibly have used or accepted the language of the First Amendment in order to accomplish the whole assortment of prohibitions which the devotees of complete separation of church and state say was the purpose expressed in the language of that amendment. As Justice Frankfurter observed in Adamson vs. California: [21] "It would be extraordinarily

21 *The United States Law Week* (June 23, 1947), p. 4742.

strange for a Constitution to convey such specific commands in such a roundabout and inexplicit way." Students of Madison will doubtless agree that it would be quite impossible in a part of a constitution in which James Madison had a hand.

Justice Rutledge further says that Madison "could not have confused church and religion or an established church and an establishment of religion." [22] Madison not only could not have confused these terms but he did not. There is no confusion in regard to this matter in any of Madison's writings and particularly in his clear statement of the purpose of the First Amendment as quoted above. The confusion, and there is a great deal of it, pervades Justice Rutledge's opinion as well as other documents, speeches, and press releases of those who find the language of the United States Constitution unsuited to their purposes.

Some of Justice Rutledge's major confusions should suffice to show how thoroughly untrustworthy his arguments are as reporting or interpreting Madison. Says the Justice: "As the *Remonstrance* discloses throughout, Madison opposed every form and degree of official relation between religion and civil authority." [23] A reading of the *Remonstrance* (Appendix C) will show that this statement is without foundation in fact. But that is not all. Justice Rutledge was using this as an argument to show that Madison meant to prohibit every form and degree of relation between religion and government by writing "Congress shall make no law respecting an establishment of religion." He clearly meant that Madison was basically and consistently so opposed, and therefore was expressing this opposition in the words used in the First Amendment. Such a reflection on Madison's ability to express his thoughts in English, is inexcusable in one who has read even a few of Madison's major papers. It is shocking to find it in a Supreme Court opinion which seeks to alter the plain and common meaning of words largely on the basis of the record of James Madison. His record totally disproves Justice Rutledge's assertion.

In the First Congress, which adopted the First Amendment, Madison was a member of the joint committee of the two houses which

[22] 330 U. S. 1 at 31.   [23] *Ibid.*, p. 39.

arranged for the chaplain system which has continued to this day, and which has always used public funds to promote religion.[24] This fact alone almost destroys practically all of the proffered support in the Rutledge opinion, much of the *dicta* of the majority opinion in the same case (the Everson case), and a large part of the total foundation offered for the decision in the McCollum case.

I have found one attempt[25] to get some backing for the Rutledge doctrine out of two veto messages[26] signed by Madison on February 21 and February 28, 1811. The first vetoed an act incorporating the Protestant Episcopal Church in Alexandria in the District of Columbia. The message said:

An act incorporating the Protestant Episcopal Church in the town of Alexandria, in the District of Columbia.
The bill enacts into and establishes by law sundry rules and proceedings relative *purely to the organization and polity of the church incorporated.* . . . *This particular church, therefore, would so far be a religious establishment by law,* a legal force and sanction being given to certain articles in its constitution and administration. [Italics mine.]

This is so clearly an *exclusive*, formal, legal arrangement between the United States government and one church (in fact, one parish) that it obviously has no bearing on equal, impartial assistance to *all religions with favor to none* (as in tax exemption). It contains the common denominator of all "establishments"—exclusiveness.

The message of February 28, 1911, vetoing a bill giving some land of the United States to a *particular Baptist church* in Mississippi, said:

Because the bill in reserving a certain parcel of land of the United States for the use of *said Baptist Church* comprises a principle and precedent for the appropriation of funds of the United States for the use and support of religious societies, contrary to the article of the Constitution which declares that "Congress shall make no law respecting a religious establishment." [Italics mine. Note misquotation of First Amendment.]

24 *Reports of Committees of the House of Representatives.* First Session, 33rd Congress (Washington, A. O. P. Nicholson, 1854), Vol. II, Report No. 124, p. 4.
25 Editorial, *Chicago Tribune*, April 16, 1947.
26 Richardson, James D:, *Messages of the Presidents* (New York, Bureau of National Literature and Art, 1908), Vol. I, p. 467.

Clearly this also concerns a particular church (a specific parish or church organization). As such it is an exclusive favor of government, not an impartial aid to all religions equally. Also it is not payment for services rendered as in Bradfield v. Roberts,[27] and other cases. This is sufficient basis for the veto. It must be admitted, however, that the phrase "appropriation for the use and support of religious societies" is ambiguous enough to bear *an interpretation* that could be used to bolster up the Rutledge doctrine. This phrase probably is the best one in all the writings of Jefferson and Madison combined for the comfort of the Supreme Court Justices in the Everson and McCollum cases. Characteristically, none of the Justices uses it! However, this phrase does not prove the validity of the positions taken in these cases for the following reasons:

1. It is ambiguous. What sort of appropriation for "use and support"—a gift or a payment for services? Madison's administration was paying out tax money for use and support of religious societies *for services rendered* on Indian reservations with no protest from Madison.

2. In its extreme interpretation, *à la* Rutledge, it would go contrary to the records of Jefferson, Madison, and practically all Congressional, Presidential, Supreme Court, and State history—up to March 8, 1948.

3. It contains (strangely, in a document signed by James Madison), a misquotation of the first clause of the First Amendment. The First Amendment says "an establishment of religion," not "a religious establishment." It is easy for one unacquainted with eighteenth-century American history to assume that "an establishment of religion" means "a religious establishment" or any religious organization or society. But this was demonstrably not the meaning of Madison and of the first Congress, in the First Amendment.

4. It is possible (all things considered, even probable) that Madison considered this exclusive favor to a Baptist church, because of its exclusiveness, at least a partial "establishment of religion" and may have meant just that by what he said. It is also possible, or probable,

[27] 175 U. S. 291 (1899).

that a clerk or secretary phrased this message and Madison signed it without carefully checking the language.

5. Anyway, this language is *not* in the Constitution. Presidential messages do not become either constitutional or statutory law.

James Madison was President of the United States for eight years. He took the oath as President to uphold the Constitution of the United States. It will probably be admitted that Madison was sufficiently informed to know what the Constitution of the United States provided and sufficiently honorable to respect his oath of office. Yet throughout his administration, public funds were used not only to support chaplains in Congress, but also in the army and navy, and for religious work on the Indian reservations. If Justice Rutledge's position is sound, either James Madison did not know what the Constitution provided or else he had no respect whatever for his oath of office. No one can deny that throughout his administration, like Jefferson, he administered the federal government, which was using federal funds in various ways to support religion, without protest, without countermanding order as commander-in-chief of the army and navy, and without any contrary recommendation to Congress to repeal the laws on this subject, or to start to amend the Constitution to clarify any ambiguity lurking in the First Amendment. It is also undeniably true that every federal administration from Washington to Truman, both inclusive, has used federal funds in aid of religion in various ways.

Unless Justice Rutledge wishes to hold that Madison was ignorant of the powers of the Congress in which he was an outstanding leader, he will have to admit that Madison could not have intended this amendment "to create a complete and permanent separation of religious activity and civil authority," [28] or to "outlaw all use of public funds for religious purposes." [29] Madison not only knew that Congress had no authority over these matters, he also believed fervently in this separation of powers.

Madison is the sponsor, the essential author, of the First Amendment. In discussing the Amendment when it was before the First Congress he clearly stated his opinion in regard to its purpose and

[28] 330 U. S. 1 at 31-32.   [29] *Ibid.*, at 33.

meaning. Why, in the face of this fact, Justice Rutledge or anyone else should seek to infer what Madison meant in the First Amendment from his political writings and speeches dealing with *something else* (such as a state religion for Virginia) is again hard to understand. This would be hard to understand even if it could be held that Madison believed that the United States Government should have the identical provisions in regard to religion which he thought proper for Virginia. Everyone at all familiar with Madison's political philosophy (which again is open to anyone who is able and willing to read) ought to know that Madison, like Jefferson, was an emphatic believer in state authority in domestic affairs. He clearly believed that the United States Government could exercise only the powers delegated to it in the Constitution and that authority in the federal government over religious matters never had been and never should be delegated to the federal government. Even if Madison had advocated legislation in the State of Virginia which totally prohibited any contact between government and religion, any support of religion by public money (which he never did), it would not follow that he believed in similar provisions in the Constitution and laws of the United States.

Into these basic theories of government and provisions for the relations of the states to the federal government, Madison fitted the First Amendment. In his clear statement in the First Congress he explained its meaning and intention. Madison's first phrasing of that part of the First Amendment dealing with established religion was "nor shall any national religion be established." This amendment, so phrased, was on July 21, 1789 referred to a committee of eleven members, on which Madison represented the State of Virginia.[30] This committee brought in version Number Two of this phrase as follows "no religion shall be established by law." There was considerable debate on this version in the course of which we find the following record:

Mr. Madison thought, if the word "National" was inserted before religion, it would satisfy the minds of honorable gentlemen. He believed that the people feared one sect might obtain a preeminence, or two combine together, and establish a religion to which they would compel others to

[30] Benton, *op. cit.*

conform. He thought if the word "national" was introduced, it would point the amendment directly to the object it was intended to prevent.[31]

Mr. Gerry did not like the term "national." He was afraid that the use of the term would indicate that we had a national rather than a federal government. In view of this position,

Mr. Madison withdrew his motion, but observed that the words "no national religion" shall be established by law, did not imply that the Government was a national one; the question was then taken on Mr. Livermore's motion, and passed in the affirmative, thirty-one for, and twenty against it.[32]

Various other phrases were suggested in the course of the debate from time to time, until finally the House on September 24, 1789, and the Senate on September 25, approved the language of the First Amendment as we have it today: "Congress shall make no law respecting an establishment of religion or prohibiting the free exercise thereof. . . ." It ought to be clear to anyone that this phraseology, although it contains neither the word "federal" nor "national," deals only with an establishment of religion for the United States *as a whole,* for which alone Congress makes laws, and that as conceived, adopted, and ratified, the First Amendment was not intended to, and did not have, any authority at all over state legislation concerning an establishment of religion. This is true regardless of how one defines "an establishment of religion." Whatever is covered by that phrase was deliberately left in the hands of the people of the several states.

To assume that James Madison did not understand all of this, or that understanding it, and believing in and ardently desiring a different provision, he accepted it without protest or argument not only in the First Congress, but later as President of the United States and throughout his life—for another forty-seven years—is not only to insult the memory of Madison; it is (in the mildest permissible characterization) a demonstration of incompetence on the part of the one who make such an assumption and tries to pass it off as valid argument.

The effect of the Fourteenth Amendment on the relation of the establishment of religion clause to the various states is covered more

---

[31] *Ibid.*   [32] *Ibid.*

fully in Chapter Ten. The position of various Justices of the Supreme Court in the Everson and McCollum cases that Madison and Jefferson *intended* the First Amendment to prohibit the States from doing anything at all about religion or education, is gross misrepresentation. The States at the time clearly had *all authority* over these matters of "domestic concern," and clearly the First Amendment only *prohibited action* by Congress, and conferred no authority on Congress *to act* in regard to anything. It follows that no rational and informed person can honestly say that Madison or Jefferson *intended* what our current Justices say was their intention. The only *possible* basis for such a position would be that Madison and Jefferson were uninformed or irrational, or both.

This fundamental and comprehensive misrepresentation of Madison and Jefferson is particularly glaring in the opinions of Justices Black, Rutledge, and Frankfurter (see pp. 287-302) and is concurred in by most of the Court. It is presented without a single accurate citation of historical fact or quoted passage to substantiate it.

Whatever effect the Fourteenth Amendment has or may have, it cannot change the *intentions* that were in the mind of Madison eighty years before this amendment was ratified. Any purpose or intention behind the First Amendment could have existed only in the thought of the men who formulated, adopted and ratified it. The intention could not have existed only in the language symbols of the thought. Madison's intentions in regard to any subject could not have been influenced by anything written by someone else twenty years after Madison's death.

Madison's *Detatched Memoranda* [33] contains some interesting passages concerning the First Amendment. However, the weight to be accorded to these passages is a bit hard to determine. The *Memoranda* was apparently written some time between 1817 and 1832, and is said by Miss Fleet to have been "hastily jotted down . . . to be corrected, expanded, and completed later." The tentative nature of this document is well-indicated by the reference in it to the chap-

[33] Fleet, Elizabeth (Ed.), *The William and Mary Quarterly*, 3rd Ser., III (October, 1946), pp. 534-568.

lains in Congress. Here Madison takes the position that the Congressional chaplains system violates the Constitution. He does this with no indication that it represents a complete change of mind on his part. He took the opposite position in 1789 when he served as a member of the joint committee to plan the chaplain system. Also as President from 1809 to 1817 he administered the federal government whose taxes were used to pay the chaplains with no word of objection or protest.

Whatever weight is to be given to the *Detatched Memoranda*, that weight is in favor of two positions: (a) Madison thought of the First Amendment as forbidding "everything like *an* establishment of *a* national religion" [34] and (b) any doubt he had about the constitutionality of the chaplain system was based on the thought that it violated *equality* among the sects and not on the thought that it impartially used public funds in support of religion in general. Of course, nothing in this *Memoranda* has any application whatever to a possible future Constitutional restriction on the powers of the individual states in the realm of religion. The principal passage on the matter of the chaplains is as follows:

Is the appointment of Chaplains to the two Houses of Congress consistent with the Constitution, and with the pure principle of religious freedom?

In strictness the answer on both points must be in the negative. The Constitution of the United States forbids everything like an establishment of a national religion. The law appointing Chaplains establishes a religious worship for the national representatives, to be performed by Ministers of religion, elected by a majority of them; and these are to be paid out of the national taxes. Does not this involve the principle of a national establishment, applicable to a provision for a religious worship for the Constituent as well as of the representative Body, approved by the majority, and conducted by Ministers of religion paid by the entire nation.

The establishment of the chaplainship to Congs is a palpable violation of equal rights, as well as of Constitutional principles: The tenets of the chaplains elected [by the majority] shut the door of worship agst the members whose creeds & consciences forbid a participation in that of the majority. To say nothing of other sects, this is the case with that of

34 *Ibid.*, p. 558.

Roman Catholics & Quakers who have always had members in one or both of the Legislative branches. Could a Catholic clergyman ever hope to be appointed a Chaplain? To say that his religious principles are obnoxious or that his sect is small, is to lift the evil at once and exhibit in its naked deformity the doctrine that religious truth is to be tested by numbers, or that the major sects have a right to govern the minor.[35]

[35] *Ibid.*

Chapter 7

CONGRESS AND THE
FIRST AMENDMENT

*B*ECAUSE the First Amendment was formulated and adopted by the Congress of the United States, and since it has been from the date of its ratification a restriction on Congress, the way in which Congress has observed that restriction, the attitude of Congress toward this Amendment, and their formal interpretations of the Amendment, ought to be helpful to anyone who is in a quandary in regard to what the First Amendment meant to its authors and has meant throughout our history.

A consideration of the language of the First Amendment and the discussion out of which the wording grew, as reported in the *Annals* of the First Congress, have been covered in Chapter Six.

When one searches the records of congressional activity for instances which show clearly the attitude of Congress toward the First Amendment's clause on religion, he necessarily has a long search for a small result. The inevitable effect of the First Amendment, expressing as it does the determination of the American people that government control over religion shall be left in the hands of the States, has meant that Congress has done relatively little. Most of what has been done in regard to legislation touching religion or religious institutions, has necessarily taken place in state legislatures. This constitutional arrangement, carefully provided for in the Bill of Rights in answer to specific requests from the individual States that this exact provision should be made, has met its first defeat in the decision in the McCollum case, which is treated at length in Chapter Twelve. It should further be borne in mind that Congress is not *the state*; Congress is not the government. When one uses the word "state" in such expressions as "separation of church and state," he means, or should mean if he is using language accurately, the state as an essential synonym for "government." The word "congress" in the United States of America is not a synonym for "government." It is the label of one of the three branches of the Federal Government, and, clearly, is no part of the government of individual states. When, therefore, we are dealing with congressional activity in regard to the First Amendment, we are dealing not with the activity of *the state* in the sense of government, but we are dealing specifically with that part of the federal government which is specifically dealt with in the First Amendment itself. The words "state," "church," and "separation" are, of course, not in the First Amendment.

However, the entire record of Congress in regard to the first clause of the First Amendment, all of the laws which Congress has passed under the aegis of that clause, support the position that the phrase "an establishment of religion," concerning which Congress was forbidden to make any laws at all, meant, and has been held to mean by Congress, only a single, formal, monopolistic union of one religion with the federal government. In all of the arguments, manifestoes, press releases, and editorials which I have been able to find in a long investigation, there is not a single citation of any action by Congress which indicates the acceptance of any other concept for the phrase "an establishment of religion."

There are two ways in which congressional action will throw a light on congressional attitude toward the slogan "complete separation of church and state" as the proper meaning of the First Amendment either as we have it, or as a desirable future substitute for the First Amendment. The *first* is congressional activity in passing laws and resolutions as a part of their ordinary routine in connection with the affairs of the federal government, and the *second* is congressional attitude toward proposals to put into the Constitution the substance of the doctrine "complete separation of church and state" as enunciated in the *dicta* of the Everson case and in the majority opinions in the McCollum case and elsewhere in the modern attack upon the First Amendment.

The First Congress demonstrated by specific actions deliberately taken that their conception of the first clause of the First Amendment was not at all what the current judges of the Supreme Court say it was. In the first place, the First Congress refused to adopt what is often spoken of as the "lost amendment"—one which was offered as a part of the Bill of Rights, and which would have restricted the freedom of the States in matters of religion. It would have prohibited any state law which would infringe the "equal rights of conscience." There is no evidence whatever that the majority of the men in the Senate of the First Congress who defeated this Amendment believed in laws that would infringe the equal rights of conscience. It seems clear from the other actions which they took that they believed simply that this was a matter for the individual States to handle. The First Congress, therefore, refused even that much of a restriction upon the freedom of the States in the field of religion. Not only that, but the position that the Amendment prohibits any law concerning religion even though it equally benefits all religion (the Rutledge doctrine) is inconsistent with various legislative acts of the First Congress which recognized and impartially aided and benefited religion.

Thus on the very day (September 24, 1789) that the House accepted the report of the Conference Committee and adopted its resolution recommending the First Amendment to the States, it also adopted a resolution

That a joint committee of both Houses be directed to wait upon the President of the United States, to request that he would recommend to the people of the United States a day of public thanksgiving and prayer, to be observed by acknowledging, with grateful hearts, the many signal favors of Almighty God, especially by affording them an opportunity to establish a Constitution of government for their safety and happiness.[1]

Again on January 7, 1790, the House adopted a resolution

that the chaplains, of different denominations, be appointed to Congress for the present session, one of each House, who shall interchange weekly.[2]

[1] Benton, T. H. (Ed.), *Annals of Congress*, Abridged by J. C. Rives (New York, D. Appleton-Century Company, 1858), Vol. I, pp. 914-915.
[2] *Ibid.*, p. 932.

Further, James Madison was a member of the congressional committee which planned the chaplain system for Congress.[3] This was implemented on the following day (January 8, 1790) by the election of the Rev. William Linn to the office of chaplain.[4] This practice of electing a chaplain as an officer of each House and paying him a salary from the national treasury was continued in the Second Congress and without deviation to the present time. During all of this period Congress has been regularly convened by prayer, not simply religious education, but religious worship. Religion and worship in this "guise, form or degree" has been regularly paid for at national expense and joined in by the Congress.

Similar action with reference to religion was taken by the adjournment of the House of April 2, 1790, in observance of Good Friday.[5]

On March 3, 1791 the First Congress passed an act for the raising of another regiment of troops and provided for the appointment among other officers of a chaplain.[6]

The Second Congress on March 5, 1792 similarly provided for chaplains in the Army [7] and the Third Congress made similar provision for the Navy on March 27, 1794.[8] Again this recognition and support of religion has been regularly extended and multiplied by every Congress, not excepting the last one.

The language of the First Amendment is not a careless or casual formulation, nor phrases borrowed from documents designed for a situation other than the one which confronted the first Congress (as were Jefferson's "Wall of Separation" letter and Jefferson's and Madison's writings concerning state laws in Virginia). The First Amendment was carefully phrased to meet a situation presented by resolutions and petitions from various States asking for a Bill of Rights. These petitions and resolutions came out of the discussions in the various States as they were considering the original Constitution.[9] Several of these conventions accompanied ratification with a

---

[3] *Reports of Committees of the House of Representatives*, Vol. II, No. 124.
[4] Benton, *op. cit.*, I (4), p. 1043.
[5] *Ibid.*, II, p. 1519.   [7] 1 U. S. Stat. L. 241.
[6] 1 U. S. Stat. L. 223.   [8] 1 U. S. Stat. L. 350.
[9] See p. 9 concerning the omission of a Bill of Rights from the original Constitution.

request for specific amendments or with resolutions setting forth declarations of principle which are relevant here. Other amendments were proposed and discussed but not formally adopted.

It is a fact of first importance that most of the States that phrased resolutions or petitions dealing with religion in regard to the desired Bill of Rights, dealt specifically with a religious provision which would prevent Congress from making it possible for *one religion nationally to be preferred over all others*. In other words, what the States asked Congress to provide was a constitutional amendment which would prevent a national "establishment of religion" in the age-old, strict, literal sense of a union between the government and a single religion.

These declarations and proposed amendments, so far as they related to religion, were as follows:

Pennsylvania (ratified December 12, 1787). An amendment proposed to the Pennsylvania convention but not adopted:

The right of conscience should be held inviolable and neither the legislature, executive or judicial powers of the United States shall have the power to alter, abrogate or infringe any part of the constitutions of the several states which provide for the preservation of liberty in matters of religion.[10]

Maryland (ratified April 28, 1788). Amendment proposed to the Maryland Convention but not adopted:

12. That there be no national religion established by law; but that all persons be equally entitled to protection in their religious liberty.[11]

New Hampshire (ratified June 21, 1788). Amendment requested:

Congress shall make no laws touching religion, or to infringe the rights of conscience.[12]

Virginia (ratified June 26, 1788). The ratifying resolution of the Virginia Convention declared, in part,

[10] Humphrey, E. F., *Nationalism and Religion in America* (Boston, Chipman Law Publishing Co., 1924), p. 461.
[11] Elliot, Jonathan (Ed.), Debates (Washington, D. C., published under the sanction of Congress by and for the Editor, 1836), Vol. II, p. 553.
[12] *Ibid.*, I, p. 326.

that, among other essential rights, the liberty of conscience, and of the press, cannot be cancelled, abridged, restrained, or modified by any authority of the United States.[13]

A proposed "declaration or bill of rights" recommended as an amendment to the Constitution was adopted the next day, June 27, 1788, and included:

20th. That religion, or the duty which we owe to our Creator, and the manner of discharging it, can be directed only by reason and conviction, not by force or violence; and therefore all men have an equal, natural, and unalienable right to the free exercise of religion, according to the dictates of conscience, and that no particular religious sect or society ought to be favored or established, by law, in preference to others.[14]

New York (ratified July 26, 1788). Its resolution ratifying the Constitution declared:

That the people have an equal, natural, and unalienable right freely and peaceably to exercise their religion, according to the dictates of conscience; and that no religious sect or society ought to be favored or established by law in preference to others.[15]

North Carolina (ratified November 21, 1789). The first convention neither ratified nor rejected the Constitution but on August 1, 1788, shortly before its adjournment, passed a declaration of rights containing a twentieth clause which was identical in form with that proposed by Virginia.[16]

Rhode Island (ratified May 29, 1790). The resolution of ratification did "declare and make known" certain principles, "declaring that the rights aforesaid cannot be abridged or violated, and that the explanations aforesaid are consistent with the said Constitution." Clause IV of this declaration was, with minor textual variations, the same as the Twentieth clause of the Virginia declaration.[17]

In determining the meaning of the words in the First Amendment, "any law respecting an establishment of religion," it is important to observe the text of the above amendments and declarations on the specific subject of an "establishment of religion"—distinguishing that subject from freedom of conscience and of religious worship.

[13] *Ibid.*, I, p. 327.
[14] *Ibid.*, III, p. 659.
[15] *Ibid.*, I, p. 328.
[16] *Ibid.*, I, p. 333; IV, pp. 244, 251.
[17] *Ibid.*, I, p. 334.

Virginia did not request the enactment of an amendment having the language of her Bill for Establishing Religious Freedom [18] but rather "that no particular religious sect or society ought to be favored or established, by law, in preference to others."

North Carolina requested an amendment in identical language.

Except that it omitted the word "particular," New York's declaration of principles was identical with the above language of Virginia.

Rhode Island, after the First Amendment had already been formulated and submitted to the states, used language identical with the language of Virginia.

The proposal for an amendment rejected by the Maryland convention was "that there be no national religion established by law."

All of the above showed simply a desire that no religious sect or society be favored or established by law in preference to others. No prohibition of equal aid to all religions, financial or otherwise, is mentioned. There is no mention of public funds, government cooperation with religion or religion in education.

The laws and resolutions which the First Congress passed on subjects other than the Bill of Rights (mentioned earlier in this chapter) further show that this Congress had no idea of preventing the use of public funds in aid or support of religion, that they had no idea of providing a wall of separation so high and impregnable between religion and the civil authority that there could be no intercourse or cooperation between them. No literate and informed person has, therefore, any right to believe that the First Congress in adopting the Bill of Rights, intended any of the effects which are claimed for it by the *dicta* in the Everson case and the decision in the McCollum case.

Congressional provisions not only for chaplains and chapels at Annapolis and West Point, but for the requirement of compulsory attendance at religious exercises by the students in these institutions, is again, of course, complete proof that no Congress has ever considered that the prohibition of an established religion in the United States means that the federal government may not recognize or sup-

[18] 12 Hening, Va. Stats., p. 86.

port religion or religious observances so long as these are not restricted to a single national religion.

It is obviously impossible in a chapter in a single volume of this sort to cover all of the laws in which, in 160 years, the Congress of the United States has recognized religion and has passed laws respecting religion or religious institutions. If the modern doctrine enunciated first by Justice Rutledge in the Everson case and essentially embodied in the decision in the McCollum case is ever universally applied, every one of these laws by Congress from the beginning down to 1948, will, of course, be unconstitutional because they are all laws respecting religion or religious institutions or organizations.

Once it is accepted that the prohibition of a law respecting an establishment of religion means prohibition of a law *about religion or a religious institution,* and if it is further accepted that the Fourteenth Amendment now places that restiction upon the states, then it follows inevitably that we will not have in this country any legislative authority, either state or national, that can pass any law at all that has to do with the subject of religion or a religious institution. All the laws favorable to religion and all those unfavorable to religion, those prohibiting funds in religious schools or supervising certain aspects of religious schools (as curriculum, teacher training, attendance, etc.) will all be unconstitutional. We shall have complete chaos throughout the nation and in all the individual states in these matters until new constitutions are adopted. If this situation is ever brought about by the edict of the Supreme Court, it will have been accomplished by avoiding the democratic process of amendment, ignoring the provisions of our Constitution, and dictating this situation to the American people in complete defiance of the expressed will of the American people every time in their history they have had an opportunity to express their will on this subject.

The Federal Government of the United States began to use federal funds in support of religion in education on August 7, 1789, when George Washington submitted to the First Congress a report [19]

[19] *American State Papers,* Class II. Indian Affairs, Lowrie and Clark, (Ed.), Vol. IV, pp. 54, 66 (Washington, Gales & Seaton, 1832).

from General Henry Knox, his Secretary of War, recommending, among other things, that missionaries be appointed to work among the Indians. On August 29, 1789, General Knox, by command of George Washington, President of the United States, sent the following instructions to the Commissioners for Trading With the Indians:

You will also endeavor to obtain a stipulation for certain missionaries to reside in the Nation providing the general government should adopt the measure.

(The measure that had already been submitted)

The object of this establishment would be the happiness of Indians teaching them the great duties of religion and morality, and to inculcate a friendship and attachment to the United States.

In these two documents of August, 1789, we have missionaries recommended by Washington's Secretary of War and the recommendation sent to the Congress by Washington himself. That Washington and the Congress realized that they were providing money to be furnished by the United States Government for this purpose is shown by the original recommendation:

The expense of such a system may be considered as a sufficient reason for rejecting it, but when this shall be compared with the system of coercion in handling the Indians, it would be found the highest economy to adopt it.

So it was not by any oversight or inadvertence that Washington's administration began spending tax money to support religion and religious education. It was a deliberate and open expression of that purpose, and it was for over a century carried out consistently.

It is interesting in view of the erroneous claims made by Justices Rutledge, Black, and others in regard to the position of Thomas Jefferson, to recall in some detail one of Jefferson's actions in his dealing with Congress which is a complete rebuttal of the truth of the allegations of the Supreme Court Justices and others united to banish religion from education. On October 31, 1803, President Thomas Jefferson sent to the Senate a treaty recently concluded with the Kaskaskia Indians by William Henry Harrison, Governor of the Indian Territory, Superintendent of Indian Affairs and Commissioner Plenipotentiary of the United States. This treaty contained the following passage: "And whereas the greater part of said tribe have been baptized and received into the Catholic Church, to which they are much attached, the United States will give annually, for seven years one hundred dollars toward the support of a priest of that religion, who will engage to perform for said tribe the duties of his office, and also to instruct as many of their children as possible, in the rudiments of literature, and the United States will further give the sum of three hundred dollars, to assist the said tribe in the erection of a church." [20]

That neither Congress nor the clergymen of the United States in the years nearest to the formulation of the First Amendment believed in the modern slogan of the "complete and absolute separation of church and state," even for the federal government, is completely demonstrated by the record of the sums of money which Congress appropriated regularly to missionaries and missionary organizations for decade after decade following the adoption of the First Amendment. On March 3, 1824, the Board of Foreign Missions applied to Congress for financial assistance for their work among the Indians. The following statements are quoted from the petition of the Board of Foreign Missions to Congress under that date:

Stating summarily what this Board and other boards of similar purpose, of different denominations, have done and are doing . . . and the encouraging proposals for the future . . . provided the means are furnished adequate to the support of their contemplated operations; and soliciting such pecuniary aid from the government as in their wisdom they shall see fit to grant . . . to extend the blessings of civilization and Christianity . . . we are happy to acknowledge with much gratitude the aid received from the government. . . . The object of the government and the board is one . . . their civil, moral and religious development [that is, the civil, moral and religious development of the Indians]. It is desirable that our Indians should receive such an education, because the Bible, and the religion therein revealed to us . . . are blessings of infinite and everlasting value, and which the Indians do not now enjoy,

[20] *American State Papers*, Class II. Indian Affairs, Vol I, *Documents of Congress, Lourie and Clarke* (Ed.), (Washington, D. C., Gales & Seaton, 1832), No. 104, 8th Congress, 1st Session, p. 687.

and again the question of how the money is to come for this support of religion and civilization:

A very small part of the profits on the many millions of acres of most valuable land purchased by the government from these would furnish ample pecuniary means for the support of as many educational establishments as would be competent to the purpose; and the religious associations of the different denominations of Christians, already formed and forming, stand ready faithfully to apply these means, when put at their disposal.[21]

This is a striking example of the cooperation of the United States government and the missionary groups in using government money to spread religion among the Indians. Federal funds raised by taxation were furnished by the United States Government for this purpose from 1789 to 1900.

In August, 1912, President William Howard Taft approved a decision of his Secretary of the Interior that the wearing of religious garb in the Indian schools conducted by the United States government did not violate the Constitution. He also approved the recommendation that the wearing of such garb should be gradually discontinued by not employing new teachers who would wear religious uniform in the school rooms, but allowing those already in the service to continue as before. By January, 1933, there were five of these "prior service" teachers wearing religious garb in the Indian schools.[22]

By 1896, Congress was appropriating annually over $500,000 [23] in support of sectarian Indian education carried on by religious organizations. This expenditure of public money appropriated by act of Congress for over a century following the ratification of the First Amendment constitutes absolute proof that for over a century neither Congress nor the religious leaders interpreted the First Amendment to mean a prohibition of the use of public funds by Congress in aid of religion and religious education.

In 1897, Congress decided upon another policy. They declared by the act of June 7, 1897 that it should be the settled policy of the

[21] Indian Affairs, Vol. II, 1st session, 18th Congress, p. 446.
[22] See Johnson, Alvin W., Church-State Relationships in the United States (Minneapolis, University of Minnesota Press, 1934), pp. 209-212.
[23] Ibid., p. 199.

government hereafter to make no appropriation whatever for education in any sectarian school. This was a declaration of policy by Congress. Whether or not a Congressional resolution can settle the policy of the government in a way to be binding on succeeding Congresses, is not a matter that should concern us here. The point is that in declaring this policy, there was no contention that Congress had been committing unconstitutional acts for the last century.

This is clearly demonstrated by the fact that in this act declaring the change of policy, Congress provided for continuing appropriations for another three years, tapering off the appropriations to end in 1900.

We have not only Congressional evidence that this was considered only a question of wisdom and expediency, and not a question of constitutionality, but the declaration of the Supreme Court of the United States in a lawsuit which grew out of the Act of 1897. This was the famous Quick Bear lawsuit,[24] decided by the Supreme Court in 1908. It resulted from a protest against public money being paid to the Catholic Board of Indian Missions. The contention was that such payments violated the declared policy of the Act of June 7, 1897. The Supreme Court ruled that the payment was not a violation of this Act because the money that was paid to the Catholic Board of Indian Missions was not tax money but "treaty funds" which belonged to the Indians. The United States was only the custodian of the treaty funds and Congress could appropriate such funds to the Catholic Board of Indian Missions. This, of course, required the Congress of the United States to pass a law about "religion or religious institutions," and the action would have been clearly unconstitutional under the Rutledge doctrine. The Supreme Court, however, in 1908 did not see it that way; in fact, it was not even argued that it was unconstitutional. The modern slogan had not been adopted at that time. Chief Justice Fuller speaking for the Supreme Court in handing down the decision said in regard to the action they were passing upon, "It is not contended that it is unconstitutional, and it could not be." [25]

---

[24] *Quick Bear* v. *Leupp*, 210 U. S. 50.
[25] For an inaccurate statement about this case, see Justice Rutledge's footnote 35. 330 U. S. 1 at 44. (Also see p. 130.)

Recently, Congress has passed the G. I. Bill of Rights, under which large sums of money are paid to religious schools and colleges throughout the United States—religious schools and colleges of various denominations. No possible violation of the First Amendment, as it was written and as it was intended to be written, can be found in this Bill, but, obviously it is in violation of the Rutledge doctrine. The same is true of the School Lunch Bill passed recently by Congress. In fact, we find Congress right up to 1948 providing funds to religious schools for work among the Indians. A letter addressed to me dated February 4, 1948, signed by Willard W. Beatty, Director of Education in the Office of Indian Affairs, Department of the Interior said that they asked Congress for a greater amount but that

Congress cut our total request for all Indian educational purposes by $725,300 and directed that the cut be distributed among the various items in the budget estimates. The application of the cut resulted in a decrease of $12,023 in the item "Mission Schools," leaving the amount of $173,477 for that purpose. These funds are "authorized only for the care of Indian children and are not applicable to the cost of their education"—"while attending mission schools."

However, the point is that today Congress is appropriating money to religious schools for the care of Indian children. This would be unconstitutional if the doctrine proclaimed by Justice Rutledge and the new organization, "Protestants and Other Americans United," were sound and accepted by the courts of the United States.

Of the institutions specified to receive the sum mentioned above, eight are Catholic, one is Episcopal, and the other is given as "nondenominational."

"A month after the decision in the McCollum case, Congress passed, and the President signed, an appropriation of $500,000 to erect a chapel for religions at the United States Merchant Marine Academy at King's Point, New York." [26] This shows that in the current Congress, the modern slogan "complete and absolute separation of church and state" or the Rutledge doctrine that there can be no cooperation of any kind between government and religion, as a con-

[26] *American Bar Association Journal* (Chicago, June, 1948), p. 484.

stitutional mandate, has no standing. At about the same time, the Senate of the Eightieth Congress voted down by a vote of eighty to five an amendment to the Federal Aid to Education bill which would have specifically excluded non-public schools from federal aid. The amendment in question would have made it impossible for any of the federal funds to be used for welfare services to parochial schools, even in states which permit such use of state funds. Such use of either federal or state funds is contrary to the *dicta* in both the Everson and McCollum cases, violates the doctrine of the manifestoes of "Protestants and Other Americans United for the Separation of Church and State," and is offensive to atheists everywhere. It is, however, in complete agreement with the provisions of the Constitution and the writings and practices of the Founding Fathers, who were the architects of the American system of religious equality and religious freedom.

In dealing with the question of an established religion or an established church, we should always keep in mind that an establishment of religion is always an act of government and can only be an act of government. Establishment is a political doctrine, to be accomplished by a political act. In this country, it takes legislative action to establish or disestablish a church or a religion. It would take the action of the legislature of an individual state to set up a state church, and it would take legislative action by Congress to set up a national church. The first clause of the First Amendment, which makes it impossible for Congress to pass any law at all concerning the subject, makes a national church for the United States an impossibility so long as we have the First Amendment.

Obviously, if the Supreme Court is not bound by the language, or the purpose behind the language, which is to be found in the Constitution of the United States, then no one knows, or can know, what constitutional provisions we have for religion or anything else. We may have some sense of security, however, from the fact that even though the Supreme Court should decide some Monday morning that they were in favor of an established church, we might still maintain our policy of religious equality through the fact that the Supreme Court could not establish a church. That would take congressional action. If the American people accept the implications of the McCollum case decision, then reliance upon the Congress of the United States as being sufficiently close to the people to express the will of the people, is the only reliance that we have left that any of the freedoms expressed in the Constitution and the Bill of Rights which we have had for 160 years will not be wiped out by the Supreme Court. This can happen whenever a majority of the Supreme Court feel that it is their function to save the American people from the ineptitude of Congress and the state legislatures, from the inadequacies of the democratic process, and from the blunders of Jefferson and Madison which have become embedded in the Constitution of the United States.

The second major way in which the record of the Congress, as the responsible representative of the American people, has completely demonstrated the subversive nature of the McCollum case decision, is the way in which Congress has treated proposed amendments to the Constitution which would limit the freedom of the States in the realm of religion or education.

In the last century the antagonisms between the Protestants and the Catholics eventually led to constitutional and statutory provisions in practically every state in the Union removing Protestantism from the programs in the public schools and prohibiting the use of public funds in the support of religious schools. Following this achievement there developed a desire on the part of a number of people to make it difficult or impossible for the states to change this situation. These people sought to put into the Constitution of the United States a provision which would take from the States their freedom of action in this area which had been guaranteed to them by the First Amendment. This last great period of attack on the First Amendment was in the period of about 1870-1888. That attack differed from the current attack which is described in detail in Chapter Four. The campaign to destroy the First Amendment in 1870-1888 was a frank and open attempt to change the Constitution according to the democratic procedure provided in the Constitution itself for its amendment. It was not like the modern strategy of avoiding the democratic process of amending and circumventing the will of the American people by putting these restrictions upon the States regardless of what the American people think of them simply by an edict of the Supreme Court. This strategy had its first success in the decision in the McCollum case of March 8, 1948.

In the earlier campaign to destroy the First Amendment, there were no fewer than eleven separate formulations of amendments to the Constitution in this area submitted to the Congress between 1870 and 1888. Five of them were introduced into the House and six into the Senate. *Congress repudiated every one of the eleven amendments.* The responsible and authoritative representatives of the American people in that period refused eleven attempts to make the Constitution say something like what the Supreme Court now says it has been saying since 1791! In other words, the American people, having refused through their responsible representatives to allow this doctrine to be put into the Constitution, the Supreme Court decides that it has become a basic constitutional principle. This is Alice-in-Wonderland constitutional law. If someday the Supreme Court wishes to be logical (I can see very little evidence of this in their recent decisions), I should suppose, following their statements in the Everson and McCollum cases, they would have to conclude that any measure which was so unfortunate as to pass both Houses of Congress and be ratified by the people of the various states according to the provisions of the Constitution, would thereby be unconstitutional, and the observance of it by the American people would be prohibited by the Supreme Court.

If the *denial of constitutional status* for a given doctrine again and again every time in history when it has come up for decision, makes that doctrine a basic constitutional principle, it seems to be fair to assume that actual adoption and ratification by the American people would remove a doctrine permanently from a position of constitutional force.

It is interesting to note that again and again propagandists for the spurious slogan of "complete and absolute separation of church and state" quote Grant's speech in favor of the doctrine and Blaine's amendment which he offered in Congress as an expression of Grant's belief, and underscore the fact that Blaine's amendment passed the House and received a majority vote in the Senate, but did not receive the two-thirds necessary to submit it to the states for ratification. Much is made of this particular incident, and no mention is made of the other ten, no one of which passed either House of Congress. In regard to Blaine's amendment, it can be said that it had considerable prestige behind it. It had the recommendation of the popular President of the United States, the great general who had won the Civil War, and who had not yet been generally recognized as a rather incompetent President in spite of his great military record. He was a President belonging to the tremendously dominant Republican party of that time, and the amendment was sponsored by James G. Blaine, one of the great congressional leaders in American history. With all this backing, and with the sentiments which this amendment expressed having very wide support—if not almost universal endorsement *as state action*—even so it was denied a place in the United States Constitution.

There is in Congressional history no evidence whatever that the people of the United States have ever changed their belief in the doctrine of the First Amendment as it was written by the First Congress, providing that governmental control in such domestic concerns as religion and education shall be the responsibility of the individual states.

These are the eleven formulations of amendments.[27] Of the eleven proposals submitted to Congress, five were introduced in the House as follows by:

Mr. Burdette of Missouri	1870
Mr. Blaine of Maine	1875
Mr. O'Brien of Maryland	1876
Mr. Lawrence of Ohio	1876
Mr. Williams of Wisconsin	1876

[27] Ames, Herman V., *Proposed Amendments to the Constitution of the United States, 1789-1889; the Annual Report* of the American History Association in the year 1896 (Washington, Government Printing Office, 1897), Vol. II, House Document No. 353, Fifty-fourth Congress, 2nd Session, pp. 277-78.

The six introduced in the Senate were by:

Senator Steward of Nevada	1871
Senator Frelinghuysen of New Jersey	1876
Senator Sargent of California	1876
Senator Christiancy of Michigan	1876
Senator Edmunds of Vermont	1878
Senator Blair of New Hampshire	1888

The three Senate proposals in 1876 were substitutes offered for the Blaine bill when it reached the Senate—three attempts to find a formula acceptable to the Senate.

"We have refused many times in the past to allow the Rutledge-Black-Frankfurter doctrine a place in the Constitution," say the official representatives of the American people exercising their Constitutional responsibility in Congress. "We have repudiated it every time it has been presented in our history. In the Eightieth Congress (1948) we allowed it to die in committee when Congressman Bryson proposed it. The unbroken record of the American people from 1789 to 1948 has been an emphatic refusal to accept the Rutledge-Black-Frankfurter doctrine."

"Therefore," says the Supreme Court, "the Rutledge-Black- Frankfurter doctrine has become a great Constitutional principle!"

Chapter 8

THE RECORD OF THE
SUPREME COURT

*W*HILE it is true that almost all provisions, constitutional or statutory, which have functioned effectively and with any significance concerning the relation of government to religion in this country, are state provisions, it is also true that today the most heated controversies arise on the federal level.

These modern controversies have to do with the relation of federal government to religion primarily in the matter of federal aid to religious schools. To a minor extent they have to do with the federal support of chaplains in the Army and Navy, with Mr. Myron Taylor's appointment to the Vatican, and even to the federal School Lunch program.

A second type of federal level controversy is brought about by the desire of certain propagandists to deprive the people of the *individual states* of their freedom to legislate on such domestic concerns as religion and education. This was guaranteed to the states by the First Amendment, so the First Amendment is now under attack.

The campaign's principal tactic has been to get the Supreme Court to distort the meaning of the phrase "an establishment of religion," either to make the word "establishment" mean simply public financial support or else to make the whole phrase mean *religion or any religious institution or organization.*

It is not possible to be specific with regard to the program of the modern attack on the First Amendment because from the very nature of the constitutional and historical facts the success of the program necessarily depends upon indefinitiveness, ambiguity and confusion. Rarely is it possible to find any serious attempt at substantiation in any of the manifestoes, public speeches, or court opinions which seek to subvert the First Amendment.

The phrases used above to state with some definiteness the exact nature of the attack are taken from the dissenting opinion of Mr. Justice Rutledge in the Everson case.[1] This is the most detailed attempt to justify the position that the First Amendment means complete, absolute, irrevocable separation of religion from government that has ever been made. It has unmerited influence because it comes from a Justice of the Supreme Court speaking from the Bench of the Supreme Court of the United States. As such it has been hailed with enthusiasm by men whose knowledge of history and Constitutional law should have saved them from making any such endorsement. Not only the above facts but the very nature of the problem (the meaning of a part of the Constitution) makes the record of the Supreme Court of primary importance. Justice Rutledge in his dissenting opinion in the Everson bus case said with fair accuracy: "This case forces us to determine squarely for the first time what was 'an establishment of religion' in the First Amendment's conception." [2] This statement is substantially accurate to the extent that it said that the establishment of religion clause was before the Court. It is inaccurate in saying that it *forced the court "to determine squarely" what this phrase meant,* because the Court succeeded in avoiding doing that. The words "for the first time" are accurate if applied to the compulsory definition idea, but not accurate if intended to say that this clause is before the Court for the first time. It was before the Court in 1899.[3] Justice Rutledge nowhere in his long opinion stated squarely or clearly what he thought an establishment of religion means. He made a good many wild statements about what the First Amendment means, but he elaborately avoided a definition of the central phrase in the whole controversy. Judge Rutledge did however suggest in one place in his text that an establishment of religion meant "religion, religious establishments, or establishments having a religious foundation, whatever their form or special

[1] 330 U. S. 1. [2] *Ibid.*, p. 29.
[3] *Bradfield* v. *Roberts*, 175 U. S. 291.

religious function." [4] He did not say this clearly but he implied it strongly. The only other place in his opinion in which we get a hint as to exactly what he thought the phrase meant, is in his footnote thirty-four,[5] in which he comes close to saying specifically that "establishment" in the First Amendment meant public financial support and nothing more.

Outside of this dissenting opinion there is practically nothing to illuminate this particular aspect of our problem because the other propagandists (including Justices Black, Frankfurter, and Jackson in the McCollum case) omit any discussion that could be called a serious attempt to defend their position. Their technique is to proclaim clearly and often that we are all bound by the great fundamental traditional constitutional principle of complete separation of church and state.

The major errors in the Supreme Court opinions in the Everson bus case, other than those made in dealing with the record of the Supreme Court itself, are discussed at length in Chapter Eleven. The meaning of an establishment of religion in the First Amendment is covered in Chapters Four to Seven. Since, however, the remarks in the Everson case are substantially the total justification offered by the judges for the decision of the Court in the McCollum case,[6] and since the McCollum case gives us the only decision in Supreme Court history which surrenders to the attack on the First Amendment and denies to a state the exact freedom of action which the First Amendment was specifically designed to preserve, it seems well to start the consideration of the record of the Supreme Court by touching upon some aspects of the references to previous Supreme Court decisions which are found in the Everson opinions.

Space does not allow comment upon all such references, but a few samples may suffice to show how completely untrustworthy is the handling of *the Supreme Court record by Supreme Court Justices* in the Everson opinions. In one of Justice Rutledge's paragraphs [7] he gave an elaborate statement of the purpose of the First Amendment. (Given in full on p. 211.) Such a list of purposes ascribed

[4] 330 U. S. 1, p. 44.
[5] Ibid.

[6] 333 U. S. 203.
[7] 330, U. S. 1, pp. 31, 32.

to a simple provision to prohibit any laws by Congress on a specific subject is startling enough to find in a Supreme Court opinion. But the concluding sentence is still more startling. It says that the "Amendment's *wording* and *history* unite with this Court's *consistent utterances* in proof*" of all the list. [Italics mine.]

Just reading the First Amendment ought to be sufficient for anyone who knows English to show that its *wording* does nothing of the sort. Anyone who knows the history of the fight against establishment in this country, the records of Jefferson and Madison (given in Chapters Five and Six), or who has read the *Annals* of the First Congress, and other congressional history (Chapter Seven) knows that *history* thoroughly disproves every single sentence in Justice Rutledge's statement of the *purpose* of the First Amendment. Bad as all this is, it seems to me that the worst offense committed in this statement is the statement that the Supreme Court's *consistent utterances* prove the positions which Justice Rutledge has taken. *No such consistent utterances are referred to. No such consistent utterances can be referred to because there are none.*

Further on, after citing various remarks of Madison and Jefferson, not about the First Amendment but about a statute in Virginia, Justice Rutledge has this remarkable little paragraph:

> In view of this history no further proof is needed that the Amendment forbids any appropriation, large or small, from public funds to aid or support any and all religious exercises. But if more were called for, the debates in the First Congress and this *Court's consistent expressions* whenever it has touched on the matter directly, supply it.[8] [Italics mine.]

Justice Rutledge is not here simply getting bogged down in early American history and biography. That is bad enough, but this is worse. This is a Justice of the Supreme Court talking about the record of the Supreme Court, and what he says is simply not true.

As will be shown, the exactly opposite position has been taken a number of times by the Supreme Court. It was not until the decision in the McCollum case thirteen months later that we have a single decision of the Supreme Court which justifies Justice Rutledge's

[8] *Ibid.*, p. 41.

position. The consistent utterances are strictly *ex post facto*. But we have some now, the echoes in the McCollum case of the Justices quoting themselves in their earlier indiscretions in the Everson case. If one must have the consolation of consistent utterances, the echo technique is almost sure fire.

Justice Rutledge does not quote from the debates in the First Congress in which the members of the First Congress were working out the language of the Amendment and in which Madison clearly explained its purpose or intent. The record of the First Congress completely disproves the Rutledge position (see p. 96). But Justice Rutledge does have a footnote attached to the passage just quoted (#32). When the reader goes to footnote thirty-two,[9] expecting to find one citation to an expression of the Supreme Court which is consistent with the Rutledge doctrine, what does he find? Not that there ever was a case in which consistent expressions were used, but the interesting fact that *Cochran v. Board of Education*, 281 U. S. 370 *was not such a case!* (Italics, exclamation point, and a few phrases not included in this text, are mine.) If Justice Rutledge wished he could have cited pages and pages of Supreme Court cases which were *not such cases*. Since there are no cases that *are* such cases, he had the total record of the Court from which to choose. No cases, however, are cited in which there are any "consistent utterances." In one instance [10] Justice Rutledge referred to a case in which expressions of the Supreme Court "confirm the Amendment's broad prohibition." Here also there is a footnote, number thirty-five. This note discusses the famous case of *Quick Bear v. Leupp*.[11] It contains two errors of such magnitude that I shall quote from it at length:

The decision most closely touching the question, *where it was squarely raised*, is *Quick Bear* v. *Leupp*. 210 U. S. 50. The Court distinguished sharply between appropriations from public funds for the support of religious education and appropriations from funds held in trust by the Government essentially as trustee for private individuals, Indian wards, as beneficial owners. The ruling was that the latter could be disbursed to private, religious schools at the designation of those patrons for paying the cost of their education. *But it was stated also that such a use of public moneys would violate both the First Amendment* and the specific

9 *Ibid.*   10 *Ibid.*, p. 43.   11 210 U. S. 50.

statutory declaration involved, namely, that "it is hereby declared to be the settled policy of the government to hereafter make no appropriation whatever for education in any sectarian school." 210 U. S. at 79. [Italics mine.]

It will be noted that Justice Rutledge does not say by whom it was stated that "such use of public moneys" would violate the First Amendment. I submit, however, that it is a fair inference considering the sentence to which this footnote is attached, and the language of the footnote itself, to conclude that Justice Rutledge was conveying the impression that *the Court* stated that such use of public money would violate the First Amendment. If this is not meant, it is difficult to understand what is meant. The truth, however, is that Chief Justice Fuller delivering the opinion of the Supreme Court in this case said nothing of the sort. He did say: "Some reference is made to the Constitution in respect to this contract with the Bureau of Catholic Indian Missions. It is not contended that it is unconstitutional, and it could not be." [12]

This is the only specific reference to the Constitution in this Court opinion. There is none on page 79. If Justice Rutledge's remark about the First Amendment is based on anything which Chief Justice Fuller said in speaking for the Court, it must be based on this passage:

But it is contended that the spirit of the Constitution requires that the declaration of policy that the Government "shall make no appropriation whatever for education in any sectarian schools" should be treated as applicable, on the ground that the actions of the United States were to always be undenominational, and that, therefore, the Government can never act in a sectarian capacity, either in the use of its own funds or in that of the funds of others, in respect of which it is a trustee; hence that even the Sioux trust fund cannot be applied for education in Catholic schools, even though the owners of the fund so desire it. But we cannot concede the proposition that Indians cannot be allowed to use their own money to educate their children in the schools of their own choice because the Government is necessarily undenominational, as it cannot make any law respecting an establishment of religion or prohibiting the free exercise thereof.

[12] *Ibid.,* at 81.

I submit that to any literate person these sentences do not say that the use of public money to pay for the education of Indian children in religious schools would violate the First Amendment.

Also Justice Rutledge's other statement that the question of "the Amendment's broad prohibition" was "squarely raised" in this case, is simply not true—as anyone can see by reading the official report of the case. Furthermore whatever was squarely raised in this case concerning the action of Congress in making a law *respecting religion or a religious organization* was squarely decided against Judge Rutledge's position. This is as close as he comes to citing a "consistent utterance" of the Court to back up his thesis, and its total effect is the exact opposite! Not much more should be needed to demonstrate the unreliability of Justice Rutledge's dissenting opinion.

Brief comments on a few other cases, however, may be helpful at this point. In 1899 *Bradfield* v. *Roberts* [13] arose over the construction of an isolation building or ward on the grounds of a hospital conducted by a Roman Catholic sisterhood in the District of Columbia. Payments were made by the District of Columbia on account of poor patients sent to the hospital by the Commissioners of the District. The plaintiff based his claim upon the contention that Congress had no power to make "*a law respecting a religious establishment.*" The Court upheld the arrangement, denying that the First Amendment was violated. In so doing Mr. Justice Peckham, writing the opinion for a unanimous Court, stated (page 297) that this was "*a phrase which is not synonymous with that used in the Constitution which prohibits the passage of a law 'respecting an establishment of religion.'*" In view of this case it is a little puzzling that Justice Rutledge said that the Everson case raised squarely for the first time the question about what an establishment of religion means. He may, however, have intended simply to say, that the question of this *definition* was raised squarely in the Everson case because the Court did not give such a definition in the Bradfield case. However, while Justice Peckham did not say what "an establishment of religion" does mean, he said it *did not* mean "a religious establishment," which is what Justice Rutledge apparently thinks is its proper meaning.

[13] 175 U. S. 291.

There is also extreme confusion in Justice Black's handling of the previous record of the Court in his majority opinion in the Everson case. In his attempt to make the First Amendment's first clause cover his large expansion of its purpose, he writes as follows:

> The meaning and scope of the First Amendment, preventing establishment of religion or prohibiting the free exercise thereof, in the light of its history and the *evils it was designed forever to suppress,* have been several times elaborated by the decisions of this Court prior to the application of the First Amendment to the states by the Fourteenth. The broad meaning given the Amendment by these earlier cases has been accepted by this Court in its decisions concerning *an individual's religious freedom* rendered since the Fourteenth Amendment was interpreted to make the prohibitions of the First applicable to state action abridging religious freedom. *There is every reason to give the same application and broad interpretation to the "establishment of religion" clause.* The interrelation of these complementary clauses was well summarized in a statement of the Court of Appeals of South Carolina, quoted with approval by this Court in *Watson v. Jones,* 13 Wall. 679, 730: "The structure of our government has, for the preservation of civil liberty, rescued the temporal institutions from *religious interference.* On the other hand, it has secured *religious liberty* from the invasions of the civil authority." [14] [Italics mine.]

A prohibition of action by Congress could not have been *designed to suppress evils.* What Justice Black means by a "broad interpretation" of "an establishment of religion" is not clear. Religious freedom is obviously a broad and general term covering a great variety of possible cases. "An establishment of religion" to Madison and the men of his time (and to innumerable historians and legal scholars dealing with the relations of government to religion both in Europe and America) was an exact, specific term. The attempt to make it mean "religion or any religious organization or institution" is not interpretation of language. It is unscholarly violation of language.

Further to imply that to allow voluntary participation in religious education classes in a public school constitutes "religious interference" because it creates "an establishment of religion" is simply an incompetent use of words. When such participation was requested by the parents of over eight hundred children, approved by the Board

[14] *Everson v. Board of Education,* 330 U. S., pp. 14-15.

of Education and sanctioned by the Supreme Court of the State of Illinois as conforming to the statutes and the state constitution, and opposed only in behalf of one child, who was of course not required to participate, the banning of the practice is obviously much closer to an interference with freedom of religion than the plan itself could possibly be. Such banning by a Supreme Court decision is, moreover, the antithesis of democratic decision and a denial of the precise freedom of action which the First Amendment was deliberately designed to preserve to the people of Illinois.

Space does not permit a full report of all of the fourteen cases Judge Black referred to in footnotes attached to this paragraph. But some sampling will show that the cases do not back up his expansion of the First Amendment. The following six cases, plus *Quick Bear* v. *Leupp* (see pp. 130-132) and *Bradfield* v. *Roberts* (see p. 132) already discussed, will doubtless suffice. *Davis* v. *Beason*, 133 U. S. 333, (1890), a criminal prosecution sought to be defended on the ground that polygamy was a matter of religious belief which was protected by the First Amendment, contains language by Mr. Justice Field, which indicated that the Court still held to Madison's meaning of the establishment of religion clause of the First Amendment as follows:

It is assumed by counsel of the petitioner, that because *no mode of worship can be established or religious tenets enforced* in this country, therefore any form of worship may be followed and any tenets, however destructive of society, may be held and advocated, if asserted to be a part of the religious doctrines of those advocating and practicing them. But nothing is further from the truth. Whilst legislation for *the establishment of a religion* is forbidden, and its free exercise permitted, it does not follow that everything which may be so called can be tolerated.[15] [Italics mine.]

The italicized passages, which obviously refer to the establishment of religion clause, are strikingly similar to the explanation given by James Madison in the Congressional Debates (see p. 96). They give no aid or comfort to Judge Black's position, but are entirely consistent with my thesis.

In *Cantwell* v. *Connecticut*, 310 U. S. 296 (1940), the first case

[15] 133 U. S. 333 at 345.

(seventy-two years after the ratification of the Fourteenth Amendment) which overruled a state court on the ground that religious freedom had been violated, the First Amendment was not involved in *the decision* as distinct from *the dicta*. The decision was that the Jehovah's Witnesses in the case had been deprived of religious liberty (as one of the basic liberties inherent in a scheme of ordered liberty) "without due process of law" as provided in the Fourteenth Amendment. But even the *dicta* are of no help to Justice Black. Mr. Justice Roberts interpreted the words, "Congress shall make no law respecting an establishment of religion or prohibiting the free exercise thereof," as follows:

The constitutional inhibition of legislation on the subject of religion has a double aspect. On the one hand, it forestalls *compulsion by law of the acceptance of any creed or the practice of any form of worship.* Freedom of conscience and freedom to adhere to such religious organization or form of worship as the individual may choose cannot be restricted by law. On the other hand, it safeguards the free exercise of the chosen form of religion. Thus the amendment embraces two concepts,— freedom to believe and freedom to act.[16] [Italics mine.]

This quotation clearly indicates that the establishment of religion clause means no "compulsion by law of the acceptance of any creed or the practice of any form of worship" and does not imply that it contained any broader prohibition. There is nothing here about *taxes* or education. The language used in this opinion of the Court is almost identical with that adopted by the United States Senate on September 9, 1789 which expressed officially the Senate's meaning of an establishment of religion: "Congress shall make no law establishing articles of faith or a mode of worship."

Terret v. *Taylor*, 9 Cranch (U. S.) 43, involved the validity of *Virginia statutes* seeking to subject to sale by the overseer of the poor the lands formerly belonging to the Anglican Church. The First Amendment to the Federal Constitution was not involved. In discussing the laws of Virginia, Mr. Justice Story said:

Consistently with the constitution of Virginia the legislature could not create or continue a religious establishment which should have exclusive

16 310 U. S. 296 at 345.

rights and prerogatives, or compel the citizens to worship under a stipu-
lated form or discipline or to pay taxes to those whose creed they could
not conscientiously believe. *But the free exercise of religion cannot be
justly deemed to be restrained by aiding with equal attention the votaries
of every sect to perform their own religious duties,* or by establishing
funds for the support of ministers, for public charities, for the endow-
ment of churches, or for the sepulture of the dead.[17] [Italics mine.]

Justice Black naturally omitted to explain how this case bolsters up
his concept of the meaning of the First Amendment.

In *Reynolds* v. *United States*, the matter before the Court, a prosecution for polygamy, did not involve the "establishment of religion"
clause of the First Amendment. The discussion of the meaning of
the First Amendment which appears in that case answered the de-
fendant's argument that he could not be punished for polygamy because polygamy was an exercise of his constitutional right to *freedom
of religion.* The case did not involve in any way the possible *financial* relationships between government and religion.

In connection with Justice Black's elaborate and erroneous *dictum*
in the Everson case (see p. 195), in which he expanded the religious
clause of the First Amendment to mean all sorts of things that it
could not possibly have been intended to mean by its authors, he
gave as his only reference this case of *Reynolds* v. *United States.*
In view of this single reference attached to a misrepresentation of
what Jefferson said in his reply to the Baptists of Danbury, it may
be interesting to see what Chief Justice Waite actually said in the
Reynolds case about Jefferson's little letter of courtesy.

In *Reynolds* v. *United States* [18] on the question of congressional
prohibition of polygamy, Chief Justice Waite delivering the opinion, in speaking of Jefferson's bill for establishing religious freedom in
Virginia, said:

In the preamble of this act religious freedom is defined; and after a recital, "that *to suffer the civil magistrate to intrude his powers into the
field of opinion,* and to restrain the profession or propagation of principles on supposition of their ill tendency, is a dangerous fallacy which
at once destroys all religious liberty," it is declared "that it is time

17 *Terret* v. *Taylor,* 9 Cranch (U. S.) 43 at 49.
18 98 U. S. 145 (1879).

enough for *the rightful purposes of civil government for its officers to interfere when principles break out into overt acts against peace and good order."* In these two sentences is found the true distinction between what properly belongs to the church and what to the state. [Italics mine.]

Further on the Chief Justice quoted from Jefferson's reply to the Committee of the Danbury, Connecticut, Baptist Association (see Appendix E):

Adhering to this expression of the supreme will of the nation [the first clause of the First Amendment] *in behalf of the rights of conscience,* I shall see with sincere satisfaction the progress of those sentiments which tend to restore to man all his natural rights, convinced he has no natural rights in opposition to his social duties.[19] [Italics mine.]

Chief Justice Waite continued:

Coming as this does from an acknowledged leader of the advocates of the measure, it may be accepted as almost an authentic declaration of the scope and effect of the amendment thus secured. *Congress was deprived of all legislative power over mere opinion,* but was left free to reach actions which were in violation of social duties and good order. [Italics mine.]

Certainly there is no support here for the new theory of the First Amendment's purpose.

On the contrary the purpose of the First Amendment's language which Jefferson said had erected a wall of separation between church and state was said by Jefferson *in his next sentence* (never quoted by the enemies of the First Amendment) to the protection of *the rights of conscience.* Since the rights of conscience of members of dissident groups are *always* interfered with by established churches, and *never* interfered with by treating all religions alike, this passage is proof (if any is needed) that Jefferson understood the purpose of the First Amendment to be exactly what Madison and the others of the First Congress said it was. If the devotees of the "wall of separation" as a substitute for the language of the First Amendment

[19] Was Jefferson at this point suggesting to the Baptists of Connecticut that he hoped these sentiments would progress in Connecticut to the point at which the Baptists of that state would enjoy the same privileges under the state that were then and, for years after, the sole possessions of the Congregationalists?

would only read one sentence beyond the metaphor, and consider it in the context of the time (1802), they could know just what kind of "separation" Jefferson had in mind. (See Appendix E.)

Watson v. Jones, 13 Wall. (U. S.) 679 (1872), did not involve the meaning of the establishment of religion clause, and the Court did not undertake to define it. What was there involved was the question of the jurisdiction of a court of equity to adjudicate a property dispute between factions of a Presbyterian congregation which had divided on the slavery issue. However the Court did express the standard Jefferson-Madison doctrine that is expressed in the First Amendment. Mr. Justice Miller in giving the opinion of the Court said:

In this country the full and free right to entertain any religious belief, to practice any religious principle, and to teach any religious doctrine which does not violate the laws of morality or property, and which does not infringe personal rights is conceded to all. The law knows no heresy, and is committed to no dogma, the establishment of no sect.[20]

The quotation given by Justice Black as quoted by the Supreme Court in *Watson v. Jones*, is from a South Carolina case, *Harmon v. Dreher*, 1 Speer's Eq. 17, 120 (1843). This is a generalized statement which has nothing to do with the specific question before the Court in the Everson case. This is clear from the fact that the *Harmon* case, from which the quotation was taken, was a suit by a minister claiming certain rights in the use of church property notwithstanding his expulsion as one of the members of the synod. The subject under discussion in the *Harmon* case was what effect should be given by the Court to the action of the ecclesiastical authority in expelling the minister. It gave full effect to such action.

This statement was simply a declaration that our law favors no one sect or religion over another. It is again a common expression of the historical twofold American doctrine of the relation of government to religion, with nothing whatever in it concerning the use of taxes for the impartial support of religion as the United States has practiced it from the beginning.

[20] *Watson v. Jones*, 13 Wall. (U. S.) 679.

Anyone who will note the contradictions between the positions taken by Justices Black and Frankfurter in the Adamson case and the positions of these same Justices in the McCollum case (see pp. 161, 180-184) will hardly be surprised at the following story in the New York Times under a Washington dateline: [21]

DEARTH OF CASES SLOWS HIGH COURT
by Lewis Wood

Faced with a dearth of cases the Supreme Court of the United States has been forced to abandon hearing arguments until new issues can be presented. Because of the peculiar situation, the Justices have used only two days of the current two weeks for hearing the legal debates, as contrasted with the usual eight or ten. . . .

The idea is suggested that because business men, convinced two or three years ago that the high court would eventually rule against them, never went to the trouble and expense of starting law suits in the lower courts. Cases begun at that time in the lower courts, would customarily be reaching the Supreme Court now.

Consulting oracles who are uninhibited by the provisions of a written constitution may well be widely recognized as too troublesome and too expensive to be worth while.

[21] *New York Times*, March 13, 1948, p. 9.

Chapter 9

THE PRACTICES OF THE SEVERAL STATES

*N*O-ONE contends that the First Amendment as adopted and ratified, had any application whatever to the actions of the individual states. There is, moreover, still considerable difference of opinion concerning to what extent the Fourteenth Amendment (1868) restricts the freedom of the states in matters of religion (see Chapter Ten). There is, apparently, no controversy concerning the statement that the earliest decision of the Supreme Court which seemed to recognize *the possibility* that through the Fourteenth Amendment the states *might be* restricted in their authority over regulations concerning personal freedoms embodied in the First Amendment was in the Gitlow case in 1925. (See pp. 172, 176, 266.)

The first case in which the Supreme Court considered a state case involving religious freedom under the Fourteenth Amendment was *Hamilton v. University of California* in 1934 (see p. 177). The first such case in which a state law was invalidated was *Cantwell v. Connecticut* [1] decided in 1940. It follows that the Fourteenth Amendment had no discernible influence on state provisions in this area until after 1925, and that it could have had no direct, controlling influence on such state action until after 1940.

The above facts (when coupled with the dates on which the various states in the Union took action forbidding the teaching of religion in public schools, and forbidding public financial support of denominational schools) makes particularly puzzling Justice Frankfurter's statement in his opinion in the McCollum case: "Separation

[1] 310 U. S. 296.

in the field of education, then, was not imposed upon unwilling states by force of superior law. In this respect the Fourteenth Amendment merely reflected a principle then dominant in our national life. To the extent that the Constitution thus made it binding upon the states, the basis of the restriction is the whole experience of our people." [2] What Justice Frankfurter means by "separation" in the field of education is not clear, but if his remark has any relation to reality he must mean the two prohibitions just mentioned: prohibiting the teaching of religion in the public school, and prohibiting funds for religious schools. If so, it is clear to any one who will look up the facts in the history of education, that this "separation" was not *imposed* upon any states, willing or unwilling, by the superior law of the Constitution of the United States. The Fourteenth Amendment had nothing whatever to do with these state provisions. State actions in these matters, prior to 1940, could not possibly have been taken in obedience to the terms of the Fourteenth Amendment.

The following table [3] shows that chronology alone proves that so far as these laws and constitutional provisions are concerned the Fourteenth Amendment might as well not have been written.

First State Action Forbidding Sectarian Instruction in Public Schools.		First State Action Forbidding Public Funds to Denominational Schools.
Up to 1868		
Alabama	1852	1854
Arkansas		1868
California	1855	1855
Connecticut		1818
Georgia		1868
Illinois	1836	
Indiana	1853	1851
Iowa		1857
Kansas		1855
Kentucky		1850

[2] 333 U. S. 203.
[3] Confrey, Burton, *Secularism in American Education* (Washington, Catholic University of America, 1931), pp. 123-125.

First State Action Forbidding Sectarian Instruction In Public Schools.	First State Action Forbidding Public Funds to Denominational Schools.
Up to 1868—Continued	
Louisiana 1855	1864
Maine	1820
Massachusetts	1810
Michigan	1835
Minnesota	1868
Missouri 1835	
Nevada 1864	
New Hampshire	1792
New York 1842	1820
Ohio	1851
Oregon	1857
Rhode Island	1843
South Carolina	1868
Texas	1845
Virginia 1847	
Wisconsin 1848	1848
The Fourteenth Amendment, 1868.	
After 1868, (Before the Gobitis decision 1925)	
Arizona 1879	1879
Colorado 1876	1876
Delaware	1897
Florida	1887
Idaho 1890	1890
Illinois	1870
Kansas 1876	
Kentucky 1893	
Maine 1916	
Minnesota 1907	1875
Mississippi 1922	
Missouri	1875
Montana 1872	1889
Nebraska 1871	1886
New Jersey	1875
New Mexico 1897	1911
North Carolina	1876

North Dakota	1887	1889
Oklahoma	1890	1907
Pennsylvania		1874
South Carolina	1871	
South Dakota	1887	1889
Tennessee		1870
Texas	1870	
Utah	1892	1895
Virginia	1847	1902
Washington	1883	1889
West Virginia		1872
Wyoming	1886	1889

The following table [4] shows the *latest dates* at which certain states in the Union specifically authorized appropriation of public money to religious schools. This again indicates that the Fourteenth Amendment did not control state action for at least some thirty years after its ratification. In fact its first definite restriction on state action in this area is expressed in the McCollum case, March 8, 1948.

The Latest Dates on which Public Money was Appropriated to Religious Schools in Certain States.

Maryland	1818	
Pennsylvania	. 1838	
New Hampshire	1845	
New Jersey	1846	
Indiana	1855	14th Amendment
California	1870	1868
New York	1871	
Texas	1874	
Mississippi	1878	
New Mexico	1897	

Every state in the Union has in its constitution a section prohibiting an establishment of religion in some words or other. All but two

[4] Brown, Samuel Windsor, *The Secularization of American Education*, Contributions to Education, No. 49 (New York, Teachers College, Columbia University, 1912), Chapter IV.

have laws or constitutional provisions prohibiting either the teaching of religion in the public schools or the support of religious schools by public funds or both.[5]

A number of the states, Iowa, Louisiana, South Carolina, and Utah, use the exact words of the federal Constitution, "no law respecting an establishment of religion." However, not a single state in the United States, when it desired to prohibit either religion in public education or public support of religious education, relied upon the prohibition of "an establishment of religion," either in these exact words of the First Amendment or in a synonymous expression, to accomplish either of these specific purposes. If this language from the First Amendment constitutes a constitutional bar to either of these practices, it is strange indeed that not a single state in the Union placed any such reliance upon it. The fact is that until the current attack began to develop on our constitutional provisions concerning governmental relations with religion prescribing complete autonomy in the individual states, it apparently never occurred to anyone that any such meaning could be gotten out of the language of the First Amendment. However, if the objectives of the modern attack are to be accomplished in the interests of secularism and atheism, it apparently became evident to the directors of the campaign that they would either have to get the First Amendment out of their way or be prepared to fight forty-nine campaigns instead of one.

It should be kept in mind that the two common state provisions mentioned above fall far short of providing for that absolute and complete separation of government and religion which is the objective of those behind the Rutledge doctrine. Today there is in the United States little denominational religion legally in the public school systems, and substantially no direct public financial support of denominational schools. There is, however, not a state that has, or ever has had, complete and absolute separation of religion and government, which I suppose is what is meant by the modern slogan, "complete separation of church and state."

[5] See Johnson, Alvin W., *The Legal Status of Church-State Relationships in the United States* (Minneapolis, University of Minnesota Press, 1934), particularly chapter XVII, pp. 273-285.

The National Education Association in a recent *Research Bulletin* [6] publishes two illuminating tables, setting forth in considerable detail the practices of the various states (a) "in aid to sectarian schools and to sectarianism in public schools" as reported by state superintendents and (b) practices "of supervision of sectarian schools by public school officials" as reported from the same source.

All of the items in both of these tables concern cooperative contacts or relations betwen state government and religion in education. Most of them obviously involve some use of public funds.

I submit that each and every one of the practices here listed would be illegal if the doctrine of separation of church and state as enunciated by Justice Rutledge in the Everson case, and by Justice Black in the *dicta* in the Court's opinion in the McCollum case, should become binding law on all the states in the Union. The result of such a calamity would be complete chaos, because then neither Congress nor any state legislature could pass any law at all concerning religion, or a religious institution, such as a denominational school. We would have complete anarchy in a large part of the educational field in the United States.

The data given in the N. E. A. bulletin are not absolutely complete because there were no returns from the superintendents in some states. Further, I am not making a distinction in this chapter between practices that are *required* and practices that are *permitted*, since both are legal.

The tables in the N. E. A. bulletin indicate the following:

Rental of church owned buildings for public school purposes—
30 states

Free textbooks furnished to parochial school students—5 states

Transportation of parochial school pupils at public expense—
19 states

Bible reading in public schools—38 states

Excusing pupils for week-day church schools—35 states

Religious instruction by church teachers inside public schools
during school hours—10 states

[6] Vol. XXIV, No. 1 (1946), pp. 36-42.

The use of public schools by religious groups after school hours
—16 states (with 11 more states in which it is said that the
law is silent, and the state superintendent did not comment
on the practice)

Equivalent school term—20 states

Certification of teachers—25 states

Registration by the state department—16 states

State-approved course of study—28 states

Prescriptions for the curriculum: American history, etc.—22 states;
Physiology and hygiene—19 states; Effect of alcohol and nar-
cotics—18 states

Standards for facilities and equipment—30 states

Attendance, records—27 states

In addition to the above list of widespread practices of cooperation
between state government and religious education in one form and
another, we have universal tax exemption of all churches, and church
school property. In other words we have clearly at least seventeen
separate breaches in the imaginary wall of separation between religion
and government. This wall of many friendly openings is the one
which the Supreme Court in the McCollum and Everson cases say
must be kept high and impregnable. Such a wall will have to be
built before it can be *kept.* Even the McCollum decision falls far
short of erecting such a wall. The Supreme Court will have to make
an effective "spite fence" out of this wall before they can require all
of the states to *keep* it high and impregnable.

In view of the force which the Supreme Court Justices in these
two recent cases tried to give to Jefferson's Bill for Religious Freedom
enacted by Virginia in 1786 and which Justice Rutledge said in his
dissenting opinion is now made binding on all the states by the
Fourteenth Amendment (see p. 202), it is instructive to notice (and
I should think might be embarrassing to the Supreme Court Justices
if they ever find it out) that the State of Virginia, in which Jefferson's Bill has been law since 1786, first took state action forbidding
sectarian education in public schools in 1847, and first took state
action forbidding public funds to denominational schools in 1902.

Further, of the seventeen practices listed above showing cooperation between government and religion in the field of education, the state of Virginia in 1946 is reported by her superintendent of public instruction to have fifteen of them! *One of the fifteen was the exact system which the Court outlawed in Champaign!*

The following shows the fantastic logic of the present Justices of the United States Supreme Court:

Says the Supreme Court:

I. "The First Amendment means complete separation of church and state (religion and government), because

    A. "This is the meaning of the Virginia statute of 1786, because

        1. "We so interpret remarks made about it by Madison and Jefferson."

These are facts:

I. The First Amendment says nothing of the sort, simply providing that Congress shall leave such matters in the hands of the various states.

    A. The Virginia statute has never been interpreted by the Virginia legislature or courts to mean anything remotely approaching this current doctrine of the Supreme Court. Virginia had on March 8, 1948, the exact practice [7] which the Court on that date declared unconstitutional in Illinois largely on the basis of what the Court thought had been the situation in Virginia since 1786. Virginia also permitted *fourteen other helpful contacts* between government and religion in education as late as 160 years after the passing of the Virginia statute.

        1. Neither Jefferson nor Madison ever anywhere interpreted the Virginia statute to mean what the Court tried to get out of some of their phrases carefully selected and inaccurately reported in some instances (see pp. 73 ff.), while

[7] See *American Bar Association Journal* (June, 1948), p. 483.

avoiding their most specific and direct remarks on the subject. (See pp. 60, 96, 148, 194.) Neither Jefferson (in the succeeding forty years of his life) nor Madison (in fifty years) ever protested Virginia's failure to observe the meaning of the statute which the Justices say Jefferson and Madison thought it meant.

I submit that this evidence is sufficiently extensive, sufficiently direct, and sufficiently weighty to refute *in toto* the interpretation recently put upon one or two fragments taken out of context by the Supreme Court Justices and others concerning the meaning and effect of Jefferson's Bill for Religious Freedom as a law in Virginia—to say nothing of the extravagant claim that their interpretation of the Virginia statute constitutes the essential meaning of the first clause of the First Amendment to the Constitution. The idea that the Supreme Court's interpretation of the meaning of that statute is valid, and yet has never occurred to the people of Virginia in 162 years, is simply silly. That Thomas Jefferson, as the leading citizen and statesman of Virginia profoundly interested in education, never observed in the forty years of his life after the adoption of his Bill for Religious Freedom that the State of Virginia was ignoring its provisions is too absurd to be taken seriously.

We have more than the same kind of negative evidence in the case of Madison. In the *Detatched Memoranda*, he wrote probably some forty years after the Bill for Religious Freedom became law in Virginia, as follows:

. . . there is one State at least, Virginia, where religious liberty is placed on its true foundation and is defined in its full latitude. The general principle is contained in her declaration of rights, prefixed to her Constitution; but it is unfolded and defined, in its precise extent, in the act of the Legislature, usually named the Religious Bill, which passed into a law in the year 1786. . . . This act is a true standard of Religious liberty; its principle the great barrier against usurpations on the rights of conscience.[8]

This Virginia law in which religious liberty "is defined in its full latitude" and which is the "great barrier against usurpations on the

[8] *William and Mary Quarterly*, 3rd Ser., IV (Oct., 1946), p. 554.

rights of conscience," has not, in the 162 years of its existence, been found in Virginia to mean what the Supreme Court now says it has always meant. This fact alone almost completely demolishes the foundation (in the Everson *dicta* and dissent) of the McCollum decision.

Throughout the United States, the establishment or disestablishment of religion has always been the exclusive function of the individual states. The federal government was kept off the subject by the First Amendment. Some of the states originally had established churches, and "many of the early constitutions of the original states set up Christianity as the state religion. Civil rights were guaranteed, but under some constitutions [New Jersey, North Carolina, South Carolina] only to Protestants." [9] "Only Rhode Island had never officially recognized a particular church nor made a religious test for office holding." [10] At the present time no state has a provision for an established religion or state church. The New Hampshire constitution, however, still authorizes "the several towns . . . within this State to make adequate provisions, at their own expense, for the support and maintenance of public Protestant teachers of piety, religion and morality." [11]

The attempt to amend the above provision by striking out the word "Protestant" was made in 1876, but failed, though at the same time the acceptance of the Protestant religion as a test for office was abolished, and the application of moneys raised by taxation for the support of denominational schools was prohibited.[12]

The handling of religious liberty *in the several states* is covered by Cooley in the following passage. Note how clearly "an establishment of religion" is treated *as a preference or favor for one sect over all the others,* and how the support of religious instruction is treated as a separate topic, not as something covered by the prohibition of an establishment.

[9] N.E.A. *Research Bulletin,* Vol. XXIV, No. 1, p. 8.
[10] *Ibid.,* p. 7.
[11] *Ibid.,* p. 8.
[12] Cooley, *Constitutional Limitations,* footnote 2, pp. 580-581.

"A careful examination of the American [state] [13] constitutions will disclose the fact that nothing is more plainly expressed than the determination of their authors *to preserve and perpetuate religious liberty,* and to guard against the slightest approach towards *the establishment of an inequality in the civil and political rights of citizens, which shall have for its basis only their differences of religious belief.* The American people came to the work of framing their fundamental laws after centuries of religious oppression and persecution, sometimes by one party or sect and sometimes by another, had taught them the utter futility of all attempts to propagate religious opinions by the rewards, penalties, or terrors of human laws. They could not fail to perceive, also, that a union of Church and State, like that which existed in England, if not wholly impracticable in America, was certainly opposed to the spirit of our institutions, and that any *domineering of one another* was repressing to the energies of the people, and must necessarily tend to discontent and disorder. Whatever, therefore, may have been their individual sentiments upon religious questions, or upon the propriety of the state assuming supervision and control of religious affairs under other circumstances, the general voice has been, that *persons of every religious persuasion should be made equal before the law,* and that *questions of religious belief and religious worship should be questions between each individual man and his Maker.* Of these questions, human tribunals, so long as the public order is not disturbed, are not to take cognizance, except as the individual, by his voluntary action, in associating himself with a religious organization, may have conferred upon such organization a jurisdiction over him in ecclesiastical matters. *These constitutions, therefore, have not established religious toleration, merely, but religious equality;* in that particular being far in advance not only of the Mother Country, but also of much of the colonial legislation, which, though more liberal than that of other civilized countries, nevertheless exhibited features of discrimination based upon religious beliefs or professions.

Considerable differences will appear in the provisions in the state constitutions on the general subject of the present chapter; some of them being confined to *declarations, and prohibitions* whose purpose is to secure

[13] In these pages where Cooley used the words "American constitutions" he means American *state* constitutions. This should be sufficiently clear from the context. If not, it is in the index (p. 866) in which these items are listed under "care taken by state constitutions." This sentence is sometimes misused to indicate that Cooley included the United States Constitutions in the phrase "American constitutions." This error is made, for instance, in the American Civil Liberties brief (Brief of American Civil Liberties Union as *Amicus Curiæ, Everson* v. *Board of Education.* Supreme Court, October Term, 1946. No. 52, p. 13) and in the N. E. A. *Research Bulletin* referred to above, p. 7.

the most perfect equality before the law of all shades of *religious belief*. While some exhibit a jealousy of ecclesiastical authority by making persons who exercise the functions of clergyman, priest, or teacher of any religious persuasion, society, or sect, ineligible to any civil office; and still others show some traces of the old notion that truth and the sense of duty do not consort with skepticism in religion.

There are exceptional clauses, however, though not many in number; and it is believed that, where they exist, they are not often made use of to deprive any person of the civil or political rights or privileges which are placed by law within the reach of his fellows.

Those things which are not lawful under any of the American [state] constitutions may be stated thus:

1. Any law respecting the establishment of religion. The legislatures have not been left at liberty to effect a union of Church and State, or to establish preferences by law in favor of any one religious persuasion, or mode of worship. There is not complete religious liberty where any one sect is favored by the State and given an advantage by law over other sects. Whatever establishes a distinction against one class or sect is, to the extent to which the distinction operates unfavorably, a persecution; and if based on religious grounds, a religious persecution. The extent of the discrimination is not material to the principle; it is enough that it creates an inequality of right or privilege.

2. Compulsory support, by taxation or otherwise, of religious instruction. . . .

3. Compulsory attendance upon religious worship, whoever is not led by choice or a sense of duty to attend upon the ordinances of religion is not to be compelled to do so by the State. . . .

4. Restraints upon the free exercise of religion according to the dictates of the conscience. . . .

5. Restraints upon the expression of religious belief. . . .

No principle of constitutional law is violated when thanksgiving or fast days are appointed; when chaplains are designated for the army and navy; when legislative sessions are opened with prayer or the reading of the Scriptures, or when religious teaching is encouraged by a general exemption of the houses of religious worship from taxation for the support of State government. Undoubtedly the spirit of the constitution will require, in all these cases, that care be taken to avoid discrimination in favor of or against any one religious denomination or sect; but the power to do any of these things does not become unconstitutional simply because of its susceptibility to abuse. This public recognition of religious worship, however, is not based entirely, perhaps not even mainly, upon a sense of what is due to the Supreme Being himself as the author of all good and of all law; but the same reasons of State policy which induce the government to aid institutions of charity and seminaries of instruction, will incline it also to foster religious worship and religious institutions, as conservators of the public morals, and valuable, if not indispensable assistants in the preservation of the public order.[14] [Italics mine.]

Cooley here follows Jefferson and Madison in expressing the double objective of America's provisions for the relations of religion and government: (1) "to preserve and perpetuate religious liberty" and (2) equality "in the civil and political rights of citizens" of all religious faiths. For generations the several states have in self-respect and constitutional freedom from outside dictation, grown in religious freedom, equality and amity under *state adopted* constitutions and laws. On March 8, 1948, the Supreme Court, following the propaganda of those who do not like the constitutional limitations so dear to Judge Cooley and the Founding Fathers, invaded this situation, wiped out the language and intent of the First Amendment and dictated to the states in terms of the "zeal" and "prepossessions" of the Justices of the Court.

[14] Cooley, *op. cit.*, pp. 576 ff.

Chapter 10

THE EFFECT OF THE FOURTEENTH AMENDMENT

*T*HE Fourteenth Amendment incorporated into the Constitution in 1868 reads in section one, the only part relative to the subject matter of this volume:

All persons born or naturalized in the United States, and subject to the jurisdiction thereof, are citizens of the United States and of the State wherein they reside. No State shall make or enforce any law which shall abridge the privileges or immunities of citizens of the United States, nor shall any State deprive any person of life, liberty, or property, without due process of law, nor deny to any person within its jurisdiction the equal protection of the laws.

I suppose no one will be disposed to question the statement that complete, absolute, unequivocal "separation of church and state" could be made a restriction on the powers of the several states by the Fourteenth Amendment only if that doctrine is found in the First Amendment. No one has ever claimed that this doctrine is enunciated anywhere else in the Constitution.

The problem of the application of the Bill of Rights by the Fourteenth Amendment as a restriction upon the power of the individual states, is still a matter of speculation, clouded by confusion and conflict in the separate opinions of the Justices and in Supreme Court decisions. The decisions not only conflict directly with each other; there are conflicting theories in regard to the authority of the Supreme Court in this matter and also in regard to the proper limitations to be observed in applying to the several states through the Fourteenth Amendment *any* of the restrictions on Congress in the

United States Constitution. As shown by the marked changes of position on the part of individual Justices from case to case, by the frequent overruling of earlier decisions by the Court, and by the elaborate arguments supporting opposing basic theories, as exhibited in *Adamson* v. *California*[1] (see Appendix G), such conflicts are found in extreme form among the judges on the Supreme Court at the present time.

This situation is covered in detail in a recent book by Professor Pritchett[2] of the University of Chicago. He publishes a table[3] showing thirty-two decisions overruled by the Supreme Court in the ten year period 1937-1947. Twenty of the decisions had been on the books for not more than twenty years, nine of them for ten years or less, and of the six newest decisions to be liquidated the most ancient was five years old. Two 1937 decisions, one by a vote of 8-0, the other 5-2, were overruled by a single case in 1939 by a vote of 7-2. The decision in the Gobitis case[4] in 1940, holding that requiring school children to salute the flag (opposed by Jehovah's Witnesses as an infringement on the Constitutional guarantee of religious freedom) did not violate the Constitution, was an 8-1 decision. Two years later, in the case of *Jones* v. *Opelika*,[5] Justices Black, Douglas, and Murphy "not only joined with Stone in dissent, but appended an unprecedented and gratuitous statement confessing repentance for their part in the flag salute decision,"[6] and one year later, in *Murdock* v. *Pennsylvania*,[7] the 8-1 Gobitis decision was overruled by a 5-4 vote.

This confusion is in part at least explained, if not excused, by some items in the history of the Fourteenth Amendment for which the Supreme Court is not responsible. This amendment was conceived in passion, partisanship, and revenge and has been the happy hunting ground of pressure groups and special pleaders throughout its history. It is the basis of more litigation than all the rest of the Constitution combined. It is the only part of the Constitution which

[1] 332 U. S. 46 (1947).
[2] Pritchett, C. Herman, *The Roosevelt Court* (New York, The Macmillan Co., 1948).
[3] pp. 300-301.
[4] 310 U. S. 586 (1940).
[5] 316 U. S. 584 (1942).
[6] Pritchett, *op. cit.*, p. 97.
[7] 319 U. S. 105 (1943).

has the blemish of the persuasions of force rather than reason on its right and title to a place in our fundamental law. In addition to this blot it has probably the unique distinction of being in the Constitution as the result of a strictly party vote. And, as has been observed many times, the protection of the rights of the recently freed Negroes under the Fourteenth Amendment has not amounted to much.

Haines writes [8] in regard to the adoption of this amendment:

By counting the reconstructed states, forcibly put under Republican control, the amendment was finally declared adopted with its meaning and intent very much in doubt. In the controversy over the adoption very little consideration was given to the significance of Section One, the only portion which has had any noticeable effect upon the relations of the federal and state governments.

Collins [9] testifies in the matter of the strict party vote:

So far as the records show, not a single Democrat in a single State in the Union voted in favor of the adoption of the Amendment.

The application, in any manner, of the establishment of religion clause of the First Amendment to the legislatures of the several states was unpremeditated, unforeseen, unintended by the men responsible for the Fourteenth Amendment. The application to the states of the Congressional restrictions mentioned *in any part* of the First Amendment was not "assumed" by the Supreme Court [10] until fifty-seven years after the ratification of the Fourteenth. So far as the relation of government to an establishment of religion is concerned, any influence that is now or ever will be exercised by the Fourteenth Amendment, is a clear constitutional accident.[11]

In the years 1868 to 1911, in cases brought under the Fourteenth Amendment, the Supreme Court decisions constituted federal intervention in state affairs fifty-five times. *None of these cases involved the religion clause of the First Amendment.*[12] Throughout

[8] Haines, C. G., "The History of Due Process After the Civil War," 3 *Texas Law Review* 1, 1924. Reprinted in Selected Essays I, p. 269.

[9] Collins, C. W., *The Fourteenth Amendment and the States* (Boston, Little, Brown and Company, 1912), p. 144.

[10] In *New York v. Gitlow*, 268 U. S. 652 (1925).

[11] See O'Neill, J. M., "Church, Schools, and the Constitution," *Commentary* (June, 1947); and Fraenkel, O. K., *Our Civil Liberties* (New York, The Viking Press, 1944), pp. 47-50.   [12] Collins, *op. cit.*, Ch. VII.

the last great period of the attack on the First Amendment (see pp. 43, 158-160) apparently it occurred to no one that the Fourteenth offered a way to get rid of the state freedom in religious affairs guaranteed by the First.

Justice Frankfurter [13] lists eighty-one cases of invalidation of state laws through the Fourteenth Amendment between 1911 and 1925 (the date on which the Court assumed that some of the personal freedoms of the First Amendment were protected from state invasion as "liberties" under the due process clause of the Fourteenth Amendment), and one hundred and eleven from 1925 through 1938. Almost all of these were "due process" cases and one or two had religious freedom aspects mixed with due process. However, since in the first case in which the Court specifically dealt with religious freedom under the Fourteenth Amendment [14] the Court upheld the state statute, there were no significant developments in this area until after 1938.

The application of the Bill of Rights through the Fourteenth Amendment to the several states is not yet completed—eighty years after its ratification. No one in the United States from the Chief Justice down to the youngest law school freshman knows today just *what parts* of the Bill of Rights are now through the Fourteenth Amendment restrictions on state legislatures, or *to what extent* any part is such a restriction. [15]

The first instance in which the Supreme Court considered the Fourteenth Amendment was in the Slaughterhouse cases in 1873. In these cases the Court laid down principles which have been followed almost without exception from 1873 to 1948 in the McCollum case. These principles are, as given consistently by recognized scholars in constitutional law, here presented in the words of Charles Warren:

The Court held that the Louisiana statute did not violate the [Fourteenth] Amendment in any particular; that if the right claimed by the

[13] Frankfurter, Felix, *Mr. Justice Holmes and the Supreme Court* (Cambridge, Harvard University Press, 1939), Appendix I, pp. 97-137.
[14] *Hamilton v. University of California*, 293 U. S. 245 (1934).
[15] See articles by Ben W. Palmer, *American Bar Association Journal*, July-October, 1948.

plaintiff to be freed of monopoly existed, it was not a privilege or immunity of a citizen of the United States as distinguished from a citizen of a State; that the Amendment in defining a citizen of the United States did not add any additional privileges and immunities to those which inhered in such citizens before its adoption; that *it was only rights which owed their existence to the Federal Government, its national character, its Constitution or its laws, that were placed under the special care of the National Government;* that it *was not intended to bring within* the power of Congress or *the jurisdiction of the Supreme Court the entire domain of civil rights heretofore belonging exclusively to the States;* and that to hold otherwise would "constitute the Court a perpetual censor upon all legislation of the States on the civil rights of their own citizens." [16] [Italics mine.]

Collins [17] remarks that the Supreme Court held in 1875 that the Fourteenth Amendment "offered no protection from individual invasion of individual rights and that Congress had no power under the Amendment to make routine and affirmative laws for its enforcement." [18]

Collins further remarks that

Mr. Justice Field delivering the opinon of the Court, spoke as follows: "Neither the Amendment broad and comprehensive as it is, nor any Amendment, was designed *to interfere with the power of the State*— sometimes termed its police power—*to prescribe regulations to promote health, peace, morals, education and good order* of the people, and to legislate so as to increase the industries of the State, develop its resources, and add to its wealth and prosperity." [19] [Italics mine.]

How far the present justices of the Supreme Court have departed from the earlier doctrine of the Court as enunciated by Mr. Justice Field in 1885 (and the dangers inherent in such departure) is indicated by the comment of *The American Bar Association Journal* [20] on the Court's decision in the Winters case.[21] In this case the

[16] Warren, Charles, *The Supreme Court in United States History* (Boston, Little, Brown & Co., 1926), Vol. II, p. 537.

[17] Collins, *op. cit.*, pp. 21-22.

[18] *United States* v. *Cruikshank*, 92 U. S. 542.

[19] *Barbier* v. *Connolly*, 113 U. S. 31 (1885) as quoted by Collins, *op. cit.*, p. 24.

[20] May, 1947, p. 390.

[21] *Winters* v. *the People of New York*, decided March 29, 1948.

Supreme Court declared unconstitutional a New York state statute of 1887 which outlawed the "massing" of pictures and stories of bloodshed, lust, and crime.

The American Bar Association Journal made the following comment under the heading "Striking Down State Laws":

All of this structure of law-making and enforcement in at least twenty-four States now is demolished, because six of the nine Judges in the Supreme Court think the procedure is vague and undefined, to such an extent as to come in conflict with what the majority in one Court think the First and Fourteenth Amendments *should mean.*[22] [Italics mine] . . . there is an obvious and increasing need for a better understanding, on the part of practising lawyers as to the reasoning and process of the Court, and on the part of the Court as to the realities of the administration of justice in the States and of the well considered laws which provide for it.

James A. Garfield, according to his official biographers and others, was an unusually careful and consistent student of congressional questions during his time in Congress: "More perhaps, than any man with whom he was associated in public life, he gave careful and systematic study to the public questions and he came to every discussion in which he took part with elaborate and complete preparation." [23]

Charles Carlton Coffin remarks that "General Garfield has participated in the discussion of almost every important question before Congress since 1864." [24]

This careful and consistent Congressional leader during the entire period of the discussion, adoption, and ratification of the Fourteenth Amendment clearly did not believe that the Fourteenth Amendment passed on to the several states any limitation whatever upon their use of tax money in the support of religion or religious education. In

[22] Note that this is what the Justices think the Constitution *should mean,* not what it *does mean* in the language and purpose of those who were responsible for formulating, adopting, and ratifying the First and Fourteenth Amendments. Enforcing what the Court thinks the Constitution should mean instead of what it says is known as "judicial legislation"—one of the most effective possible ways of ending "government by the people."

[23] Smith, Theodore Clark, *Life of James Abram Garfield* (New Haven, Yale University Press, 1925), Vol. II, p. 700.

[24] Coffin, Charles Carlton, *Life of James A. Garfield* (Boston, 1880), p. 224.

Garfield's letter accepting the nomination for the Presidency by the Republican party, July 10, 1880, he wrote:

But it would be unjust to our people and dangerous to our institutions to apply any portion of the revenues of the nation or of the states to the support of sectarian schools. The separation of the church and the state in everything relating to taxation should be absolute.

It is doubtless unnecessary to document the statement that this recommendation of Garfield did not result in the altering of the Constitution of the United States to carry his recommendation into effect. In the decade immediately preceding Mr. Garfield's recommendation, Congress had refused to allow this doctrine a place in the Constitution *ten times*. In the succeeding decade Congress took the same position *once more*. (See p. 124.)

General Grant was elected President in 1868 as a candidate of the Republican party. This was the year in which the Fourteenth Amendment, written and adopted by the Republican party in Congress, became part of the Constitution of the United States. The proof that Grant, as an outstanding Republican leader of that exact period, did not believe that the Fourteenth Amendment limited the powers of the state to do as they pleased regarding the support of religion or religious schools, is attested by the following quotation from Grant's message to Congress, December 7, 1875:

I suggest for your earnest consideration, and most earnestly recommend it, that a constitutional amendment be submitted to the legislatures of the several states for ratification, making it the duty of each of the several states to establish and effectively maintain free public schools adequate to the education of all children in the rudimentary branches within their respective limitations, irrespective of sex, color, birthplace or religion, forbidding the teaching in said schools of religious, atheistic or pagan tenets, and prohibiting the granting of any school funds or school taxes or any part thereof either by legislative, municipal, or other authority, for the benefit or in aid, directly or indirectly of any religious sect or denomination, or in aid or for the benefit of any other object of any nature, or kind whatever.

President Grant immediately followed the foregoing recommendation with one for taxing all church property "exempting only the last resting place of the dead and possibly, with proper restrictions, church edifices." Grant's message resulted in the Blaine proposal for an amendment, which was one of the eleven repudiated by Congress between 1870 and 1888.

Flack's [25] careful, step by step, account of the adoption of the Fourteenth Amendment contains no reference to the first clause of the First Amendment. In all of the discussion in Congress apparently no one had in mind a change that would have any effect at all on any question of religion or religious education. This is not surprising when one considers that in the first century after the adoption of the Bill of Rights we find no evidence either in public discussion or legislative debate that anyone thought that "an establishment of religion" meant anything other than what it had meant to Jefferson, Madison, and the men who wrote, adopted, and ratified the First Amendment. Further, by 1868 any proposal to establish a religion, whether nationally or in any state, would probably have received about the attention that would be given today to a proposal to restore Negro slavery. The last established church (the Congregational in Massachusetts) had not held the exclusively favored position for over a quarter of a century. The threat of a possible national establishment no longer frightened or angered the people of the country. Probably more important than any of the above, the modern slogan of atheists, secularists, and others united for the divorce of religion and education, through "the complete separation of church and state," had not yet been put forward as a substitute for the language of the Constitution.

The growth of the totalitarian idea, of dictatorship supplanting the democratic process, had in the eighteen sixties so far as is discoverable, no acceptance in America among men and women of any influence. Most important public leaders of America in the nineteenth century, of all parties, all creeds, and all sections, would have repudiated in strong terms the propaganda we face today which is deliberately trying to change the Constitution to get rid of the First Amendment's first clause by Supreme Court decision, thus avoiding the democratic process and the will of the American people.

[25] Flack, Horace Edgar, *The Adoption of the Fourteenth Amendment* (Baltimore, The Johns Hopkins Press, 1908).

A recent illuminating discussion of the application of the Four-teenth Amendment is found in the opinions of the various judges of the Supreme Court in the case of *Adamson v. California*.[26] Appendix G contains excerpts from the opinions which show in some detail the two theories concerning the manner in which the Fourteenth Amendment applies the Bill of Rights to the several states.

The first theory which is expounded by Justices Reed and Frank-furter expresses the historic position of the Supreme Court. This is that the Fourteenth Amendment does not apply to the States "a shorthand summary of the first eight amendments," but rather that it protects from invasion by the States through the due process clause only those basic freedoms which are "implicit in the concept of or-dered liberty." Mr. Justice Frankfurter phrases it in another place as "those canons of decency and fairness which express the notions of justice of English-speaking peoples."

The second theory which Mr. Justice Black presented at great length in a dissenting opinion is essentially that the Fourteenth Amendment applies the Bill of Rights completely to the States. This "shorthand summary" of the Bill of Rights guarantees the citizens of each state protection against invasion of the exact freedoms, and the enjoyment of the precise privileges, guaranteed to them as against the federal government in the Bill of Rights. In his words: "To guar-antee that hereafter no State could deprive its citizens of the priv-ileges and protections of the Bill of Rights."

This theory has never been openly accepted by the majority of the Court. It does not underlie, even as an essential but *unexpressed* assumption, any decision of the United States Supreme Court in its entire history, before the McCollum decision. It is an essential part of any possible theory of *constitutional* validity of that decision. How-ever, since none of the Justices in that case argued or defended their positions in terms of accurately cited history or constitutional law, there is no way of knowing that the Justices were even aware that they were assuming a theory of application of the Fourteenth Amend-ment which had been consistently denied by the Court since 1873 and explicitly repudiated in *Adamson v. California* in June of 1947.

[26] 332 U. S. 46.

An attempt to fit the decision in the McCollum case into either of the theories so fully and emphatically expounded in June, 1947, leads to bewildering but, I believe, inescapable conclusions.

I. Under the long established Supreme Court theory, as given by Justices Reed and Frankfurter in the Adamson case (if the Court should ever seek by well-grounded argument to justify the decision in the McCollum case presented for the Court by Justice Black), the Court would have to take the position that the simple provision of the First Amendment leaving laws about "an establishment of religion" (regardless of how they define this term!) in the hands of the states, is a provision violative of certain minimal standards "implicit in the concept of ordered liberty."

To state this position should be enough to show its complete absurdity. If any Justice of the Supreme Court is ever so unaware of the meaning of words, the history of liberty, and the Constitutional arrangements in these United States, as to take such a position openly and clearly, I trust he will not ascribe his aberrations to his respect for the principles of Thomas Jefferson!

II. Under the theory presented by Justice Black in the Adamson case (if the Court should ever attempt a reasoned defense of the McCollum decision) the Court would have to hold that Illinois had, in the June, 1947 words of Justice Black, deprived "its citizens of the privileges and protections of the Bill of Rights." The privileges and protections of the Bill of Rights under the "establishment of religion" clause, were the privileges and protections *against a nationally established religion*—not against a "state establishment." The five state establishments existing at the time were untouched—and not even adversely criticized in the Bill of Rights. To hold that the Fourteenth Amendment protects the people of Illinois from a *national* establishment of religion to be created by the legislature of Illinois is again a complete absurdity which probably no justice of the Supreme Court will ever express in so many words.

Under any theory that was alive in the Supreme Court in June of 1947, the McCollum decision of March, 1948 is indefensible. This is doubtless the reason why the Court *assumed* rather than *defended* its position.

If the Court ever clearly decides that "an establishment of religion" in the First Amendment means "religion or any religious institution or organization," that decision will make unconstitutional a great many acts of Congress, and the practices under them, that reach back to the first Congress, and that have been administered without objection, countermanding order, or contrary recommendation to Congress by every President from Washington to Truman—including both Jefferson and Madison.

If the Court decides, further, that since 1868 it has been unconstitutional for any state to make or enforce any law about "religion or any religious institution or organization," that decision will invalidate many laws and constitutional provisions in every state including the laws in practically all states concerning religious freedom, religious schools, religion in the public schools, tax exemption, and many other state concerns, including the Illinois provisions and regulations upon which Mrs. McCollum originally relied!

The chaos which such a decision would create in various departments of the federal government, the army, the navy, the penal institutions, and in every state, *would be incurable,* pending the ratification of new amendments to the United States Constitution, because neither Congress nor any state would then have the power to make or enforce *any laws at all* concerning religion or any religious institution or organization.

If the people of the country want this situation they should bring it about in the orderly fashion provided by the Constitution by adopting and ratifying some such proposal as that contained in the Bryson Constitutional amendment bill in the Eightieth Congress. The Constitution should not be so sweepingly amended by a judicial decision 157 years after the adoption of the First Amendment.

As shown above it has been consistently held that the "privileges and immunities" protected by the Fourteenth Amendment are those of *national,* not state, citizenship. The privileges and immunities clause of the Fourteenth Amendment, therefore, furnishes no basis for granting legal force and effect to the slogan "the separation of church and state." It is obviously impossible to show that the objectives pursued by the devotees of this slogan are the privileges and immunities of *national citizenship*. Neither freedom from an established religion or freedom of worship in this country were ever privileges of *national* as distinct from *state* citizenship. Freedom of worship in the First Amendment had no qualification on it. It was endorsed. Congress could not "restrict it." Invasions of freedom of religion were condemned. But "an establishment of religion" was not condemned. The only "establishments" this country had ever known, state establishments, were left untouched and some of them went on for years. The First Amendment made a national establishment impossible and so protected the people of a state against a national establishment only. If it is argued that, therefore, there is a privilege or immunity here that is an aspect of national citizenship, it is clearly and inevitably only an immunity from a *national* establishment of religion, and cannot be applied to protect the people of Illinois from a *state* establishment of religion. This should be sufficiently clear from the simple and specific language of the clause itself, according to the meaning of the words in eighteenth-century America and the constitutional situation in which the clause was framed. For the reader unfamiliar with the language of the subject, we have Madison's very definite statement (made when the wording of the Amendment was under discussion in the first Congress) that this was its exact purpose (see p. 96).

Illustrative of the privileges and immunities which belong to *citizens of the United States* as distinct from those of the *citizens of an individual State*, are the following: [27]

> right to demand protection on the high seas or abroad
> right to use navigable waters
> rights secured by treaty
> right to pass freely from state to state
> right to vote for national officers
> right to enter public lands
> right to engage in interstate and foreign commerce
> right to appeal in proper cases to the national courts.

[27] See Corwin, Edward S., *The Constitution and What it Means Today* (Princeton, Princeton University Press, 1947), 9th ed., pp. 187-188; Guthrie, William D., *The Fourteenth Amendment* (Boston: Little, Brown and Company, 1898) pp. 56-65.

For over a century after the ratification of the First Amendment the citizens of each state were free to have any laws they wanted dealing, either pro or con, with religion or established churches. If they had not been so free the state-established churches could not have been disestablished. No state could have made a law respecting its "establishment of religion."

The individual states were free to establish or to disestablish state religions or churches. But the individual states were never free, *for lack of jurisdiction, even without the First Amendment,* to establish (or make any law concerning) a *national* religion. It follows that the Fourteenth Amendment (if it applies this phrase to the states at all) gives to the citizens of any state on this subject only an immunity which they have always had.

When the Fourteenth Amendment, therefore, is held to channel the First Amendment to the several states in such a way as to deprive them of their freedom to do as they please in regard to a state establishment of religion *through state constitutions and state laws, each applicable only in the individual state concerned,* it takes away from people of the several states the precise freedom which the First Amendment was explicitly designed to preserve. The preservation of this precise freedom has been specifically defended by Congress many times (see p. 124).

Not only did the first Congress refuse to allow any invasion of the authority of the states in this respect by voting down the "lost amendment" (see p. 110), but Congress has taken the same position every time the question has been raised in our history. The chief period of the attack on the First Amendment preceding the current one came just after the Civil War and the adoption of the Fourteenth Amendment. In the atmosphere following the ratification of that amendment (which was a clear reversal of our former policy of keeping the federal government much more rigidly out of any part of the domestic concerns of the people of the various states) there was a determined drive to reduce state freedom in the area of the relations of government to religion and education. It seems not even to have occurred to anyone for some sixty years after 1868 that there was a possibility of bringing about such interference through the Fourteenth Amendment. The Supreme Court did not recognize the possibility until 1925. [28]

By about 1870 most states had removed "Trinitarian Protestant Christianity" from its historic position of support by taxation in the public school systems, and had forbidden the use of public funds for religious schools (see p. 141). But believers in these arrangements (or one of them) then, as now, were not content to leave these matters where Jefferson, Madison, and the Constitution had placed them—in the hands of the people of the states. The attackers of that day also wanted these measures frozen into the Constitution. The propagandists for secularism in the former period, however, differed markedly from their modern counterparts—such as "Protestants and Other Americans United." The earlier attack on the First Amendment was openly carried on according to the democratic tradition and the Constitutional provisions, by seeking an amendment to the Constitution to put their new doctrine of outside dictation to the individual states into the fundamental law of the nation. They did not seek, as do their successors today, to avoid the democratic process of amendment, and to circumvent the will of the American people, by knocking out the First Amendment by an edict of the Supreme Court.

Between 1870 and 1888, Congress had before it no less than eleven separate formulations of proposed amendments to put at least a large part of the program of "Protestants and Other Americans United" into the Constitution by specific amendment. Congress repudiated all of them. Only one so much as passed one house of Congress. In spite of the fact that the responsible representatives of the American people have consistently refused to allow the doctrine of the Protestants and Other Americans (such as most of the Justices of the Supreme Court) to go into the Constitution, these people keep on proclaiming (without any valid evidence whatever to bolster up the claim) that this doctrine is *a great constitutional principle,* and is endorsed by the American people. The propagandists of today, however, refuse to allow a test of their proclaimed faith. They were opposed to supporting the Bryson Bill before the Eightieth Congress to

[28] *New York* v. *Gitlow,* 268 U. S. 652 (1925).

amend the Constitution to express their doctrine. In fact, "Protestants and Other Americans United" are, probably, according to one of their leaders, in part responsible for this bill being allowed to die in committee (see p. 47).

I realize that the question of how we should at the present time prevent an establishment of religion in state or nation is an academic question. No one in America is now, apparently, interested in advocating an established religion in any state, or in openly advocating any restriction on religious freedom.

The Court's decision in the McCollum case (March 8, 1948) in spite of history, the English language, and the doctrine of *stare decisis*,[29] reversed the total relevant record of the Court up to date. This great reversal was accomplished under the theory that the Fourteenth Amendment channeled the doctrine of complete separation of church and state from the First Amendment to the Constitution and laws of the several states. It was done with little attempted justification except in the erroneous *dicta* in the Everson case and the Justices' "zeal" and "prepossessions" (see p. 236) in the realms of religion and education.

An example of the extreme to which it is possible to go, under the Fourteenth Amendment with success in our present Supreme Court, in destroying ancient and honored practices of education and the democratic control of public education for generations in the American states, is given by the McCollum case. The brief of the Attorney General of Illinois presented the following (without avail):

Appellant [Mrs. McCollum] would read the Fourteenth Amendment as categorically prohibiting the instant Board of Education from even permitting the purely *optional* study of the Bible by any child upon publicly-owned school property during school hours.

Illinois' Attorney General asks this Court to consider the implications of appellant's proposition the more carefully because it embodies

29 The maxim, *stare decisis et non quieta movere,*—to stand by precedents and not to disturb what is settled. . . . is founded on the principle that stability and certainty in the law are of first importance. When a point of law is once clearly decided by a court of final jurisdiction, it becomes a fixed rule of law to govern future action. The certainty of the law is regarded as of more importance than the reason of it. It is better to have a bad law with certainty of its meaning than a good law whose scope of operation is indefinable and unknown. (Collins, p. 110.)

an interpretation of the Fourteenth Amendment that has never before, so far as we are aware, found utterance upon the part of any litigant in this Court in the history of the Union and because it is opposed to scholastic traditions throughout the nation that are older than the federal or any state constitution.

The Bible is all but universally recognized as of prodigious literary and historical importance in the world's culture. It has informed and inspired the art and letters of the world's civilizations for thousands of years.

But if appellant's constitutional thesis is correct, although children may be compelled to study the history of the Western World, a history that has been dominated in many of its aspects by the writings in question, nevertheless they may not be even *permitted*, much less compelled, to read those writings themselves on school property. And this is true, according to appellant, notwithstanding the fact that the parents (whose responsibility for their children's tutelage must remain primary among a free people) desire that their children be tutored in this great literary work.

If appellant's constitutional doctrine is correct, a state university may not give a course in Biblical letters or even a course in comparative religion if the Bible is one of the texts.

Illinois' Attorney General briefly but strongly emphasizes the historical demonstration developed in appellees' brief (pp. 94-100) that Thomas Jefferson himself was the author of a plan for voluntary religious education upon the publicly-owned grounds of the University of Virginia; and that this plan found approbation in the times and among the people who wrote and ratified the First Amendment.

The important question as to whether the Bible may comprise a part of the elective curriculum of the public schools should, we submit, be left to the states, whose governments are, with this Court, custodians of constitutional liberty and guardians of civil rights.

The part of the Fourteenth Amendment which bears directly upon our problem, in addition to the phrase concerning "privileges and immunities of citizens of the United States," is the phrase about "due process of law."

Edward S. Corwin, Professor of Jurisprudence at Princeton University, sums up the status of due process at the present time:

Originally, "due process of law" meant simply the mores of *procedure* which were due at the common law, especially in connection with the accusation and trial of supposed offenders. It meant, in short, the kind

of procedure which is described in detail in the more definite provisions
of Amendments V and VI. [See appendix A.] Today, "due process of
law" means "reasonable law" or "reasonable procedure," that is to say,
what a majority of the Supreme Court find to be *reasonable* in some
or other sense of that extremely elastic term. In other words, it means,
in effect, *the approval of the Supreme Court;* but, as will be pointed
out presently, this approval will sometimes be extended on easier terms
than at others.[30]

Summing it up: In consequence of the modern doctrine of due process
of law as "reasonable law," *judicial review ceases to have definite, statable
limits;* and while the extent to which the Court will recanvass the factual
justification of a statute under the "due process" clauses of the Constitution often varies considerably as between cases, yet this is a matter which in the last analysis depends upon the Court's own discretion,
and nothing else.[31]

Let us see how this change came about and what bearing it has on
our present subject. The phrase "due process of law" has a history in
our law dating from the English Statute of Westminster 1354. It
has commonly been held to be substantially synonymous with the
phrase "the law of the land" coming to us from the Magna Carta,
1215.[32] Throughout the centuries down to relatively recent American
court history, these phrases have meant roughly "according to law,"
or "through proper legal procedure." That is, the governments could
not imprison or execute a person or take away his property without
proceeding against him, according to the laws and procedures which
were known and applicable to the person in question. Kelly and
Harbison give the year 1850 as approximately the end of the period
in which due process was accepted by the Supreme Court as "a
procedural rather than a substantive restriction upon governmental
authority." [33] The *substantative* theory of due process of law, as
against the ancient *procedural* meaning of the phrase, is that the
substance of the law, the content of the law, that is, the law itself,
must be "reasonable" (in the opinion of the Court).

According to outstanding legal scholars generally the changing
of the meaning of "due process" from its centuries-old significance
(clearly the only meaning it had to those who wrote and ratified the

---

[30] Corwin, *op. cit.,* pp. 155-156.   [32] *See* Kelly and Harbison, pp. 500-501.
[31] *Ibid.,* p. 193.   [33] p. 501.

Constitution and the Bill of Rights), was not due to the influence of radical forces seeking to have their way regardless of the Constitution. This change was brought about by Supreme Court Justices committed to the conservative economic theory generally covered by the familiar label *laissez-faire*. The specific object, however, was much more pointed and practical than the preservation of an economic theory. What the Supreme Court Justices in the period from about 1870 down to 1925 were concerned about, was the protection of the property of American corporations from the onslaughts of State legislatures seeking to make effective social legislation on such subjects as taxes, minimum wages, rates charged by public service corporations, maximum hours of labor, and conditions of labor for women and children. In order to make possible such protection of the "property" of the corporations in spite of the provisions of the Constitution of the United States and the laws of the several states, the Supreme Court did violence to both history and language in taking the following two positions.

First, the Court in 1886 [34] announced that a corporation was a "person" within the meaning of the Fourteenth Amendment, and that therefore the corporation as a person could not have its life, liberty or property (especially property) taken from it without "due process of law." "This decision sounded the death knell of the narrow 'Negro-race theory' of the Fourteenth Amendment. . . . By so doing it cleared the way for the modern development of due process of law and the corresponding expansion of the Court's discretionary powers over social and economic legislation." [35] In this way the property of the corporation (person) could not be taken from him by the new social legislation of the individual states unless the Supreme Court approved of the new laws as *reasonable* measures.

This situation led Kales to refer to the Supreme Court as the American substitute for the British House of Lords.

The time has come when the political scientists of the country should recognize in the decisions of the Supreme Court under the due process

[34] *Santa Clara County* v. *Southern R. R.*, 118 U. S. 394 (1886).

[35] Graham, H. J., "The 'Conspiracy Theory' of the Fourteenth Amendment," 47 *Yale Law Journal* 371 (1938). Reprinted in Selected Essays, I, p. 237.

clause the functioning of a second chamber, organized to defeat the popular will as expressed in legislation when that will appears to endanger what the court may regard as a fundamental requirement of the social structure itself.[36]

The accuracy of this observation is not diminished by Kales' opinion that this veto power of the Supreme Court over both national and state laws is rather a good thing.

Second, the Court in further bending law and language in defense of corporation property, played havoc with the word "liberty" in the due process clause in the Fifth and Fourteenth Amendments.

The right which was originally guaranteed by this term was physical liberty, freedom from illegal detention, a right which the writ of *habeas corpus* exists to protect and violation of which is redressible by an action for false imprisonment. But in the Lochner Case,[37] decided in 1905, we find "liberty" to mean the right of males twenty-one years of age to work in a bake shop more than ten hours a day and sixty hours a week; while in the Coppage Case,[38] decided in 1915, it meant the right of an employer to fire an employee for belonging to a labor union; and in the late District of Columbia Minimum Wage Case,[39] decided in 1923, it meant the right of women to work for less than a living wage.[40]

Charles Warren in discussing the Supreme Court's juggling with the word "liberty" has some striking passages.

Thus the single word "liberty" will have become a tremendous engine for attack on state legislation—an engine which could not have been conceived possible by the framers of the first ten amendments or by the framers of the Fourteenth Amendment itself.[41]

Warren, in 1926, seems to have prophesied the specific calamity of the McCollum decision. He wrote:

Those framers of the Constitution (1787) believed that they should impose few limitations upon the authority of the State Legislatures, except such as were necessary from a national standpoint. In matters of

[36] Kales, A. M., "New Methods in Due Process," 12 *American Political Science Review* 241 (1918). Reprinted in Selected Essays, Vol. I, p. 488.
[37] 198 U. S. 45.   [38] 236 U. S. 1.   [39] 261 U. S. 525.
[40] Corwin, Edward S., *Court Over Constitution*, p. 109.
[41] Warren, Charles, "The New Liberty under the 14th Amendment," 39 *Harvard Law Review*, 431 (1926). Reprinted in Selected Essays, Vol. II, pp. 263-264.

local interest, the relations between a State and its own citizens, were jealously preserved against National interference, protection, or restriction. Clearly, if anything can be said to be purely a local matter and of no national concern it would be the relation of the State to subjects to be taught in its schools. Certainly, if anything has no need of National protection, it is the relation between a State and its own pupils.[42]

In 1833, John Marshall, in the much quoted case of *Barron* v. *Baltimore*,[43] accepted the literal language of the First Amendment as meaning exactly what it said, and declared that the Bill of Rights in the Federal Constitution imposed no restrictions on the individual states. This position was held consistently until after the adoption of the Fourteenth Amendment in 1868.

Following the adoption of the Fourteenth Amendment, the question was raised from time to time as to whether or not the Fourteenth Amendment transferred as restrictions upon state legislatures the various items in the First Amendment: freedom of speech, religion, press, etc.

From 1868 to 1925 the Court many times and without a single exception refused to recognize that any part of the First Amendment had been made a restriction on the legislative powers of the states. As late as 1922 the Supreme Court, in the Prudential Insurance Company case (259 U. S. 530), speaking through "Judge Pitney, expressly stated that: neither the Fourteenth Amendment nor any other provision of the Constitution of the United States imposes upon the States any restriction about 'freedom of speech.' "[44]

Three years later in the Gitlow case Judge Sanford for the Court said

For present purposes, we may and do assume that freedom of speech and of the press—which are protected by the First Amendment from abridgment by Congress—are among the fundamental personal rights and liberties protected by the due process clause of the Fourteenth Amendment from impairment by the States.[45]

This flat assumption on the part of the Supreme Court in 1925 departed without explanation from all relevant Supreme Court de-

[42] *Ibid.*, p. 238.
[43] 7 Peters 243.
[44] Warren, *op. cit.*, p. 239.
[45] *New York v. Gitlow*, 268 U. S. 652 (1925).

cisions of the previous fifty-seven years. It should be noted, however, that this was not a decision that said that the First Amendment was transferred to the state by the Fourteenth; only that "fundamental personal rights and liberties" were protected from state invasion by *the due process clause* of the Fourteenth.

Chief Justice Hughes, giving the decision of the Court, repeated this doctrine a few years later. "It is no longer open to doubt that the liberty of the press and of speech is within the liberty safeguarded from invasion by state action." [46]

Professor Robert E. Cushman of Cornell University in commenting on this situation recently wrote:

Since that time the Court has added freedom of religion [47] and freedom of assembly [48] to the list of liberties protected by the due process clause. Thus, by a complete judicial about-face, the Supreme Court quietly imposed on the states at least some of the guarantees of civil liberty in the federal Bill of Rights. *It did this, furthermore, without disturbing Chief Justice Marshall's ruling that the Bill of Rights itself does not limit state action.* [Italics mine.]

Only those civil liberties, however, have been thus read into the term "liberty" in the Fourteenth Amendment which the Court regards as fundamental . . . of the very essence of a scheme of ordered liberty.[49] On the other hand, some of the guarantees of the federal Bill of Rights are held not to be of this vitally important nature and are, therefore, not protected by the due process clause. These are mainly those which relate to criminal procedure. The Court has held that the due process clause of the Fourteenth Amendment does not require a state to give a person accused of crime a grand jury indictment [50] or a jury trial [51] or to refrain from subjecting him to compulsory self-incrimination,[52] or double jeopardy.[53] In referring to these guarantees of criminal procedure, Mr. Justice Cardozo observed: "Few would be so narrow or provincial as to maintain that a fair and enlightened system of justice would be impossible without them." [54]

[46] *Near* v. *Minnesota*, 283 U. S. 697 (1931).
[47] *Hamilton* v. *University of California*, 293 U. S. 245 (1934).
[48] *De Jonge* v. *Oregon*, 299 U. S. 353 (1937).
[49] *Palko* v. *Connecticut*, 302 U. S. 319 (1937).
[50] *Hurtado* v. *California*, 110 U. S. 516 (1884).
[51] Dictum in *Maxwell* v. *Dow*, 176 U. S. 581 (1900).
[52] *Twining* v. *New Jersey*, 211 U. S. 78 (1908).
[53] *Palko* v. *Connecticut*, 302 U. S. 319 (1937).
[54] *Ibid.*

It will be seen that the Court has divided the guarantees of the federal Bill of Rights into two classes, those which are essential to the preservation of "the fundamental principles of liberty and justice which lie at the base of all our civil and political institutions, and those which require particular forms of judicial procedure." [55]

It is clear that at least until after the Palko decision in 1937 (sixty-nine years after the Fourteenth Amendment became a part of the Constitution), the Supreme Court had not considered that the Fourteenth Amendment transferred the First Amendment to the states as a list of restrictions on state power. The Court had simply assumed since 1925 that certain fundamental personal rights and liberties "of the very essence of ordered liberty" (which were also mentioned in the First Amendment as restrictions on Congress) had been made restrictions on the states by the due process clause of the Fourteenth Amendment.

To do this they gave to the word "liberty" a meaning which it could not possibly have had to the authors of the Fifth Amendment, and therefore could not properly be the sense of the word in the phrase in the Fourteenth Amendment. This phrase *was copied from the Fifth* (and so stated by Representative John A. Bingham of Ohio, the chief author and sponsor of the first section of the Fourteenth Amendment, speaking in Congress on February 26, 1866 when that amendment was under debate).[56] In this way the Court essentially makes the Bill of Rights say: "Congress shall make no law abridging the freedom of speech unless the Supreme Court of the United States approves of the abridgment in any particular instance."

I submit that a logical and literate person has to grant that this juggling with the word "liberty" in the Fourteenth Amendment either (a) so reads the Fifth Amendment in the Bill of Rights as to make the First Amendment redundant and ridiculous, or (b) makes necessary the belief that *identical words* copied from the Fifth Amendment into the Fourteenth mean one thing in the Fifth and something else in the Fourteenth. All this in spite of the fact that

[55] Cushman, Robert E., *New Threats to American Freedoms* (New York, Public Affairs Committee, 1948), Pamphlet No. 143, pp. 23-25.

[56] *Congressional Globe*, Thirty-ninth Congress, Washington Congressional Globe Office, 1866, Part 2, pp. 813 ff.

"the Supreme Court has more than once said that the due process clause in the Fourteenth Amendment has the same scope as the similar clause in the Fifth Amendment." [57]

One more prophetic passage from Warren is well worth repeating. It took only twenty-two years for the Supreme Court to achieve the enormity which Warren envisaged in 1926.

If, as is now assumed, the right of Freedom of speech as contained in the First Amendment to the Federal Constitution, is a part of a person's "liberty" protected against State legislation by the Fourteenth Amendment, then the right of free exercise of his religion contained in the First Amendment must also be a part of a person's "liberty," similarly protected against State action. And on this ground, the United States Supreme Court may be called upon to pass on State laws as to religion and religious sects—a subject which, of all others, ought to be purely the concern of the State and its own people, and in no wise subject to interference by the National Government.[58]

The petitions and resolutions of the various states in response to which the first clause of the First Amendment was written (see pp. 112 ff.), show that the prevention of this exact "interference by the National Government" was the precise purpose of this clause which was liquidated by the Supreme Court in the McCollum case.

A brief tracing, case by case in chronological order, will best show the casual, almost absent-minded way in which the Justices of the Supreme Court have let fall from time to time a few phrases which mark their wanderings from 1920 to 1948. They have moved backwards and forwards, and in circles, sometimes arriving at a position held earlier, then abandoned, and then arrived at again. It is a clear case of "Now you see it, and now you don't." At no time is there any explanation, argument, or defense of any sort of the new doctrine, or even any evidence that the Justices realize that a long established position is being abandoned and a new one being assumed—or later that the new one is being given up and the old one reoccupied.

Here only the more important cases can be mentioned. Since the story of the destruction of the maps and compasses (in the "substantive due process," "corporation-person," and "meaning of liberty"

[57] Warren, op. cit., p. 244.   [58] Ibid., p. 260.

debaucheries) has already been covered, only the key cases in this strange story from 1920 to 1948 will be listed here.

In 1920 Justice Brandeis in a dissenting opinion remarked sharply, after having seen the word "liberty" stretched to protect various economic privileges from state legislative control: "I cannot believe that the liberty guaranteed by the Fourteenth Amendment includes only liberty to acquire and to enjoy property." [59]

This prodding of his colleagues on the Supreme Bench bore fruit in a short time. In 1925, full fifty-seven years after the First Amendment was ratified, the Supreme Court first "assumed" that some of the freedoms mentioned in the First Amendment had been made restrictions on the states. In that year in the Gitlow case Justice Sanford for the Court said:

> The precise question presented, and the only question which we can consider under this writ of error, then is, whether the statute, as construed and applied in this case by the state courts, deprived the defendant of his liberty of expression in violation of the due process clause of the Fourteenth Amendment. . . .
>
> For present purposes we may and do assume that freedom of speech and of the press—which are protected by the First Amendment from abridgment by Congress—are among the fundamental personal rights and "liberties" protected by the due process clause of the Fourteenth Amendment from impairment by the States.[60]

In this case the Court upheld the New York statute in question, Holmes and Brandeis dissenting. The Gitlow case did not decide that the *First Amendment* had been made a restriction on the states, but only that freedom of speech and press are protected by the due process clause of the Fourteenth Amendment, as "fundamental personal rights and liberties."

In 1931 the Supreme Court for the first time held a state law unconstitutional under the theory enunciated in the Gitlow case. A California law which prohibited the display of the red flag was invalidated.[61] The issue was one of the right of free speech under the due process clause of the Fourteenth Amendment. The Court (Chief

[59] *Gilbert v. Minnesota*, 254 U. S. 325 (1920).
[60] *Gitlow v. New York*, 268 U. S. 652 (1925).
[61] *Stromberg v. California*, 283 U. S. 359 (1931).

Justice Hughes speaking) held that the law "was worded so broadly as conceivably to impose penalties upon peaceful and orderly opposition to government." [62] The First Amendment was not involved.

Also in 1931 the Court held unconstitutional a Minnesota statute [63] "providing for the suppression of any malicious, scandalous, or defamatory newspaper" [64] also under the due process clause of the Fourteenth Amendment. Still no First Amendment decision.

The first case in which the Supreme Court considered religious freedom as one of the personal liberties protected from state violation by the Fourteenth Amendment raised the question [65] whether compulsory military training imposed on religious and conscientious objectors, as a condition of attending the University, deprived them of freedom of religion without due process of law.

The Court decided without dissent that the religious freedom of the students as guaranteed by the due process clause had not been violated. The First Amendment *per se* was not involved. Federal protection of religious freedom from invasion by state power was first brought into this status, like freedom of speech and press, through the due process clause.

However, Justice Cardozo in a concurring opinion, in brief passages of clear *dicta* (since only the due process clause had been involved), assumed conditionally that the First Amendment as a whole had been, or might be, applied bodily to the states. These are the passages.

Cardozo concurring,

I assume for present purposes that the religious liberty protected by the First Amendment against violation by the nation, is protected by the Fourteenth Amendment against invasion by the states.

The First Amendment, if it be read into the Fourteenth Amendment,
  Neither directly nor indirectly is government establishing a state religion.

In this historic case in the history of the relation of our government to religion, Justice Cardozo goes no further than to express in

---

[62] Kelly and Harbison, *op. cit.,* p. 703.
[63] *Near* v. *Minnesota,* 283 U. S. 697 (1931).
[64] Kelly and Harbison, *op. cit.,* p. 703.
[65] *Hamilton* v. *University of California,* 293 U. S. 245 (1934).

dicta a tentative presumption "for present purposes," and, apparently, a doubt as to whether the First Amendment is to be read into the Fourteenth. The third passage, however, is arresting on two counts. First, it seems to take for granted that the First Amendment is transferred to the states by the Fourteenth. Otherwise any remark about California "establishing a state religion" could have no possible bearing on the case he was discussing. No one, so far as I am aware, has ever yet gone so far out of bounds as to suggest that an arrangement explicitly leaving legislation about "an establishment of religion" in the hands of the states (where it had been implicitly left by the Constitutional Convention in Philadelphia) violated any fundamental human freedoms implicit in the concept of ordered liberty.

If the whole First Amendment has been carried to the states by the Fourteenth, there must have been a "carrier clause." What is it? The Supreme Court has consistently held that the privileges and immunities clause covers only matter inherent in national citizenship— not in state citizenship. It seems to me impossible for any orderly and informed mind to believe that immunity from "an establishment of religion" (however defined) to be set up *by a state* is an immunity that comes from national citizenship as distinct from state citizenship. Consequently, unless there is a clause in the Fourteenth Amendment expressed in some secret writing discernible only to Supreme Court Justices, the Court was demonstrably wrong either in the Everson and McCollum decisions (which assumed the whole First Amendment applicable to the states) or in the whole line of decisions from the Slaughterhouse·cases in 1873 down through and including the Adamson case in June 1947—three months *after* the Everson decision! The Justices cannot have it both ways indefinitely. In the name of common sense, *stare decisis*, and good government, they ought "to light someplace" and stay there. As Professor Corwin puts it, in regard to an earlier crisis, "The question arises, how far is a court entitled to indulge in bad history and bad logic without having its good faith challenged?" [66]

The second interesting aspect of Cardozo's third *dictum* above is that he understood the language of the First Amendment and knew

[66] Corwin, Edward S., *Court Over Constitution*, p. 188.

that it related to the setting up of *a religion* by government, and not to the support of religion in general.

The next episode in our story takes place in 1940. In the Cantwell case [67] the Court invalidated for the first time a state statute as an abridgment of religious freedom, as protected by the recently discovered meaning of the due process clause of the Fourteenth Amendment. Justice Roberts speaking for a unanimous Court held unconstitutional *under this clause* a Connecticut statute which required solicitors for a religious cause to get approval of the secretary of the public welfare council. Since this official could refuse approval the Court decided that this was censorship of religion and so an abridgment of religious freedom under the Fourteenth Amendment. The First Amendment was not involved.

In the next case [68] along the trail, we discover the first trace of the application of the First Amendment to the states through the Fourteenth Amendment. In a perfect example of an *obiter dictum*, in a decision that was specifically reversed three years later, we find the first statement in Supreme Court history that the Fourteenth Amendment "absorbed" the First.

The First Amendment was not involved in the Gobitis case, but a reference to it slipped in, evidently quite inadvertently as we shall see. This was a Jehovah's Witnesses "flag salute" case. The Witnesses claimed that requiring school children to salute the flag violated rights guaranteed by the Fourteenth Amendment.

Justice Frankfurter, speaking for the Court (Justice Stone alone dissenting) said: "We must decide whether the requirement of participation in such a ceremony, exacted from a child who refused upon sincere religious grounds, *infringes without due process of law the liberty guaranteed by the Fourteenth Amendment.*"

The Court decided that the due process clause of the Fourteenth Amendment *was not violated* by the compulsory flag salute law. Again the First Amendment was not involved. Justice Frankfurter, however, delivered a *dictum* which it is interesting to compare with later Frankfurter statements. He said:

[67] *Cantwell v. Connecticut*, 310 U. S. 296 (1940).
[68] *Minersville School District v. Gobitis*, 310 U. S. 586 (1940).

The First Amendment, and the Fourteenth *through its absorption of the First,* sought to guard against repetition of those bitter religious struggles by prohibiting the *establishment of a state religion* and by securing to every sect *the free exercise of its faith.* [Italics mine.]

Note the three italicised phrases here. When Judge Frankfurter said the Fourteenth Amendment had *absorbed* the First, I think that he should be held to have said that it had absorbed *all of the First.* He argued at length, and on the prevailing side, against this view in *Adamson v. California.*[69] The decision in the Adamson case is based on the idea that the Fourteenth Amendment *does not* transfer the Bill of Rights *per se* to the states, and Frankfurter there pleads for preserving the doctrine that the only "carrier" clause in the Fourteenth Amendment is the "due process of law" clause.

We are, consequently, left in doubt as to just what he means. Is he saying anything more than Sanford said in the Gitlow case (discussed above) in "assuming" that the due process clause of the Fourteenth Amendment carried to the states some of the freedoms which were mentioned in the First Amendment—and that their position in the First gave them a special standing? Or is he saying that the Fourteenth by "absorption" carried the First as a whole to the states? While this seems the most natural interpretation of this phrase, it is vitally inconsistent with Justice Frankfurter's whole argument in the Adamson case. There he wrote a strong concurring opinion fervently endorsing the doctrine of the famous Twining[70] and Palko[71] cases. (See appendix G.) These cases repeated and emphasized the unvarying doctrines of the Court up to that time: viz. (a) that the due process clause of the Fourteenth Amendment "does not draw all of the rights of the Federal Bill of Rights under its protection," but that only "such provisions of the Bill of Rights as were 'implicit in the concept of ordered liberty' became secure from state interference by the clause," and (b) the privileges and immunities clause of the Fourteenth Amendment applied only to privileges and immunities arising from *United States citizenship,* and not those

[69] 332 U. S. 46. (1947)
[70] *Twining* v. *New Jersey,* 211 U. S. 78 (1908).
[71] *Palko* v. *Connecticut,* 302 U. S. 319 (1937).

"flowing from state citizenship." The Palko case reaffirmed both of these doctrines as did the Adamson case [72] in 1947.

If Justice Frankfurter believed in 1940, and in February 1947 (Everson case), that the Fourteenth Amendment absorbed the whole of the First, he seemingly overruled himself in June 1947 in the Adamson case. If not this, then he has some undisclosed theory by which he holds that the Fourteenth Amendment transfers the First *in toto* as written, but does not so transfer the other amendments in the Bill of Rights.

The short-lived Opelika [73] decision is famous for a number of reasons. Its five to four decision was formally vacated one year later in the Murdock [74] case by a five to four vote the other way. The Opelika case raised the question whether "a non-discriminatory license fee, uncontested in amount, from those selling books or papers . . . abridges the freedom of worship, speech, or press." In this case the books were religious books. The Court answered "No." Chief Justice Stone dissented ("because the license is revocable in the unrestrained and unreviewable discretion of the license commission"). He was joined by Justices Black, Douglas, and Murphy who "appended an unprecedented and gratuitous statement confessing repentance for their part in the [Gobitis] flag salute decision of two years previously." [75]

The Court's opinion, by Justice Reed, does not say whether it is based on the due process clause or on an assumption that the Fourteenth Amendment carries the First as a whole to the states. This reference to the First Amendment appears: "The First Amendment does not require a subsidy in the form of fiscal exemption." Quite obviously true, but not indicative of the type of Constitutional application on which the decision was based.

Chief Justice Stone's dissenting opinion contains another of those casual, revolutionary remarks with no explanation of when, how, or

[72] In the Palko case Justice Cardozo spoke for the Court (Hughes, McReynolds, Brandeis, Sutherland, Stone, Roberts, and Black). Justice Butler dissented. In the Adamson Case Justice Reed spoke for the Court (Vinson, Frankfurter, Burton, and Jackson). Black, Douglas, Murphy and Rutledge dissented.

[73] *Jones* v. *Opelika*, 316 U. S. 584 (1942).

[74] 319 U. S. 105.   [75] Pritchett, *op. cit.*, p. 97.

by whom "came the revolution." He wrote: "The First Amendment, which the Fourteenth makes applicable to the States. . . ."

The year 1943 had numerous Jehovah's Witnesses cases. The first of the more important ones [76] overruled the Opelika case by a five to four vote, when Justice Rutledge who had replaced Justice Byrnes on the Court swung the balance the other way.

In the Murdock case the question was again whether selling books and pamphlets, again religious books, without a license fee required by an ordinance deprived the sellers "of the freedom of speech, press, and religion, guaranteed by the First Amendment." Here for the first time we have the question phrased specifically in terms of the First Amendment alone. But whether deliberately or thoughtlessly we have no way of knowing. And if deliberately, we do not know *why*.

Justice Douglas, for the Court, used these passages:

"The First Amendment, which the Fourteenth makes applicable to the states, declares that . . .", etc. We have here again the now familiar phrase, with the also familiar total absence of explanation, or even indication of the users' exact meaning.

"This form of religious activity occupies the same high estate under the First Amendment as do worship in the churches and preaching from the pulpits." (See Corwin's comment p. 184.)

The judgment in *Jones* v. *Opelika* has this day been vacated. Freed from that controlling precedent, we can restore to their high, constitutional position the liberties of itinerant evangelists who disseminate their religious beliefs and the tenets of their faith through distribution of literature.

Note that Justice Douglas mentions only the year-old precedent which is abandoned, but evidently does not even think of the precedents running back through about half the history of the Court which he is (perhaps without realizing it) also throwing into the discard.

Confusion is added here by Justice Reed's remark in a dissenting opinion:

The real contention of the witnesses is . . . taxation of the occupation of selling books and pamphlets . . . would be contrary to the due

[76] *Murdock* v. *Pennsylvania*, 319 U. S. 105 (1943).

process clause of the Fourteenth Amendment, which now is held to have drawn the contents of the First Amendment into the category of individual rights protected from state deprivation.

To Judge Reed this was evidently not yet the revolution, but only the due process pattern of recent years badly phrased by Judge Douglas. Justices Frankfurter, Jackson, and Roberts also dissented.

Later in 1943, the Gobitis flag salute case of 1940 was overruled by a much-quoted case.[77] Here Justice Jackson speaking for the Court said:

> The Board of Education moved to dismiss the complaint . . . alleging that the law and regulations are an unconstitutional denial of religious freedom, and of freedom of speech, and are invalid under the "due process" and the "equal protection" clauses of the Fourteenth Amendment to the Federal Constitution.
> Whether the First Amendment to the Constitution will permit officials to order observance of ritual of this nature does not depend upon whether as a voluntary exercise we could think it to be good, bad or merely innocuous.

While Justice Jackson worded the question to be decided in terms of the due process clause, he *seems to assume* that the First Amendment governs as if transferred bodily, and not simply that some of the items mentioned in the First Amendment have been transferred by the due process clause as "fundamental personal freedoms."

Justices Roberts, Reed and Frankfurter dissented. Justice Frankfurter adds to the confusion by the following in another of his most famous dissents.

> I cannot bring my mind to believe that the "liberty secured by the due process clause" [sic] gives this Court authority to deny to the State of West Virginia the attainment of that which we all recognize as a legitimate end, namely, the promotion of good citizenship by employing the means here chosen.

And a bit later: "Moreover, since the First Amendment has been read into the Fourteenth, our problem is . . .", etc. He does not say when, where, or by whom this reading was done. It seems clear, however, that in this case Justice Frankfurter is standing on both the

[77] *West Virginia State Board of Education* v. *Barnette*, 319 U. S. 624 (1943).

theory which he attacked in the Adamson case in June, 1947, after having approved it in the Everson case in February, 1947, and on the theory which he expounded in the Adamson case in June 1947 and abandoned in the McCollum case in March, 1948.

This record of drifting first one way and then the other, of error and repentance, contradictions and counter contradictions, and of introducing, consciously or unconsciously, revolutionary doctrines with no explanation, argument, or defense, moved Professor Corwin to the following comment on the Court's record on religion under the law—even before the superlatives of "bad history and bad logic" had been written in the Everson and McCollum opinions.

Another "liberty" over which the Court has in recent years sought to spread a protecting wing in the name of the "due process" clause of Amendment XIV is religious freedom. It cannot be said, however, that the results it has so far achieved by these endeavors are characterized by self-consistency, stability, or a conspicuous adherence to common sense. The Court got off to a bad start in 1940 in the leading case of Cantwell v. Connecticut. Three members of the sect calling itself Jehovah's Witnesses were convicted under a statute which forbade the unlicensed soliciting of funds on the representation that they were for religious or charitable purposes, and also on a general charge of breach of the peace by accosting in a strongly Catholic neighborhood two communicants of that faith and playing to them a phonograph record which grossly insulted the Christian religion in general and the Catholic church in particular. Both convictions were held to violate "the constitutional guarantees of speech and religion," "the clear and present danger" rule being invoked in partial justification of the holding, although it is reasonably inferable from the Court's own recital of the facts that the listeners to the phonograph record exhibited a degree of self-restraint rather unusual in the circumstances. Two weeks later the Court, as if to "compensate" for its zeal in the Cantwell Case, went to the other extreme, and urging the maxim that legislative acts must be presumed to be constitutional, sustained the State of Pennsylvania in excluding from its schools children of the Jehovah's Witnesses, who in the name of their beliefs refused to salute the flag. The subsequent record of the Court's holdings in this field is singularly erratic. A decision in June, 1942, sustaining the application to vendors of religious books and pamphlets of a non-discriminatory license fee was eleven months later vacated and formally reversed; shortly thereafter a like fate overtook the decision in the "Flag Salute" Case. In May, 1943, the Court found that

an ordinance of the city of Struthers, Ohio, which made it unlawful
for anyone distributing literature to ring a doorbell or otherwise summon the dwellers of a residence to the door to receive such literature,
was violative of the Constitution when applied to distributors of leaflets
advertising a religious meeting. But eight months later it sustained the
application of Massachusetts' child labor laws in the case of a nine-
year-old girl who was permitted by her legal custodian to engage in
"preaching work" and the sale of religious publications after hours.

The Court, one suspects, has not thought its problem quite through,
if indeed most of these cases presented a problem. In this connection
a statement by Justice Douglas in Murdock v. Pennsylvania appears to
be especially significant. "This form of religious activity," that is,
proselytizing by the distribution of tracts, etc., he there asserts, "occupies the state estate under the First Amendment as do worship in the
churches and preaching from the pulpits." In other words, the right
of religious enthusiasts to solicit funds and peddle their doctrinal wares
in the streets, to ring doorbells and disturb householders, and to accost
passersby and insult them in *their* religious beliefs stands on the same
constitutional level as the right of people to resort to their own places
of worship and listen to their chosen teachers! If, as is generally understood, one man's right to swing his fists stops just short of where
another man's nose begins, a somewhat similar rule must be presumed
to hold in the field of religious activities. As Justice Jackson sensibly
suggests in his dissenting opinion in the Murdock and Struthers Cases,
the Court ought to ask itself what would be the effect "if the right
given these Witnesses should be exercised by all sects and denominations." Unfortunately, in United States v. Ballard (see p. 155) Justice
Jackson himself takes leave of common sense to indulge some high-
flown doubts that were evidently suggested to him by a perusal of William James's The Will to Believe.[78]

I have two final comments before leaving the subject of due process
in the Fourteenth Amendment.

First, the contention by both attorneys and Justices in the Everson
case that transportation to a religious school at public expense violated the "due process" clause of the Fourteenth Amendment, over-
looked fundamental facts or elementary logic or both. If compulsory
education laws are "reasonable" laws and are as completely satisfied
by attendance at a parochial or private school as at a public school,
and if the purpose of the compulsory school attendance laws is a

[78] *Ibid.,* pp. 199-201. Quoted by permission of author and publisher.

"reasonable" public purpose (which can hardly be denied), then it follows that the private and parochial schools which satisfy these laws serve a "reasonable" public purpose. The public service performed by religious schools is obviously the sole justification for tax exemption of such schools. No one who believes that it is "reasonably" lawful under the United States Constitution to have tax exempt religious schools which meet the requirements of the compulsory school laws of the various states, can logically believe that furnishing public transportation to the pupils of such schools violates the "due process" clause of the Fourteenth Amendment, regardless of his standard of "reasonableness" or his theory of "due process."

Second, the Oregon School case [79] is frequently (I believe without warrant) considered simply a "due process" case. It is not clear in the unanimous opinion of the Court that it was so considered by the Justices. True, due process was mentioned both in connection with the "liberty" of parents in the education of their children and in the matter of depriving the proprietors of private schools of their "property" without due process of law. But the Court was evidently also thinking of those rights "which are in their nature fundamental; which belong, of right, to citizens of all free governments".[80] Indeed some of the Justices doubtless had in mind the "inalienable rights which are the gifts of the Creator, which the law does not confer, but only recognizes." [81] After speaking of rights which "may not be abridged by legislation which has no reasonable relation to some purpose within the competence of the state," the Court said in the Oregon case: "The fundamental theory of liberty upon which all governments in this Union repose excludes any general power of the state to standardize its children by forcing them to accept instruction from public teachers only."

It seems reasonable to conclude that in view of this language the Court could have, and would have, invalidated the Oregon statute if the Fourteenth Amendment had never been written. In addition to such opinions as those of Washington and Field just quoted, the

79 *Pierce v. Society of Sisters*, 268 U. S. 510 (1925).
80 *Justice Washington in Corfield v. Coryell*, 4 Washington C. C. 371 (1825).
81 *Justice Field in Cummings v. Missouri*, 4 Wallace 277 (1886).

Court would have found sufficient grounds well within the power granted to the Court by the Constitution and the Congress as expounded by John Marshall and accepted for generations.

The Fourteenth Amendment seems universally held to be the weakest section of the Constitution. It is by a tremendous margin the source of more litigation than any other part of the constitution. Its basic purpose, to create and protect the citizenship of the Negroes, has been almost wholly neglected. Its loose, vague language gives free scope to that appetite for dictatorial power which seems to be latent in many members of the human race. Some men who carry the germ of this disease apparently sometimes get on the Supreme Bench. If the specific provision of the other parts of the Constitution are all by the Fourteenth Amendment essentially rendered subject to the discretion of Justices, this makes the Constitution only an interesting historical document illustrating the futile aspirations of those who thought constitutional democracy could be made to work. In 1877 Mr. Justice Miller, for the Court, said:

But while it has been a part of the Constitution as a restraint upon the powers of the States, only a very few years, the docket of this Court is crowded with cases in which we are asked to hold that State Courts and State Legislatures have deprived their own citizens of life, liberty, or property without due process of law. There is here abundant evidence that there exists some strange misconception of the scope of this provision as found in the Fourteenth Amendment. In fact, it would seem from the character of many of the cases before us, and the arguments made in them, that the clause under consideration is looked upon as a means of bringing to the test of the decision of this Court the abstract opinions of every unsuccessful litigant in a State court of the justice of the decision against him, and of the merits of the legislation on which such a decision may be founded.[82]

The situation reported by Collins in 1912 has grown worse in the intervening thirty-six years, and markedly worse in the last few terms of the Supreme Court.

Only a very unpractical mind could conjure up a political philosophy that would hold it to be an issue of national concern whether the operating of barber shops on Sunday in Minnesota be a work of necessity or

[82] *Davidson* v. *New Orleans*, 96 U. S. 103, quoted by Collins, pp. 26-27.

188 RELIGION AND EDUCATION UNDER THE CONSTITUTION

the practice of a handicraft for gain, or what damages should be given a man in Michigan when his neighbor's dog jumps through the front gate and bites him on the leg! To justify this phase of the operation of the Fourteenth Amendment would set up a theory of abstract justice which has been many times repudiated by the Supreme Court itself. A people born and bred in the high ideals of liberty and independence can but resent the encroachment of this new paternalism.[83]

I submit that today "the high ideals of liberty and independence" which have characterized so much of the thinking and the legislation of the people of the several states, are severely threatened by the Supreme Court following an unpredictable, Constitutionally uncharted, historically and semantically indefensible course, under the shelter of the Constitutional anarchy of the Fourteenth Amendment.

[83] *Ibid.*, p. 34.

Chapter 11

THE EVERSON BUS CASE (NEW JERSEY)

*T*HE justices of the Supreme Court of the United States in the decision in the New Jersey bus case (Feb. 10, 1947) indulged in what was probably the strangest argument ever offered by the Court up to that time. This was particularly true of Justice Rutledge's dissenting opinion, concurred in by Justices Frankfurter, Jackson, and Burton. Historical facts bearing on the issue before the Court, so important as to be practically controlling, were not so much as mentioned. One of Jefferson's oratorical figures of speech was taken from its context, given a meaning it could not possibly have had either to Jefferson or to the men to whom it was addressed, and given priority over the language of the Constitution in both the majority and minority opinions. Some misquotations and plain misstatements of fact crept in. Footnotes were furnished which flatly contradict the main thesis to which they were attached. The basic positions of both Jefferson and Madison were grossly misrepresented. It would be difficult to find another set of arguments of similar length from any responsible source containing so many instances of ignoring and misinterpreting relevant facts of history and the language of pertinent documents.

The important question in this case, the one that received most of the attention of the Court was: Does the New Jersey law authorizing payment from public funds for the transportation of pupils to parochial schools violate the First Amendment to the Constitution of the United States? The provision of the First Amendment which had to be applied (with the Fourteenth Amendment) in this case reads "Congress shall make no law respecting an establishment of religion, or prohibiting the free exercise thereof." The issue here raised has deep roots in American political and judicial history, and has tremendous significance to all Americans interested in civil liberties, education, or religion, and ultimately to all interested in the democratic process and constitutional government.

I. The Majority Opinion

The majority opinion, delivered by Justice Black, with Chief Justice Vinson, and Justices Douglas, Murphy, and Reed concurring, upheld the New Jersey law. As has been shown (previously) this is the only possible decision which is consistent with the language and meaning of the First Amendment and with the clear intention of Madison, Jefferson, and the men of the first Congress who were responsible for drafting the First Amendment. However, the majority in arriving at this correct decision indulged in false history and biography, garbled quotations, and fallacious reasoning. In fact about the only sound argument in the *minority* opinion is found in the passages in which Justice Rutledge attacks the majority for apparently believing in the doctrine of "complete separation of church and state" as a constitutional mandate while upholding the New Jersey law,[1] and the majority's further position that in this law New Jersey has reached the "verge" of its power under the United States Constitution.[2]

In stating the issue in this case Justice Black misquotes the First Amendment three times—all the same misquotation, and one that is quite common among those who are currently trying to twist the First Amendment to mean something it clearly could not have meant to its authors. I quote the Justice: "The New Jersey statute is challenged as a 'law respecting the establishment of religion' "; "the expression 'law respecting the establishment of religion' "; "Whether this New Jersey law is one respecting the 'establishment of religion' requires an understanding of the meaning of that language, particularly with respect to the imposition of taxes." The First Amend-

[1] 330 U.S. at 50.   [2] *Ibid.*, p. 51.

ment says "*an* establishment of religion" not *the* establishment of religion. It is obviously easier to get people to believe that what the First Amendment forbade Congress to make laws about was *public support of all* religion (which is false) rather than *exclusive public favors of various kinds, including public support, to one religion only* (which is true) if one promulgates the idea that the Amendment speaks of *the* establishment of religion, not *an* establishment of religion. (See Chapter Six.) Madison might have written, or accepted as good English adequately expressing a thought: "a law respecting *the* support of religion." In fact he would have if he had had any such thought in mind. However, Madison could not have written or accepted "Congress shall make no law respecting *a* support of religion." Spreading the idea that the Amendment was designed to prohibit public support of religion rather than an established national religion, is clearly easier if we start by substituting "the" for "an." As his entire record shows, Madison was not concerned with taxes or the support of religion *per se.* He wanted an amendment, in answer to specific requests from a number of the states, which would prevent Congress from setting up *a* national establishment of religion. He said this was his exact intention. (See p. 96.)

Justice Black in opening referred briefly and with substantial accuracy to the situation which brought about the First Amendment.[3]

A large proportion of the early settlers of this country came here from Europe to escape the bondage of laws which compelled them to support and attend government favored churches. The centuries immediately before and contemporaneous with the colonization of America had been filled with turmoil, civil strife, and persecutions, generated in large part by *established sects* determined to maintain *their absolute political and religious supremacy.* With the power of government supporting them, at various times and places, Catholics had persecuted Protestants, Protestants had persecuted Catholics, Protestant sects had persecuted other Protestant sects, Catholics of one shade of belief had persecuted Catholics of another shade of belief, and all of these had from time to time persecuted Jews. In efforts to force loyalty to *whatever religious group happened to be on top* and *in league with the government* of a particular time and place, men and women had been fined, cast in jail, cruelly

[3] *Ibid.*, p. 8.

tortured, and killed. Among the offenses for which these punishments had been inflicted were such things as *speaking disrespectfully of the views of ministers of government-established churches*, *non-attendance* at those churches, expressions of *non-belief* in their doctrines, and *failure* to pay taxes and tithes to support them.

(Note *four* items of offenses against the established churches. All italics mine.)

These practices of the old world were transplanted to and began to thrive in the soil of the new America. The very charters granted by the English Crown to the individuals and companies designated to make the laws which would control the destinies of the colonials authorized these individuals and companies to erect *religious establishments* which all, whether believers or non-believers, would be required to *support* and *attend*. An exercise of this authority was accompanied by a repetition of many of the old-world practices and persecutions. Catholics found themselves hounded and proscribed because of their faith; Quakers who followed their conscience went to jail; Baptists were peculiarly obnoxious to certain dominant Protestant sects; men and women of varied faiths who happened to be in a minority in a particular locality were persecuted because they steadfastly persisted in worshipping God only as their own consciences dictated. And all of these dissenters were compelled to pay tithes and taxes to support *government-sponsored* churches whose ministers preached inflammatory sermons designed to strengthen and consolidate the *established* faith by generating a burning hatred against dissenters.[4]

(Note the correct use of "establishment" and "established" here wholly inconsistent with Black's basic position both here and in the McCollum case, Chapter Twelve. Italics mine.)

The whole argument would have been sharpened and clarified if Justice Black had added at this point a brief passage of specific and unquestionable historical fact covering the following matters:

1. The "religious establishments" out of which these abuses arose were single, specific religions or churches, having (one in each country) an official, legal, formal *union* with the government, enjoying a monopoly of government force and favor. The monopoly of government *force* was the distinguishing characteristic of "establishments of religion" both Catholic and Protestant throughout Europe and in

<hr />

[4] *Ibid.*, p. 910.

most of the American colonies. The government punished those who did not conform to the "established" or "state" religion.

2. The majority of the very early settlers who came here to escape the bondage of established churches came principally from Great Britain, and therefore came to escape from the Anglican and the Presbyterian established churches of England, Ireland, and Scotland. *They were not opposed to religion, nor to the religion of the Anglican and Presbyterian Churches.* They were opposed to "establishment" in all its features.

3. By the beginning of the Revolution there were established churches in nine of the thirteen colonies—the Anglican in six, the Congregational in three.[5]

The fight against established churches in the states was being won when the First Amendment was written. Four had been eliminated; five remained. Many new state constitutions prohibited establishments, but others kept the old establishments or provided for an established religion in new terms. South Carolina in 1778 included in its constitution: "The Christian Protestant religion shall be deemed and is hereby constituted and declared to be, the established religion of this state." [6]

4. For years before 1789 a fight had been going on in the various colonies and states against established churches. Disestablishment in the states was on its way. There was an ardent desire to have Congress leave this situation alone, keep out of it, and above all things to prevent Congress attempting to set up a "nationally established religion" to replace the dying state establishments. As Judge Story expressed it in his *Commentaries:* [7]

the real object of Amendment I was not to countenance, much less to advance Mohammedanism or Judaism or infidelity by prostrating Christianity; but to exclude all rivalry among Christian sects and to prevent any national ecclesiastical establishment which should give to any hierarchy the exclusive patronage of the national government.

[5] Sweet, William Warren, *The Story of Religions in America* (New York, Harper & Brothers, 1930), 1st ed., p. 274.
[6] Thorpe, F. N., *American Charters, Constitutions and Organic Laws* (Washington, Government Printing Office, 1909), Vol. VI, p. 3255.
[7] Story, Joseph, *Commentaries on the Constitution of the United States* (Boston, Hilliard, Gray & Co., 1833), pp. 690 ff.

By this amendment the federal government "deliberately deprived itself of all legislative control over religion."

The whole power over the subject of religion is left exclusively to the state governments to be acted upon according to their own sense of justice and the State Constitutions; and the Catholic and the Protestant, the Calvinist and the Armenian, the Jew and the Infidel may sit down at the common table of the national councils without any inquisition into their faith or mode of worship.

A clear and accurate definition of the phrase "an establishment of religion" as used in the First Amendment should have been supplied right here. But there is no such definition to be found in either the majority or the minority opinions. Such a definition according to the meaning of the words to the men who used them, as shown by other use of the same words by the same men, and by the context of the times, would have, or certainly should have, made the Court's opinion short, simple, and unanimous. It seems incredible that anyone at home in the English language and familiar with the important documents of historical relevance could believe that the New Jersey bus law (or any other state law that does not set up "an establishment of religion" *as the phrase was used in* 1789) is in violation of the First Amendment. Both the majority and the minority opinions omit the most pertinent passages from Jefferson and Madison showing what they meant by establishment and disestablishment, and instead repeat at great length political documents advocating or discussing *state legislation* in Virginia, which is not binding on any other state. And both miss the point that even the Virginia contest was over "*an* establishment of religion"—not over simply impartial state support of religion.

All of Justice Black's and Justice Rutledge's discussion of Virginia legislation, and of Jefferson's and Madison's remarks concerning that legislation, is invalid on three counts: (1) It was legislation for a single state and as such neither the laws themselves nor speeches for or against them had any bearing on the laws of any other state, as New Jersey. (2) The assumption that Jefferson or Madison ever believed that the Constitution of the United States should contain the same provisions as a law of the state of Virginia, is a pretty wild assumption

for which there is not a shred of proof. (3) The assumption that either
Jefferson or Madison ever believed that the Constitution of the United
States contained, or should contain, any restriction on the individual
states regarding state laws "respecting an establishment of religion
or prohibiting the free exercise thereof" is an assumption that could
exist only in a mind thoroughly ignorant of the words and records
of these two Founding Fathers.

By a selective, circuitous, and largely irrelevant recital, the majority
opinion arrives at this *obiter dictum*:

The "establishment of religion" clause of the First Amendment means
at least this: Neither a state nor the Federal Government can set up a
church. Neither can pass laws which aid one religion, aid all religions,
or prefer one religion over another. Neither can force nor influence a
person to go to or to remain away from church against his will or force
him to profess a belief or disbelief in any religion. No person can be
punished for entertaining or professing religious beliefs or disbeliefs,
for church attendance or non-attendance. No tax in any amount, large
or small, can be levied to support any religious activities or institutions,
whatever they may be called, or whatever form they may adopt to teach
or practice religion. Neither the state nor the Federal Government can
openly or secretly, participate in the affairs of any religious organizations or groups and *vice versa*. In the words of Jefferson, the clause
against establishment of religion by law was intended to erect "a wall
of separation between Church and State." [8]

Obviously setting up *a* church, aiding *one* religion only, using force
or punishment on account of dissident belief or failure in attendance
at *the* "established" church, compelling support of *one* religion, were
all removed by the clause in question from the power of *the Congress
functioning for the United States as a whole*. However, the First
Amendment, by the universal agreement of courts, Congress, state
legislatures, historians, and legal scholars, did not restrict in any way
the *individual states' freedom to do all of these things* if they chose.
Further, there is not an item *in the last three sentences* of this elaborate expansion of the First Amendment which on the same universal evidence restricts even Congress acting for the United States as
a whole. Such an "interpretation" is inconsistent with its plain

[8] 330 U.S. 1 at 15-16.

language, with any passage accurately quoted or referred to by the Court as showing any such purpose or intent on the part of the framers or adopters of this amendment, with the context of the times out of which the First Amendment came, and with over 150 years of United States history.

The *meaning* of the "establishment of religion" clause cannot be affected by whatever power the Fourteenth Amendment (see Chapter Ten) has to make that clause a restriction on the states. The First Amendment means nothing at all concerning "a state" or "the Federal Government." It says and means that Congress cannot make a law about a specified subject. The only question which Justice Black had to deal with here was what Madison and his colleagues in the First Congress meant by "an establishment of religion."

Had Justice Black addressed himself to the exact question, an hour or two spent in reading early American history would have saved him from writing the elaborate nonsense of this *dictum*.

Since both the majority and the minority in this case tried to make Jefferson and Madison father their attack on the First Amendment, it is too bad that the Justices did not read, and quote accurately, the most illuminating and relevant passages from the *Annals of Congress*, Jefferson's remarks about the "wall of separation," and Eckenrode's *The Separation of Church and State in Virginia*. All of these are referred to in a spurious display of the appearance of scholarship. But the most relevant passages are either omitted entirely (see p. 96) or fragments of sentences are selected to garble the clear meaning of the passages referred to (see pp. 60, 209, 286).

A good example of the unwisdom of this attempt to substitute for the specific, literal language of the First Amendment, the vague, ambiguous language of the modern slogan, "the separation of Church and State," is shown by Justice Black's use of the word "church" in three different and distinct meanings in this paragraph: "set up a church," "remain away from church," "between Church and State."

Constitutions written by such literate and competent statesmen as James Madison are not written in ambiguous, or figurative language. Documents in which accuracy and clarity are of first importance, as constitutions, laws, and court opinions, should never be expressed in figurative language. "Walls of separation" are wholly out of place in all such writing.

We have in this *dictum* of Judge Black and in Justice Rutledge's dissenting opinion, a clear attempt to insert into the Constitution a vague, figurative principle which is new as a constitutional provision. No Congress, no President, no Supreme Court decision, had ever recognized or promulgated "the complete separation of Church and State" as a principle operative in either the federal or the state government, until February 10, 1947. But the Judges lacked the frankness and the courage to say this. So they tried to place their illegitimate offspring on the ultra-respectable doorsteps of Jefferson and Madison. In commenting on this stealthy attempt to amend the Constitution without consulting the American people, Mr. John L. Franklin writes the following sharp comment: [9]

What is most appalling to the logical mind is the way the Court almost insidiously introduced into an otherwise unexceptionable statement, the words, "aid all religions," thus proscribing equal non-discriminatory aid to all religions, while at the same time recognizing that it was preferential treatment that the Amendment prohibited.

This the court said without a reference to what Madison had said of the meaning of the amendment and without a single relevant citation of judicial authority or appeal to philology. It was as though the Amendment meant this so plainly as to be obvious or as though this was a tribunal that could issue ukases without being restricted by logic or accountable at the bar of public opinion.

Particularly the last three sentences of Black's *dictum* are in direct opposition to the writings and the responsible actions, in Congress and in the Presidency, of Jefferson and Madison. (See Chapters Five and Six.) This fact is of prime importance when we come to examine the argument that it was the *intention* of Madison or Jefferson, or the *purpose* of the First Amendment, to accomplish all of these things.

The majority opinion expressed a belief that the New Jersey law "approaches the verge of the states' power," because "New Jersey cannot consistently with the 'establishment of religion clause' of

[9] "Education and Religion," *Phi Delta Kappan*, Fulton, Mo. (May, 1948), p. 367.

the First Amendment contribute tax-raised funds to the support of an institution which teaches the tenets and faith of any church." [10] As we shall see, this position (which is obviously not explicitly stated in the language of the Amendment) is flatly contrary to the controlling facts of history. The *opposite position* was taken without a single exception by the Supreme Court, Congress, and the legal scholars for over 150 years after the ratification of the First Amendment, and has been practiced consistently by the United States government from 1789 to 1948. (See p. 115.) It is impossible, granting them ordinary competence, to believe that Madison, Jefferson, and the other men behind the First Amendment could have intended or expected any such results to flow from that Amendment. Madison could not have meant "any religious institution" by the words "an establishment of religion" in the First Amendment.

Further, the majority opinion says that Madison in his *Memorial and Remonstrance* "eloquently argued . . . ; that no person, believer or nonbeliever, should be taxed to support a religious institution of any kind." [11] Madison argued nothing of the sort—as anyone can see by reading the *Memorial* (Appendix C). The nearest he came to it was opposition to taxes in support of "an establishment," i.e., *a single "established" state church or religion.* He was opposed to every feature of an established religion, including tax support. He worked to prohibit *an established religion* in the state of Virginia; and in the Congress he helped to prevent an established religion for the nation as a whole in the First Amendment. The latter purpose was accomplished by prohibiting *any law* by Congress in regard to "an establishment of religion" *at a time when Congress had not yet set up a national religion.*

By requiring Congress to keep hands off the subject of established religion the specific objective of preventing an established religion for the United States as a whole was accomplished. This was done by language which at the same time made support of the proposed amendment possible by all the people who objected to Congress taking over areas such as religion, which they considered matters for *state* control, as well as the many people in the various states who

[10] *Ibid.*, p. 16.   [11] *Ibid.*, p. 12.

wanted the state established churches to continue free from federal interference. A number of state establishments continued years after 1791, one until 1833. But all had disappeared by state action before the Fourteenth Amendment (1868). By state provisions, not through the effect of the Fourteenth Amendment, no state can now set up an established church or religion. That is the whole story. The rest is simply "judicial legislation" based on either ignorance of, or distortion of, relevant and unambiguous facts of history.

For the discussion of Justice Black's elaborate misrepresentation of Jefferson in the matter of the famous metaphor, the "wall of separation between church and state," see Chapter Five. In writing the majority opinion in this case (as also in the McCollum case, Chapter Twelve) Justice Black clearly preferred the freedom of the figurative language of the rhetoric of courtesy to the restrictions of the literal language of the United States Constitution. So he dealt at some length with an imaginary wall of separation instead of with a "law respecting an establishment of religion" which was actually the matter before the Court.

However, the majority does not keep consistently to the doctrine found in its excursion into the realm of oratorical figures of speech. Later on, it speaks favorably of state requirements of local transit companies "to provide reduced fares to school children including those attending parochial schools," and of municipal transportation systems carrying "all school children free of charge." It mentions police, fire, sewage, sidewalk, and highway service available at public expense to parochial schools and their pupils. The majority conclusion on this part is that "cutting off church schools from these services, so separate and so indisputably marked off from the religious function . . . is obviously not the purpose of the First Amendment." [12] (Note that the word "separate" is not given the same meaning in this statement concerning state services and religious functions that is given to it by the Court in dealing with "the wall of separation.") The Court, however, omitted any mention of even more directly applicable state services that are commonplace in government cooperation with parochial schools; tax exemp-

[12] *Ibid.*, pp. 17-18.

tion, compulsory attendance procedures, licensing of teachers, training of teachers, school inspection, curricular requirements, state accrediting of individual schools, state examinations, and the accepting of credits from church schools in all public schools and colleges (see Chapter Nine). In the face of all this it seems that the Court must have been a bit fanciful in referring to the figurative wall as one that *must be kept* so "high and impregnable" that it could not suffer "the slightest breach." [13]

The Supreme Court's magnification of Jefferson's wall is fantastic. It has no relation to any reality of either law or fact. No such wall has existed for a single day in any state in the union or in the United States as a nation. From the beginning of our existence we have had tax exemption, established churches persisting for many years in some states after the adoption of the First Amendment, numerous laws creating legal "relations" between state governments and church schools, federal support of chaplains in the Army and Navy, in Congress, in military and naval academies, federal support of religious missions and schools on the Indian reservations, federal and state contribution to religious activity in hospitals and penal institutions, and in recent years the federal lunch program in parochial schools, the G. I. Bill of Rights paying vast sums to religious schools and colleges, and so on *ad infinitum*. As Senator Aiken recently remarked: "The old argument of separation of church and state falls down when under the G. I. Bill of Rights the United States is paying today to educate priests, Protestant ministers, and rabbis." [14] The argument fails to stand up whenever it is examined in the light of fact and law.

The word "old," however, may well be questioned here. The slogan "complete separation of church and state" was not much used until comparatively recent years. It was not common in argument in the period from 1791 well into the twentieth century. Throughout this time the non-Protestant Americans of all kinds were numerically small and had little or no weight in the settlement of public policies regarding religion, education, the use of public funds, and other important subjects. All through this long period the teachings of "Trini-

[13] *Ibid.*, p. 18.   [14] *New York Times*, May 15, 1947.

tarian Protestant Christianity" were generally included as an integral part of the public school program (see pp. 26-27) and Congress furnished tax money not only for chaplains in Congress, the Army, Navy, etc., but also for religious missionaries and religious schools (largely Protestant of course) to promote religion and education on the Indian reservations. The slogan "the complete separation of church and state" was certainly not widely invoked in an effort to put a stop to any of these practices. It was appealed to occasionally by small groups in attempts to stop congressional support of chaplains. But Congress either promptly tabled such petitions or, as in 1852,[15] answered them by carefully pointing out that "an establishment of religion" meant to the men who wrote it and who administered it in the first half-century after its adoption—*a union of one church or religion with the government,* to the exclusion from equal government favor of all other churches or religions.

II. THE DISSENTING OPINION

The dissenting opinion written by Mr. Justice Rutledge, and concurred in by Justices Frankfurter, Jackson, and Burton, is an almost incredible document. After quoting two paragraphs from a Bill for Establishing Religious Freedom, for the State of Virginia, enacted by the General Assembly of that state in 1786, Justice Rutledge writes: "I cannot believe that the great author of those words [Jefferson] or the men who made them law, could have joined in this decision." Anyone is entitled to his belief as to what Thomas Jefferson would do were he a Justice of the Supreme Court in 1947. But in any such speculation we should keep in mind (if we want a rational result) some basic and indisputable facts such as those cited above, plus those which follow.

It is too bad that Justice Rutledge, in his speculation regarding Jefferson's probable decision in this case, did not follow Jefferson's advice on the way in which the Constitution should be construed by the Supreme Court, "according to the plain and ordinary meaning

[15] See *Reports of Committees of the Senate of the United States.* Second Session, 32nd. Congress. 1852-1853. No. 376. (Washington, Robert Armstrong, 1853).

of its language, to the common intendment of the time, and of those who framed it." [16]

"On every question of construction, carry ourselves back to the time when the constitution was adopted, recollect the spirit manifested in the debates, and instead of trying what meaning may be squeezed out of the text, or invented against it, conform to the probable one in which it was passed." [17]

"It should be left to the sophisms of advocates, whose trade it is, to prove . . . that a power has been given because it ought to have been given." [18]

Certainly Jefferson and Madison, and probably most of the members of the Virginia Assembly and later the members of the First Congress of the United States, knew enough about the relations of the state and federal governments to know that any expressions used in or about a Virginia statute could not control the interpretation of a law of New Jersey or any other state except Virginia.

Following all of this speculation which was made possible only by ignoring the relevant facts of Jefferson's life and works, Justice Rutledge mounted the figurative great wall and delivered the following *dictum*: "Neither so high nor so impregnable as yesterday is the wall raised between church and state by Virginia's statute of religious freedom and the First Amendment, now made applicable to all the states by the Fourteenth." [19] This sentence, as punctuated, says that the Virginia Law of 1786 is now applicable to all of the states under the Fourteenth Amendment of 1868. This of course may be merely bad punctuation or a printer's error. However, the conclusion that the sentence is intended to mean what it says, as punctuated, certainly gets great support from the elaborate substitution in the minority opinion of the political writings of Jefferson and Madison (in circumstances far removed from the formulation and adoption

[16] "The Solemn Declaration and Protest of the Commonwealth of Virginia, on the Principles of the Constitution of the United States of America, and on the Violations of them, December, 1825." Padover, *The Complete Jefferson*, p. 134.
[17] "The Usurpation of the Supreme Court," in a letter to William Johnson, June 12, 1823, Padover, *The Complete Jefferson*, p. 322.
[18] *Ibid.*, p. 323.
[19] 330 U.S. 1, at 29.

of the First Amendment) for the exact language of that amendment and the circumstances specifically relevant to its meaning.

Granting the complete legitimacy of reference to antecedent writings in order to clear up ambiguous passages, the misinterpretation of the plain and simple language of the First Amendment in the dissenting opinion can have no such justification. This misinterpretation is arrived at only (1) by ignoring the most important facts in the setting in which Madison and Jefferson carried on their fight for religious freedom and against established churches (or by assuming that they were themselves ignorant of these facts), and (2) by ignoring or misinterpreting the plain language these men used, which is, some of it (but not the most important), quoted or referred to in this opinion, and (3) by assuming an incompetence on the part of Madison in the use of the English language which should not be the position of anyone who has read so much as two paragraphs of Madison's orderly, grammatical, meticulously worded, clear, and often brilliant prose.

These three basic weaknesses of the argument in the dissenting opinion show up in the handling of two problems: the meaning of the phrase "an establishment of religion," and the intent or purpose of the first Amendment.

The Meaning of "An Establishment of Religion"

The treatment in the minority opinion of the meaning of this phrase in the First Amendment is bewildering in view of the fact that it is apparently the responsible argument of a Justice of the Supreme Court, concurred in by three other Justices of that Court. The facts of the general history of establishments of religion in Europe and America, the statements of many historians and commentators on these establishments, and especially the accounts of the fight against established churches in America, are all available in any fairly good library. Particularly the writings of Madison and Jefferson, *frequently alluded to by Justice Rutledge*, are plain on the meaning of this phrase.

Obviously "an establishment of religion" must mean in the Constitution just what it means in the writings of Madison, Jefferson, and the others engaged in the controversy over establishments, and in the writings of the scholarly commentators and historians who have made a study of that period. In these writings it means a SINGLE CHURCH OR RELIGION ENJOYING FORMAL, LEGAL, OFFICIAL, MONOPOLISTIC PRIVILEGE THROUGH A UNION WITH THE GOVERNMENT OF THE STATE. That is the meaning given in the *Encyclopaedia Britannica*.[20] The phrase has been used this way for centuries in speaking of the established Protestant churches of England, Scotland, Germany, and other countries, and of the established Catholic Church in Italy, Spain, and elsewhere. There is not an item of dependable evidence offered in the dissenting opinion which shows that the term means, or ever has meant, anything else.

"Not simply an established church, but any law respecting an establishment of religion is forbidden" says the minority opinion. But you cannot make a law respecting an establishment of religion unless you have, in existence or in prospect, an establishment of religion respecting which you make the law. So first we have to know what "an establishment of religion" is. In fact Justice Rutledge says, "This case forces us to determine squarely for the first time what was an establishment of religion in the First Amendment's conception; and by that measure to decide whether New Jersey's action violates its command." [21] This was, of course, the exact, and essentially the only, question that was properly before the Supreme Court in this case. But Justice Rutledge elaborately avoids determining squarely what this key phrase means in the Constitution. Nowhere does he give a direct answer.

The passages which seem to indicate what Justice Rutledge thinks "an establishment of religion" means in the First Amendment are two, one in his text and one in footnote 34. In the first he says that a threat to maintaining that complete and permanent separation of religion and civil power which the First Amendment commands is through the use of the taxing power to support religion, religious establishments, or establishments having a religious foundation, whatever their form or special religious function.[22]

20 Ed. 14, Vol. VIII, p. 726.   22 *Ibid.*, p. 41.
21 330 U.S. at 29.

Here Justice Rutledge may mean either of two things: (1) that "establishment" means "*taxing power* to support religion or religious establishments," or (2) that "an establishment of religion" means "religion, religious establishments, or establishments having a religious foundation, whatever their form or special religious function"—in other words any religious organization or institution or establishment (as a commercial establishment, an educational establishment, a financial establishment).

The first possible meaning of this passage from Judge Rutledge's text, that "establishment" means taxing power or "public support by public funds" is like the *second fragment* on which we can base a guess as to what Justice Rutledge would have said had he "determined squarely" the only question in the case. This fragment is in footnote 34, "showing unmistakably that 'establishment' meant public 'support' of religion in the financial sense." This one is easily disposed of. An establishment of a religion obviously *includes* public support of the religion established. It always has both in Europe and America and everywhere else. Support by taxation is inevitably, universally *one of the features* of an establishment. But it is also inevitably and universally *only one of the features of establishment. Establishment means tax support but tax support does not mean establishment.* Horses are quadrupeds but quadrupeds are not (necessarily) horses. This elementary logic applied to this case should have resulted in an unanimous decision that would have avoided all further argument on the meaning of the First Amendment. It is greatly to be regretted that the Supreme Court in this first case which forced the question upon them did not "determine it squarely" instead of muffing it so completely.

Tax support of religion or religious education certainly did not mean "establishment" to Thomas Jefferson as shown by the following list of facts which are all reported in detail in Chapter Five.

1. Jefferson recommended a school of theology for the training of clergymen in the public education system of the State of Virginia.

2. He approved rather elaborate arrangements in the University of Virginia for students for "institutions in religion" which might be

set up by the various denominations "within, or adjacent to, the precincts of the University."

3. He recommended a large room in the University of Virginia "for religious worship."

4. As President, Jefferson used tax funds of the United States for
   a. Chaplains in the Army and Navy
   b. Chaplains in Congress
   c. Religion and religious education among the Indians

5. He did not protest Virginia's continuing to use tax money in various ways to promote religion and religious education in the forty years he lived as a leading citizen of Virginia after the passage of his Bill for Religious Freedom, in 1786.

Tax support did not mean establishment to James Madison. The following items from Madison's record are all covered more fully in Chapter Six.

1. Madison said, in the First Congress, that the word meant a single, national religion which Congress should establish and to which it would enforce legal observance by law.

2. He so used the term "establishment" in his *Memorial and Remonstrance.*

3. As a member of the First Congress, almost coincident with the writing of the First Amendment, Madison served as a member of the joint committee which set up the Chaplain system in the House of Representatives, and in the Senate, which has used tax money from that day to this.

4. As Commander-in-Chief of the Army and Navy, Madison used tax money to support chaplains and religion in both of these services.

5. Throughout his administration, he used tax money to promote religion and religious education among the Indians.

Tax support did not mean establishment to the First Congress of the United States when they formulated and adopted the First Amendment (see Chapter Seven), or to succeeding congresses when the First Amendment was said to mean a *single religion* united with the Government; or when the Congress used tax money for chaplains in Congress, in the Army and Navy and among the Indians.

Tax support has never meant establishment in any state in the

United States, as shown in Chapter Nine. Every state in the Union has used tax money in helpful contacts with religion and religious education in a number of ways in addition to universal tax exemption throughout our history.

Tax support has never meant establishment to any President of the United States. All presidents, from Washington to Truman, both inclusive, have presided over administrations which used tax money in the ways suggested above by both Madison and Jefferson. Using the funds of the United States to support religious education started in the administration of George Washington, in August, 1789, and Harry Truman, as President in the spring of 1948, signed a bill passed by Congress appropriating $500,000 to build a chapel for religions at the United States Merchant Marine Academy at King's Point, New York.

Tax support does not mean establishment in such countries as Holland and Switzerland where, according to the histories in the encyclopedias, there are no established churches, but where both Catholic and Protestant schools have public support. The one universal and all-important feature of establishment is *exclusiveness*, monopoly. *Exclusive* support by taxation of one religion constitutes partial establishment. Such establishments are hard to find in the pages of history. The dying American established churches in New England became practically that sort of establishments before they expired. They are frequently referred to as "partial establishments." Equal, impartial support by taxation is in no way establishment, and is not so considered by scholarly historians, religious or lay. The idea has been common only in the speeches and press releases of relatively irresponsible modern propagandists until the Supreme Court Justices in the Everson case began to prefer it to the ideas of Jefferson and Madison expressed in the outmoded Constitution of the United States!

In the exhilaration of their new freedom from Constitutional provisions the Justices made one big mistake. They tried to make Jefferson and Madison responsible for their betrayal of Jefferson and Madison. That was an error—of a sort. At the same time it was a cautious thing to do. Imagine the situation had the justices said: "This is what the Constitution provides because we like it this way;

we are quite unimpressed by what Jefferson and Madison thought or said; we are not concerned with the provision the American people have approved or disapproved for inclusion in the Constitution of the United States." Then the situation would have been very different. Then the American people would have answered with probably substantial unanimity something like this: "We disagree completely; we regret your inaccurate reading of history and of the Constitution of the United States, and we shall rejoice in your return to private life!"

The first clause of the First Amendment cannot legitimately have the slightest bearing on any law that treats all religions alike in the matter of taxation or anything else. Equality of all religions and freedom in the exercise of all religions *nationally* were the two objectives of the First Amendment, and the only objectives in the purpose of its creators.

As is plain from the discussion reported in the *Annals of Congress*,[23] while there was difference of how to accomplish it in suitable language, there was apparently no difference of opinion as to the desirability of preventing, in Judge Story's words, "any ecclesiastical establishment which would give to any hierarchy the exclusive patronage of the federal government." [24]

But accomplishing this purpose by the use of the language chosen not only won the support of some who favored the existing established state churches, and who feared that any national church might be of some denomination other than theirs, but also expressed much better than a specific banning of an established religion *per se* a basic principle in Jefferson's philosophy of government with which Madison seems wholly to have agreed but which he expressed less frequently and with less passion. Leaving the problem of establishments "without prejudice" in the hands of the several states also fitted better into the thinking of all who took their theories of Constitution making from Alexander Hamilton. (See p. 92.)

This basic Jeffersonian principle is frequently referred to as the principle of "states rights." It involves the doctrine of delegated

[23] Vol. I, pp. 729 ff.   [24] *Commentaries*, p. 600.

powers (the Tenth Amendment) and Jefferson's frequent insistence that the states are supreme in "domestic concerns" and the federal government *only* in "foreign concerns" (the coinage of money alone excepted). This principle also harmonizes well with the consistent doctrine of the Supreme Court up to the McCollum case in distinguishing (when applying the Fourteenth Amendment) the freedoms and immunities of national citizenship from the freedoms and immunities of state citizenship.

Jefferson not only objected to but feared usurpation of power by Congress and the Supreme Court. He wanted the whole federal government kept in its place.[25] He wanted guarantees against the abuses of federal power. Some constitutional amendment that would prevent a national church in the future, phrased in words which said that Congress should leave the subject alone, was generally satisfactory to Americans of all shades of political and religious opinion in the eighteenth century. This satisfaction with the purpose and language of the First Amendment remained substantially unbroken for a century or more. In recent years, however, especially since the Supreme Court recognized, some fifty years after the fact, that the Fourteenth Amendment could apply some of the First (in some circumstances, to some extent—all still undefined) in the area of personal liberties, to the individual states, this century of peace has been shattered by controversies. Some people have sought to win certain objectives (which they have a wholly unquestioned right to believe in and to advocate) by the simple device of *assuming* (never proving) that the First Amendment means all of the extravagant phrases Justice Rutledge uses: "complete and permanent separation," which would prevent "every form and degree of official relation between religion and civil authority."

It is interesting, if not thoroughly diverting under the circumstances, to observe the many instances in which Justice Rutledge himself uses the terms "an established church" and "an establishment of religion" (or simply the words "establishment" and "disestablish-

25 See the following in Padover's *Complete Jefferson*: "Comments on the Federal Constitution (1787)," p. 120; "Letter to Madison (1789)," p. 123; "The Usurpation of the Supreme Court (1823)," p. 320; "Solemn Declaration and Protest (1825)," p. 134.

ment") in the accurate, historic meaning of Jefferson, Madison, and the historians, legal scholars, and lexicographers. When he is off his guard Justice Rutledge uses the vocabulary of other educated persons speaking the English language. Here are some of Justice Rutledge's expressions: [26]

> "the existing Virginia establishment"
> "the prevailing establishment"
> "he linked this with disestablishment"
> "the fight over establishments"
> "fragment of establishment"
> "the life blood of establishment"
> "the great fight over establishments"
> "against establishment in 1776"
> "the time of disestablishment"
> "the prohibition of establishments"
> "had an established religion and dissident groups"

These are all Justice Rutledge's phrases, not quotations from others. To substitute in any of them for the word "establishment," the words "religious organization," "religious institution," or "religion in any guise, form or degree" (which Justice Rutledge seems to say is the meaning of "an establishment of religion" in his squarest answer to the question which he said was the essential issue in the case before him) is to make complete nonsense of the Justice's sentences. To do the same in the writings of Jefferson and Madison would be to make nonsense of the writings of these superlatively literate statesmen.

The dissenting opinion has a narrative footnote [27] which alone almost completely demolishes the basic argument of the minority. The story, gathered from the *Annals of Congress* and Madison's writings, is this: A Connecticut Representative was afraid that the Amendment as worded might interfere with compelling a man to keep his engagement to contribute to the expense of supporting ministers or building a meeting house " 'for a support of ministers or building of places of worship *might be construed into a religious*

*establishment.' To avoid any such possibility Madison suggested in-
serting the word 'national' before 'religion.' "* (Italics mine.) The
dissenting opinion concludes from this little story that it shows "unmistakably that 'establishment' meant public 'support' of religion in
the financial sense." Obviously establishment includes support, but
support does not include establishment. The story shows that Madison made this distinction—not a great feat for one who had been
fighting an established church for years, but who was evidently not
concerned with public support of religious enterprises that was other
than a feature of an established church.

Madison's response to the man from Connecticut showed further
that he was interested in the matter before Congress only on the
national scale, not at all in its aspects in the several states, as Connecticut and New Jersey, and *that he did not want either the support
of ministers or the buildings of a place of worship to be construed as
"an establishment of religion!"* Yet this incident is offered to us to
prove that it was Madison's *purpose* to have such a law as one allowing the public to pay for bus rides for pupils to parochial schools
outlawed as "a law respecting an establishment of religion."

The Intent or Purpose of the First Clause
of the First Amendment

The position of the dissenting opinion on the purpose of the First
Amendment is expressed in these passages:

> The Amendment's purpose was not to strike merely at the official
> establishment of a single sect, creed or religion, outlawing only a formal
> relation such as had prevailed in England and some of the colonies.
> Necessarily it was to uproot all such relationships. The object was broader
> than separating church and state in this narrow sense. It was to create
> a complete and permanent separation of the spheres of religious activity
> and Civil authority by comprehensively forbidding every form of public
> aid or support for religion.[28]
> The prohibition broadly forbids state support, financial or other of
> religion in any guise, form or decree. It outlaws all use of public funds
> for religious purposes.[29]

[28] *Ibid.,* pp. 31-32.   [29] *Ibid.,* p. 33.

Such is the thesis of the dissenting opinion. Justice Rutledge purposes to carry the burden of forcing on the First Amendment this brood of illegitimate offspring in three ways. He writes: "In proof the Amendment's wording and history unite with this Court's consistent utterances whenever attention has been fixed directly upon this question." [30] Nothing more should be needed than an elementary understanding of the English language, to know that the *wording* of the Amendment does not say, or imply, or faintly suggest, the meaning of a single sentence in this thesis. *History* refutes the thesis. Any *consistent utterances of the Court* which are not consistent with the language of the Constitution, illuminated, when necessary, by history antecedent to, or concurrent with, the putting of the language into the Constitution, are nothing more than unfortunate and irrelevant utterances. The less said about them the better.

This, however, is not the whole story concerning Justice Rutledge's references to "this Court's consistent utterances." He has another one: "this Court's consistent expressions, whenever it has touched on the matter directly." [31] He gives no references at all in connection with the first phrase. But he has a footnote on the second one. Hunting it out in the fine print with the thought that now at last *some basis* for the Rutledge doctrine would be discovered, we are told only that *Cochran v. Board of Education* 281 U. S. 370 (the Louisiana text book case) "was not such a case!" In neither instance does the Justice cite one case in which the Supreme Court has in 160 years taken a position "consistent" with his own revolutionary rewriting of the First Amendment. But he has a good defense. He "could do no other." There are no such cases.

History is the only possible prop for the thesis of the Rutledge dissenting opinion. Here (as elsewhere when no other help is available) history is summoned to the witness stand to testify that the *intention* of the framers and adopters of the First Amendment was something quite other than anything expressed by its language. It's an old technique. When confronted by unyielding language, going around it and somehow discovering accommodating *intentions* of

[30] *Ibid.*, p. 32.   [31] *Ibid.*, p. 41.

dead men and Congresses that have passed away, has long been the last refuge of legislating judges.

This opinion's statements concerning "merely the official establishment of a single sect, creed or religion" and "outlawing only a formal relation such as had prevailed in England and some of the colonies" [32] are certainly not history. It was exactly the "formal relation" of a single church and government in both England and America which "official establishment" created and maintained, that the whole fight was about. The relation could only be formal and official because it was the deliberate, constitutional or statutory, act of government. This was precisely the object of attack of the opponents of establishment in England and Scotland, and of Madison, Jefferson, Witherspoon, John Adams, Sam Adams, Isaac Baccus, and others in America.

John Adams said, "If Parliament could tax us, they could also establish the Church of England." [33] Sam Adams said, "The establishment of a Protestant Episcopacy in America is also zealously contended for. . . . We hope to God such an establishment will never take place in America." [34] Judge Story in his *Commentaries* wrote: "The real object of Amendment I was to prevent any ecclesiastical establishment which would give to any hierarchy the exclusive patronage of the federal government." [35] Dr. Conrad Moehlman says of the First Amendment: "Any established church meant a repetition in the United States of all the political-religious quarrels of Europe . . . sectarian antipathy could express itself with much less damage to the commonwealth under religious liberty than under an establishment." [36] Judge Cooley in his *Constitutional Limitations* in discussing the First Amendment wrote: "There is not complete religious liberty where one sect is favored by the State and given an advantage by law over the other sects." [37] Corwin says, "An establishment of religion means a state church, such as for instance existed

[32] *Ibid.*, p. 31.
[33] *See* Moehlman, C. H., *School and Church* (New York, Harper & Brothers, 1944), p. 39.
[34] *Ibid.*
[35] P. 600.
[36] Moehlman, *op. cit.*, p. 43.
[37] P. 584.

in Massachusetts for more than forty years after the adoption of the Constitution." [38]

Furthermore, it was precisely "separating church and state in this narrow sense" of breaking up or preventing unity of the government with one church or religion, that had been fought for through the years. There is not a scrap of evidence cited here, which shows that Madison or Jefferson ever desired, or tried to provide for "a complete and permanent separation of the spheres of religious activity and civil authority." [39] On the other hand, the use of the phrase "separation of church and state" in the "narrow sense," the only sense which has validity as stating an American policy, is quite common among careful writers. It is so used by William Warren Sweet in his *The Story of Religions in the United States*,[40] by Morrison and Comager in *The Growth of the American Republic*,[41] and others. Cardinal Gibbons was clearly using the phrase in this exact sense in his *A Retrospect of Fifty Years*:

The separation of church and state in this country seems to Catholics the natural, the inevitable, the best conceivable plan, the one that would work best among us, both for the good of religion and of the state. . . . American Catholics rejoice in our separation of church and state; and I can conceive of no combination of circumstances likely to arise which should make a union desirable either to church or state.[42]

Even the citation of V. T. Thayer's *Religion in Public Education*, 1947, by Justice Rutledge [43] in support of the thesis concerning the "complete division of religion and civil authority which our forefathers made," is an error. Dr. Thayer takes the *opposite* position. He writes "of the First Amendment, which prohibits an established church and guarantees freedom of worship. This left each state free, however, to determine its own policies in matters of religion." [44] True, Dr. Thayer argues in favor of keeping religion out of the public schools as a *policy*, a current problem, but not as a matter that was decided by "our forefathers."

[38] *The Constitution—What It Means Today*, 9th ed., pp. 155-156.
[39] 330 U. S. 1 at 31.   [40] Pp. 105, 274-275.   · [41] Pp. 200-204.
[42] (Baltimore, J. Murphy Co., 1916), Vol. I, p. 211.
[43] 330 U.S. 1 at 63.
[44] Thayer, V. T., *Religion in Public Education* (New York, The Viking Press, 1947), pp. 21, 22, 25.

The dissenting opinion tells us that the First Amendment "outlaws all use of public funds for religious purposes." [45] Since the language of the Amendment says nothing of the sort, this is clearly a conclusion in regard to *intention* from the testimony of history. On cross-examination, we find that history admits the truth of all of the following:

(1) Various types of institutions under religious auspices (schools, colleges, orphanages, hospitals, etc.), in the support of which public funds were used at least in part, were common in eighteenth-century America. [46]

(2) Madison, Jefferson, and their contemporaries in Congress could not possibly have been ignorant of the existence of these institutions and the circumstances of their support.

(3) Particularly, about the only kind of education of their day, or before it, in either Europe or America, was education partly or wholly under church control. [47]

(4) Our system of public education, while getting its embryonic start in the religio-educational enactments of the Massachusetts Bay Colony around 1640, took on the features of a general system only near the middle of the nineteenth century, and was in no sense "separated" from religion until long after Jefferson and Madison were dead. [48]

(5) Jefferson's elaborate plans for a public education system for Virginia included partial support of sectarian schools of religion [49] and *a school of theology* for the training of clergymen. [50]

(6) There has never been in any state in the United States or in the federal government "a complete and permanent separation of the spheres of religious activity and civil authority by comprehensively forbidding every form of public aid and support for religion" [51] or an instance of a single state observing a prohibition of "every form

[45] 330 U.S. 1 at 33.
[46] See Beale, Howard K., *op. cit.*, Chs. I to IV inclusive.
[47] *Ibid.*   [49] Padover, *Complete Jefferson*, pp. 957-958.
[48] *Ibid.*   [50] *Ibid.*, p. 1067.
[51] See references to chaplains in Army and Navy, and in Congress, and religious work at public expense on Indian reservations, and in hospitals and penal institutions in the index.

and degree of official relation between religion and civil authority" in the area of government, religion, and education.[52]

(7) Neither Jefferson nor Madison (both prolific writers and speakers on government, education, the establishment of religion, and kindred topics) left a single sentence which says, in the direct, clear, unambiguous language which both men used habitually and with distinction, that he was opposed to the use of public funds for religious purposes *except as a feature of "establishment"*; no such sentence is quoted or referred to in this opinion or in similar arguments.

(8) Madison like Jefferson served eight years as President of the United States. Everything said above in regard to Jefferson's record as President (see pp. 116, 206), applies equally to Madison. Neither his actions as Commander-in-Chief of our Army and Navy nor his messages to Congress show any dissatisfaction with either the national or the all-state failure to observe that "complete separation" of church and state which Justice Rutledge says was Madison's purpose in the First Amendment. Again if Justice Rutledge is right, Madison must have had small respect in general for his responsibilities as President, and in particular for his oath of office in which he swore to uphold and enforce the Constitution.

Throughout Sections III and IV in his dissenting opinion, Justice Rutledge assumes that the *preamble* of Jefferson's Bill for Religious Freedom has the force of a provision in the Constitution of the United States. The fact is that the language of the Virginia law as enacted, and as interpreted and enforced in Virginia for 162 years, did not make binding, even on the people of Virginia, Rutledge's interpretation of certain fragments he finds in the preamble.

In these sections also Judge Rutledge in talking about our compulsory *public school* machinery, misses the whole point of the compulsory school laws of the various states, just as Justice Black misses the same point in the McCollum case. In the absence of state laws compelling attendance at such institutions as the Y. M. C. A., Sunday Schools, or the Epworth League, the remark about public transpor-

[52] *See* Beale, *op. cit.*, Chs. I-IV; also N. E. A. *Research Bulletin*, XXIV, No. 1 (1946), pp. 36, 42.

tation to the meetings of such organizations is wholly irrelevant. Children in America are compelled to go to some school—public or private, religious or secular. Any school that serves the public purpose of furnishing the type or standard of education required by the state laws satisfies the provisions of the constitutions and the laws. This is one of the vital points in the Pierce case in Oregon.[53] That case was not decided, as Justice Rutledge reports, on the "basis of the private character of the function of religious education." An excellent discussion of the confusion in the Everson case concerning state school laws on the part of Justices Rutledge, Jackson, Frankfurter, and Burton, will be found in *Supreme Court Oversight*,[54] by Edward J. Heffron.

If "state support, financial or other, of religion in any guise, form or degree" means "establishment of religion," then we have always had "establishment of religion" nationally in the United States and in every state in the union from the day of the beginning of the nation and of each state. Under this "interpretation," the First Amendment was a dead letter from the minute it was adopted, and *was so treated by the men who formulated and adopted it*. Anyone—Supreme Court justice, bishop, editor, educator, or congressman—who asks us to believe such a thesis ought to offer *some* accurate, credible evidence to support it, or he ought to be challenged and repudiated by all informed Americans regardless of their religion or their theories of government.

Obviously in all of this Justice Rutledge is trying hard to be a friend to the American people and to save them from the stupidities of their legislatures and of Congress to which democracy leaves them constantly exposed. In the devoted exercise of that friendship he simply wants to put into the Constitution of the United States a doctrine which the responsible representatives of the people have (apparently without protest or reproof) officially, publicly, definitely refused many times to allow in the Constitution! Since the American people if allowed to choose will have none of the doctrine, he will make it a "great constitutional principle." That is just what he did. With

[53] 268 U. S. 510 (1925).
[54] *The Commonweal* (April 18, 1947), pp. 9-11.

218 RELIGION AND EDUCATION UNDER THE CONSTITUTION

the aid of some fragments from the unhistorical *dicta* from the Court's decision in this case, he got his doctrine substituted for the First Amendment's first clause in the McCollum case without the necessity of citing accurately any foundation in history, language, or previous Supreme Court cases.

With his finger in the dyke, cheered on by Justices Frankfurter, Jackson, and Burton, Mr. Justice Rutledge held back the tides of Constitutional democracy until in the McCollum case a new wall of separation (architect unknown) was erected between the people of a state and their democratic control of education within their borders. The faith of the people of Illinois, of Jefferson and Madison, of the American people for more than a century and a half, that the Constitution preserved such democratic control, has been wiped out by a Supreme Court decree that such control never existed. From now on for some time at least, the Supreme Court will doubtless decide each case as it sees fit, on the sole basis of the justices' "zeal" and "prepossessions" (see p. 236) as measurements of what is wise and good for the people of any state in matters of religion and education. For how long a time? Probably until we have a majority of justices on the Supreme Court who are thoroughly competent in understanding, interpreting, and writing the English language, and who know American history, especially constitutional and Supreme Court history. The time will probably be long or short as the American people express pleasure or displeasure at the substitution of life under a dictatorship for democracy and constitutional government.

Chapter 12

THE McCOLLUM RELIGIOUS
EDUCATION CASE (ILLINOIS)

*I*N THE McCollum case[1] the School Board of Champaign, Illinois, acting under the authority given them by the laws of the state, allowed the Champaign Council of Religious Education, a voluntary association of Jewish, Roman Catholic, and Protestant faiths, to conduct classes in religious education in the public school buildings during school hours. Pupils were admitted on the written request of parents to classes designated by the parents. They were excused by the Board from regular school activities for forty-five minutes each week while attending the religious education classes. Pupils representing thirty-one different denominations participated in these classes in the year before this case was tried in Illinois. In five years of operation no resident of the school district other than Mrs. McCollum registered any complaint about the religious classes. About eight hundred fifty children, over eight hundred of them Protestant, about twenty Catholic, were in the religious classes at the time this action was started.

Mrs. McCollum is an atheist. Her child Terry did not attend the classes in religious education. The hundreds of children who did attend were apparently well satisfied. But Mrs. McCollum objected to the plan and started suit to end it. The Illinois Courts upheld the Champaign practice under the Illinois law, and the case was appealed to the Supreme Court·of the United States.

[1] *People of the State of Illinois*, ex. rel. *Vashti McCollum* v. *Board of Education of School District No. 71, Champaign County, Illinois*, et al., No. 90, October Term, 1947. 333 U. S. 203.

The opinions of the Supreme Court Justices in this case are in some ways worse, in their disregard of the history and meaning of the First Amendment, than those in the Everson case.[2] True, in this case, the Justices have not committed so many errors of flat misstatement concerning the words and records of Jefferson and Madison, or so many striking omissions of controlling historical facts which were directly pertinent to the statements they were making, or so many gross errors in logic. But this faint praise is made possible only because the Justices in this case almost wholly avoided even the pretense of discussing the First Amendment and the facts of history which could be legitimately called upon to make clear its meaning.

Obviously, if judges, or others, are not sufficiently at home in the English language and the facts of early American history to be able to understand the provision: "Congress shall make no law respecting an establishment of religion," they should seek enlightenment in the dictionaries, histories, biographies, and the records of the courts and the Congress. In the McCollum case, however, these steps were not taken. The ordinary procedures of careful definition and interpretation were omitted or bungled. The language of the First Amendment was almost wholly avoided. The Justices discussed instead the language of the ancient figure of speech "the wall of separation," and the modern slogan "the separation of church and state."

The basic question before the Court—the one most specifically presented by the briefs on both sides in this case—was whether the practice in Champaign, Illinois, violated the "establishment of religion" clause of the First Amendment.

1. *Brief for Appellant* by Walter F. Dodd:

Errors Relied Upon

The Supreme Court of Illinois erred in sustaining a plan of religious education in public schools which deprives of due process of law and denies equal protection of the laws, through a law "respecting an establishment of religion and prohibiting the free exercise thereof," in violation of the Fourteenth Amendment; . . .

[2] 330 U.S. 1.

Summary of Argument

The assignment of errors summarizes the argument in this case. To such assignment may be added the statement of the Supreme Court of Illinois that appellant, a resident and taxpayer, "seeks to prohibit the teaching of religious education in the public schools during the hours when the public schools are regularly in session." In this respect it is argued that the state makes a law respecting an establishment of religion, in violation of the Fourteenth Amendment, by the development of sectarian groups in the public schools, and that such a development violates freedom of religion.

2. *Brief of American Civil Liberties Union as Amicus Curiae* by Kenneth W. Greenawalt:

Point I

The teaching of sectarian religion by religious teachers to public school students in public school buildings during school hours violates the First Amendment of the Federal Constitution as applied through the Fourteenth Amendment and the basic doctrine of separation of church and state inherent therein.

We respectfully submit that the action of the Appellee Board of Education, in permitting and in aiding and cooperating in the teaching of sectarian religion to pupils of public schools in school buildings during regular school hours by religious teachers sent in for that purpose is a clear violation of the fundamental American principle of separation of church and state and the constitutional prohibition respecting an establishment of religion.

3. *Motion and Brief of Amicus Curiae: The Joint Conference Committee on Public Relations Set Up by the Southern Baptist Convention, the Northern Baptist Convention, The National Baptist Convention Inc. and the National Baptist Convention* by E. Hilton Jackson:

First. It is now well established that the mandate of the First Amendment applies to the states as well as to the Federal Government; that the rights guaranteed in the amendment are of the kind protected by the Fourteenth Amendment which is applicable to the states and therefore that a law respecting an establishment of religion or prohibiting the free exercise thereof by any state would be a violation of the Federal Constitution.

Second. The "establishment of religion" provision is just as much a mandate to the states as the provision for "free exercise of religion."

Third. The First Amendment, now applicable to the states, is not limited to restrictions upon the exercise of religious liberty, but embraces aid in any form to religious organizations.

Fourth. The provisions of the First Amendment, both as to aid and restrictions, apply not alone to the churches or religious organizations but to other religious activities, including schools and other educational activities of religious bodies. The absolute separation of church and state thus means that in states there must be that separation in the public schools operated by the states.

4. *Brief of Amici Curiae and Motion* by Henry Epstein for Synagogue Council for America:

THE ISSUE

In more general terms the question presented to this Court is whether a statute or regulation permitting religious instruction in public school classrooms during school hours is a law respecting an establishment of religion within the prohibition of the First and Fourteenth Amendment.

5. *Motion for Leave to File Brief as Amicus Curiae and Brief as Amicus Curiae on Behalf of General Conference of Seventh-Day Adventists* by Homer Cummings, and William D. Donnelly:

1. The resolution and plan of the Champaign school board constitute State action respecting an establishment of religion.

6. *Appellees' Brief* by John L. Franklin, and Owen Rall:

. . . . we feel that it is necessary that we present to the Court a carefully detailed and historically accurate statement of the background and environment of the establishment-of-religion clause of the First Amendment as well as its legislative history and the legislative debates attending its passage.

We are the more impelled to do this because of the historical inaccuracies that have surrounded current public discussion, and the fact that the first direct judicial construction of the establishment of religion clause of the First Amendment has been delayed for nearly 160 years following its adoption.

The principal question in this case, therefore, boils down to the meaning in the First Amendment of the term "an establishment of religion." I grant that it would be going too far, even considering the linguistic ineptness of the Justices in the Everson and McCollum cases, to assume that they were stumped by the English words "Congress shall make no law respecting." The only possible question is *"What is the subject concerning which Congress was forbidden to make a law?"* This is the exact question posed by Justice Rutledge, and thereafter elaborately avoided in the Everson case. Just why the language of the Constitution of the United States should not be discussed by the Supreme Court when it is presented to them by both sides in a given case is a bit hard to understand. After all, it is in the defense and enforcement of the Constitution to which the Justices are committed by their judicial oaths—not the editorials of *The Christian Century,* or the manifestoes of "Protestants and Other Americans United for the Separation of Church and State."

Justice Rutledge stated with complete accuracy in the Everson case (one of the relatively few key statements in his dissenting opinion to which such a remark can be justly applied), "This is not therefore just a little case over bus fares." [3] So here, this is not just a little case to relieve a "maladjusted problem child" [4] from embarrassment. Both of these cases involve the integrity of the Bill of Rights, the validity of the democratic process of amending the Constitution, and the authority of the Constitution itself.

How did the Justices of the Supreme Court discharge their obligations to their oaths of office, to the Constitution, and to the American people in the McCollum case?

THE MAJORITY OPINION

Mr. Justice Black, speaking for the Court, in the deciding opinion, avoided any discussion of the specific language of the First Amendment which was his whole problem. In opening he posed the question in general terms as involving "the power of a state . . . as that power may be restricted by the First and Fourteenth Amendments to the Federal Constitution." Clearly, since neither religion nor educa-

[3] 330 U.S. 1, p. 29.
[4] So viewed by his teachers and his mother according to the testimony in the trial in the lower court. See Transcript of Record, *McCollum* vs. *Board of Education,* U. S. Supreme Court, pp. 134-135, 177, 198, 208-209.

224 RELIGION AND EDUCATION UNDER THE CONSTITUTION

tion is so much as mentioned in the Fourteenth Amendment, the power of *a state* over religion and education can be thus restricted only if the restriction dealt with can be found in the First Amendment. The Fourteenth can be only a channel.

Justice Black's later remarks, particularly his quotation of his erroneous *dicta* in the Everson case (see p. 195) carrying his substantial misquotation of (and gross misrepresentation of) Jefferson, show that the issue here (however dimly conceived) is the meaning of "an establishment of religion" in the First Amendment. But not by so much as a single sentence does he discuss the specific issue, or seek to justify historically or semantically either his own rewriting of the First Amendment or Justice Rutledge's unrestrained rhetoric (which he quotes here in footnotes) in the Everson case.

The record in the trial court showed:

Lesson materials and curriculum were to be selected by a committee representative of all groups participating and in a manner to avoid any offensive, doctrinal, dogmatic, or sectarian, teaching (Transcript 102-107, 156, 159, 162). The teaching was to be of the content of the Bible without interpretation or attempt at influencing belief in the doctrines or creeds of any church. (*Ibid.*, 105-161.)

This Justice Black sums up as follows:

"This is beyond all question a utilization of the tax-established and tax-supported public school system to aid *religious groups to spread their faith*" [5] (italics mine). This I submit is a *loaded* and inaccurate summary. But suppose it were literally true. What has the First Amendment to do with it? If the Constitution forbids it, how does it? The Justice's summary here represents the exact plan followed throughout the country in practically every public school system in America up to the Civil War in making Protestantism an integral part of the public school program. In many of them this was continued long after the ratification of the Fourteenth Amendment in 1868. It also represents the practice of the federal government in supporting religion in various ways with public funds from Washington's Administration down to the present day. Change the phrase "tax-established and tax-supported" to "tax-exempt" and it expresses

[5] *Law Week* (March 9, 1948), p. 4226.

the exact situation we have today and always have had in all states, in all private and religious schools, and in all churches, synagogues, and all other religious institutions and organizations. Unless Justice Black is ready to defend the position that the First Amendment is concerned with the mere bookkeeping techniques involved in differentiating between *tax-support* and *tax-exemption*, the position he takes here (even if held to be accurate reporting) makes no sense at all.

I am not arguing here that tax-exemption is wise or unwise. The American people have through their responsible representatives in state and nation universally provided for it. If this plan is ever changed, it should be changed by the American people, not by the Supreme Court. However, the essential conflict between tax-exemption and the doctrine which the court upheld in this case was specifically presented to the court in the brief for the appellees, and was covered by direct questions and answers between Justice Black and Attorney John L. Franklin in the oral argument [6] on December 8, 1947:

MR. JUSTICE BLACK. Do I understand you to take the position that if the State of Illinois wanted to contribute five million dollars a year to religion they could do so, so long as they provided the same to every faith?

MR. FRANKLIN. Yes, and the State of Illinois does contribute five million dollars annually to religious faiths, equally, and more than five million dollars, and has during its entire history.

MR. JUSTICE BLACK. How does it do it?

MR. FRANKLIN. By tax exemptions specifically granted to religious organizations.

MR. JUSTICE BLACK. Your position is that they could grant five million dollars a year to religion, if they wanted to, out of the taxpayer's money, so long as they treated all faiths the same?

MR. FRANKLIN. Yes, Your Honor. That is our interpretation of the meaning of the first clause of the First Amendment.

The same avoidance of the specific realities of both constitutional language, and universal state and national practice for 160 years un-

[6] *Oral Arguments* (McCollum case). Althea Arceneaux, reporter. 1033 National Press Bldg. Washington, D. C., pp. 50-51.

der the First Amendment, is characteristic of this whole opinion: Consider the following statements of Justice Black.

The foregoing facts, without reference to others that appear in the record, show the use of tax-supported property for religious instruction and the close cooperation between the school authorities and the religious council in promoting religious education.[7]

What of it? The United States Constitution makes no reference whatever to such practices or to anything which covers such practices. The use of tax-supported property for religious instruction was substantially universal until stopped by state constitutional provisions (see pp. 144, 149). And not one of the states in stopping it relied on the prohibitions of *"an establishment of religion" in the Federal Constitution *or in the state constitutions!* Further, tax support of religion or religious organizations is now, and always has been, provided by the Federal Government from the beginning in West Point, Annapolis, and on Indian reservations. It was endorsed not once but many times by Thomas Jefferson, and administered without question by Jefferson and Madison as well as all other Presidents of the United States.

The operation of the state's compulsory education system thus assists and is integrated with the program of religious instruction carried on by separate religious sects. Pupils compelled by law to go to school for secular education are released in part from their legal duty upon the condition that they attend the religious classes.[8]

Each state's compulsory education system assists religious education in exactly this way in all religious schools throughout the country, and pupils in these schools "compelled to go to school for secular education" attend religious classes part of the time.

If Justice Black, in spite of history and the meaning of words, wishes to say that the First Amendment forbids these practices, he should say so openly and specifically, and he should make some attempt to prove it. If he does not mean to say this, what does he mean?

However, one can hardly take exception to Justice Black's highly

[7] *Law Week* (March 9, 1948), p. 4226.   [8] *Ibid.*

specialized summary of all the above: "It falls squarely under the ban of the First Amendment (made applicable to the States by the Fourteenth) *as we interpreted it in Everson v. Board of Education,* 330 U. S. 1." [9] (Italics mine.) How thoroughly both the majority and the minority mangled history, the English language, and the words and records of Jefferson and Madison, in the Everson case, is shown in Chapter Eleven. The Everson case is substantially the only support cited for the decision in this case. In both cases the discussion of the issue before them, the meaning of "an establishment of religion" in the First Amendment, is avoided with a completeness that must have taken careful planning. This, obviously, is the only safe strategy for anyone who is emotionally or ideologically committed to destroying the First Amendment by "judicial legislation."

The attitude of reverence for their own words rather than for those of the Constitution or of Madison and his colleagues, is not confined to Justice Black. It pervades both the questions in the oral arguments and the opinions in this case.

MR. JUSTICE RUTLEDGE. What does the First Amendment of the Constitution prohibit?

MR. FRANKLIN. It prohibits the preferment by law in any degree of one religion over another and one sect over another.

MR. JUSTICE RUTLEDGE. Is that the ruling of the Everson case? [10]

MR. FRANKLIN. I believe the decision [discussion?] in the *Everson* case was only *dicta.*

MR. JUSTICE RUTLEDGE. Does the Everson case say that, or something else?

MR. FRANKLIN. I do not understand that the case was decided on that ground, so I believe that question still to be an open one for decision by Your Honors.

Justice Black continues:

"The majority in the Everson case, and the minority as shown by quotations from the dissenting views in our Notes Six and Seven, agreed that the First Amendment's language, properly interpreted, had erected a wall of separation between Church and State." [11] This violates the proper canons of interpretation. To substitute ambigu-

[9] *Ibid.*   [10] *Oral Arguments,* pp. 51-52.
[11] *Law Week* (March 9, 1948), p. 4226.

ity for specificity, figurative language for literal language, is the antithesis of legitimate interpretation. The Supreme Court substituted the general, ambiguous word "state" for the specific term "Congress"; the ambiguous word "separation" for the specific phrase "make no law"; the figurative "wall of separation" for the specific "law." After making this outrageous list of substitutions, the Court gives to the selected figure of speech a meaning which must necessarily be held to be false by any rational person who knows Jefferson, knows that the First Amendment had no bearing on state legislation at least up to 1868, and who knows to whom Jefferson addressed the figurative language in 1802 (see p. 83). It is shocking to find the Supreme Court calling such procedure "interpretation" of the Constitution.

Perhaps the enormity of the distortion masquerading as "interpretation" will be made most clear by presenting it in this tabulated form.

"Congress	Shall Make No Law Respecting		an Establishment of Religion." (The First Amendment)
The state (the government)	shall be completely separated	from	the church, or religion (Supreme Court)
The state (the government)	shall be separated by a wall	from	the church, or religion (Supreme Court)
A wall of separation	is hereby erected	between	church and state (Supreme Court)
State support, financial or other	is prohibited	to	"religion in any guise, form, or degree" (Rutledge, Everson dissent)

This is reversing, rewriting, amending the Constitution, and promoting uncertainty and confusion where none need exist for anyone willing to do a bit of reading to find out what an "establishment of religion" meant in the vocabularies of eighteenth-century Americans, especially in those of Jefferson and Madison. An hour in any good library should suffice for this task for anyone familiar with the use of a library.

Finally Justice Black sums up the basic contentions of the attorneys for the appellees as follows:

Recognizing that the Illinois program is barred by the First and Fourteenth Amendments *if we adhere to the views expressed both by the Majority and the minority in the Everson case* [italics mine], counsel for the respondents challenge those views as *dicta* and urge that we reconsider and repudiate them. They argue that historically the First Amendment was intended to forbid only government preference of one religion over another, not an impartial governmental assistance of all religions. In addition they ask that we distinguish or overrule our holding in the Everson case that the Fourteenth Amendment made the "establishment of religion" clause of the First Amendment applicable as a prohibition against the States.[12]

This again is not an accurate summation. The appellees' position, as shown by their brief, was that the First Amendment forbade the *Federal Congress*, not *government*, to make *any law at all* about (i.e., either for or against) an establishment of religion. This had the necessary effect of preventing a *national established religion*, because at that time there was no established religion in the nation (though there was in five of the states). This prevented the Federal Government from preferring *one* religion or *one* church to all others, *because that is what "an establishment of religion" meant* to the men who used the phrase, had meant for centuries, and still does mean to scholars, historians, and others who use the expression competently. Impartial *government* assistance could not possibly have been proscribed if we assume that the First Amendment expressed the thoughts of Jefferson and Madison and other literate Americans of their time.

All Americans of that day who were aware of the conditions in which they were living, and of the educational history of their cultural tradition, had to know that Congress had nothing whatever to do with the universal and immemorial custom of government aid to religion. Government aid to religion and religious education as practiced in all of the states at that time (and still today in 1948, see Chapter Nine) was not in any way under the authority of Congress. If Madison, Jefferson, Story, Cooley, Corwin, and innumerable his-

[12] *Ibid.*, p. 4226.

torians, both lay and religious, are dependable authorities, the preservation of this situation was the exact purpose of the first clause of the First Amendment. It is beyond intelligent doubt that neither Jefferson nor Madison was opposed to the impartial support of religion by government. (See Chapters Five and Six.)

The Appellees' brief furnished the Court with many pages of accurate citation and quotation supporting their fundamental positions. Justice Black dismisses it all, without explanation, without argument, without courtesy, in this one sentence: "After giving full consideration to the arguments presented we are unable to accept either of these contentions."

Justice Black concludes with the complaint that under the Illinois practice "the State also affords sectarian groups an invaluable aid in that it helps provide pupils for their religious classes through the use of the state's compulsory public school machinery. This is not separation of Church and State." [13] The Justice is in error again in referring to the "compulsory *public* school machinery." There is no such machinery in the United States. A Justice of the Supreme Court ought to be familiar with the Oregon school case.[14] Any Justice so familiar knows necessarily that in the Oregon case the unanimous Supreme Court declared "compulsory public school machinery" unconstitutional.

Such gross errors in the name of the Supreme Court of the United States are not trivial matters on account of their patent untruth. They are taken seriously by some people who should know better. For instance, the office of the Superintendent of Public Instruction of the State of Illinois, recently issued a bulletin on *Religious Education in Public Schools*. In this the Superintendent relied on two of Justice Black's major errors, (1) the one just mentioned and (2) the statement that "the use of tax-supported property for religious instruction and the close cooperation between school authorities" and religious education [15] is prohibited by the First Amendment.

Relying on the above irresponsible language, the Illinois Superintendent issued the following paragraphs:

13 *Ibid.*   15 *Law Week* (March 9, 1948), p. 4226.
14 *Pierce* v. *Society of Sisters*, 268 U.S. 510 (1925).

A School board may not help to provide pupils for religious education classes in any manner whatsoever or take any active part through its teachers or superintendents in the supervision of or provision for classes in religious education.

Certainly if a school board may not do these things, then the states' whole educational machinery may not. This destroys all state provision for compulsory school attendance, requirements for teachers, curriculum, equipment, examinations, etc., in all private and religious schools in all the states.

There may be doubt as to some seasonal Christmas or Easter program. However, where there is no resentment in a community, school boards would seem to be justified in demanding further word from the Supreme Court before abandoning these traditional programs.

From now on, if any public school in Illinois wants to have a Christmas program, the principal should call up the Supreme Court of the United States to get permission!

Since sessions of Congress are regularly opened with a religious invocation, there can be no objection to the same practice at graduation exercises.

This is extreme disobedience. If the actions of Congress, the Presidents, the state governments, the Supreme Court (previous to March 8, 1948) are to be followed instead of the ukase of March, 1948, then Illinois may ignore the McCollum decision entirely and continue to exercise the freedom which the First Amendment, in purpose and in words, guaranteed to all the states.

Finally the superintendent, with a daring which the Supreme Court (in its new found freedom from the restraints of the "fuddy-duddy" old Constitution) could easily call treason, grants sweeping freedom of teaching in the fields of literature, history, and music.

The Bible as well as mythology can be called upon to provide a background for the study of English literature.

A course in history can include a study of the Crusades, the Reformation, and other examples in which religion has played a vital role in history.

Music is not banned because it happens to have been originally written for religious purposes. The High School Choral Group can still sing the Hallelujah Chorus.

So Justice Jackson's fear that the McCollum decision (in which he concurred!) might leave "public education in shreds," may be averted in part in Illinois. The High School Choral Group will not have to bootleg the Hallelujah Chorus. At least the superintendent of Public Instruction is now estopped from reporting their offense to the Supreme Court of the United States for "proceedings not inconsistent with this [the McCollum] opinion."

Not only do compulsory school laws apply to all schools alike both public and private, religious and secular, but all states have, in addition, many laws regarding various aspects of private and religious education and educational institutions. What Justice Black declares unconstitutional (probably without knowing its import) is precisely the universal practice in providing pupils for religious education in all Catholic, Protestant, Jewish and other religious schools, and in seeing to it that such education meets state standards. Neither the nation nor any state has ever taken action against these practices. Whether or not they conform to "separation of church and state" depends wholly on what is meant by that superlatively ambiguous phrase. But what difference does it make? Neither the Federal Constitution nor the constitution of any state says anything at all about "separation of church and state." It is to be deeply regretted that the Justices of the Supreme Court are apparently not familiar with the forty-nine constitutions which the American people have adopted.

The opinion of the Court as presented by Justice Black is substantially (a) a refusal to discuss the language of the Constitution which was at the heart of this case, (b) a refusal to discuss the evidence and argument presented by the appellees, (c) a reiteration of the errors of the Everson case, which were based (d) almost wholly on clear misrepresentation of the words and records of Jefferson and Madison.

THE JACKSON OPINION

In his concurring opinion Mr. Justice Jackson did not so much as mention the language of the First Amendment on which he was presumably passing judgment. Perhaps this is just as well since in the first question in the following quotation from the Oral Arguments in this case [16] he demonstrated that he had no understanding of what "an establishment of religion" means in the Constitution, meant to Jefferson and Madison, and has meant to historians and legal scholars for some centuries.

MR. JUSTICE JACKSON. Do I understand your contention is that you can establish religions, but you can't prefer one over another? [This is like asking a man if he believes in a monopoly of the automobile field provided the monopoly is granted equally to every automobile company requesting it.]

MR. FRANKLIN. No. Perhaps in my flight of oratory I did not make myself clear. I believe the phrase "establishment of religion" had as well defined a meaning at that time as now, namely, the establishment of one particular church or religion, creating a monopoly. The framers could not have selected a better clause than "establishment of religion" if they had searched all the lexicons.

MR. JUSTICE BLACK. In your judgment, can this practice stand under the Constitution and be consistent with what was said, either in the majority or minority opinion, in the *Everson* case?

MR. FRANKLIN. Yes.

MR. JUSTICE BLACK. How?

MR. FRANKLIN. For the reason that the farthest the *dicta* have gone in that case is to say that if a tax is actually levied that is for the benefit of religion, it cannot stand in the face of the first clause of the First Amendment. But Your Honors did not say that once public facilities are established, religious organizations cannot enjoy the benefits of them. Thank God that was not said!

MR. JUSTICE FRANKFURTER. Your flight of oratory did not seem to me to be too flighty. I am led to ask this: Suppose everything you say is so about the place of religion in this country, another question arises of *whether the public schools of the United States, bearing the relation that they do to the democratic way of life, are a good place to introduce it?* [Italics mine.]

MR. FRANKLIN. This is not a group of legislative censors before whom I am arguing today. Your Honors have only the constitutional questions.

[This reminding of the Court that its function was not that of a super-legislature for the State of Illinois failed to stop Justice Frankfurter from considering the *wisdom* of the Illinois practice (which

[16] *Op. cit.*, p. 54.

was not his responsibility) to the total neglect of the constitutional question which was his responsibility.]

MR. JUSTICE FRANKFURTER. I put my question again: We have a school system of the United States on the one hand, and the relation it has to the democratic way of life. On the other hand we have the religious beliefs of our people. *The question is whether any kind of scheme which introduced religious teaching into the public school system is the kind of thing we should have in our democratic institutions.* [Italics mine.] [Still wisdom!]

MR. FRANKLIN. That is a proper question to ask. May I ask, though, that you depend to some extent on the record in this case for what is the proven result of this program. Variations of this program are in effect in at least one thousand school districts in forty-six states, and there is nothing in this record or any actual facts pointed out in the briefs of the friends of the court to support the proposition—

MR. JUSTICE FRANKFURTER. You have a half dozen religious groups opposing this *as offensive.* [But not proving it unconstitutional!] [Italics mine.]

MR. FRANKLIN. Your Honor knows I am not permitted to argue the extent to which the briefs represent the feeling of those they purport to represent.

MR. JUSTICE FRANKFURTER. The very fact you raised this question shows that *this kind of thing projects the public schools into religious controversy.* [Claimed but not proved—and purely a question of wisdom for the legislature, not of constitutionality.] What I am saying is that we have these briefs by the religious bodies. We can't go behind them. They purport to speak for those sects.

MR. FRANKLIN. May I ask you to consider only the law in those briefs and not consider them a supplement to the record?

This was a bull'seye shot by Mr. Franklin, but no bell rang in the mind of Mr. Justice Frankfurter.

Justice Jackson's opinion is open to the same criticism he made of the majority opinion in the Everson case. He argues one way and decides the other. Why he has adopted this Janus-like attitude is an unexplained mystery. He doubts whether the Supreme Court has jurisdiction in this case. He doubts "whether the Constitution . . . can be construed . . . to protect one from the embarrassment that always attends noncomformity, whether in religion, politics, behavior or dress." He says that "any cost of this plan to the taxpayer is incalculable and negligible." He writes the following paragraphs—and then votes to concur in a decision that accomplishes this elaborate debauchery of the First Amendment:

What is asked is not a defensive use of judicial power to set aside a tax levy or reverse a conviction, or to enjoin threats of persecution or taxation. The relief demanded in this case is the extraordinary writ of mandamus to tell the local Board of Education what it must do. The prayer for relief is that a writ be issued against the Board of Education "ordering it to immediately adopt and enforce rules and regulations prohibiting all instruction in and teaching of religious education in all public schools . . . and in all public school houses and buildings in said district when occupied by public schools." The plaintiff, as she has every right to be, is an avowed atheist. What she has asked of the courts is that they not only end the "released time" plan but also ban every form of teaching which suggests or recognizes that there is a God. She would ban all teaching of the Scriptures. She especially mentions as an example of invasion of her rights having pupils learn and recite such statements as, "The Lord is my Shepherd, I shall not want." And she objects to teaching that the King James version of the Bible "is called the Christian's Guide Book, the Holy Writ, and the Word of God," and many other similar matters. This Court is directing the Illinois courts generally to sustain plaintiff's complaint without exception of any of these grounds of complaint, without discriminating between them and without laying down any standards to define the limits of the effect of our decision.

To me, the sweep and detail of these complaints is a danger signal which warns of the kind of local controversy we will be required to arbitrate if we do not place appropriate limitation on our decision and exact strict compliance with jurisdictional requirements. Authorities list 256 separate and substantial religious bodies to exist in continental United States. Each of them, through the suit of some discontented but unpenalized and untaxed representative, has as good a right as this plaintiff to demand that the courts compel the schools to sift out of their teaching everything inconsistent with its doctrines.[17] If we are to eliminate everything that is objectionable to any of these warring sects or inconsistent with any of their doctrines, we will leave public education in shreds. Nothing but educational confusion and a discrediting of the public school system can result from subjecting it to constant law suits.[18]

[17] *See* discussion of taxes to propagate opinions the taxpayer "disbelieves and abhors," pp. 76-78.
[18] *The United States Law Week*, (March 9, 1948), pp. 4227, 4228.

Justice Jackson remarks further that "The task of separating the secular from the religious in education is one of magnitude, intricacy and delicacy." [19] Why he did not continue with the observation that this task is clearly one for the legislative and educational machinery of the several states, and that no really informed person can honestly assert that it is comprehended in either the purpose or the language of the First Amendment, is the second great mystery in this opinion.

However, Justice Jackson achieves contact with reality in the following passages:

> To lay down a sweeping constitutional doctrine as demanded by complainant and apparently approved by the Court, applicable alike to all school boards of the nation, "to immediately adopt and enforce rules and regulations prohibiting all instruction in and teaching of religious education in all public schools," is to decree a uniform, rigid, and, if we are consistent, an unchanging standard for countless school boards representing and serving highly localized groups which not only differ from each other but which themselves from time to time change attitudes. It seems to me that to do so is to allow zeal for our own ideas of what is good in public instruction to induce us to accept the role of a super board of education for every school district in the nation.
>
> It is idle to pretend that this task is one for which we can find in the Constitution one word to help us as judges to decide where the secular ends and the sectarian begins in education. Nor can we find guidance in any other legal source. It is a matter on which we can find no law but our own prepossessions.[20]

"Zeal" for their "own ideas of what is good in public education," no law but their "own prepossessions," and a deep reverence for their own words in the unscholarly distortions of American constitutional history in the Everson case are the basis for the further twisting of the First Amendment in this case. The contact with reality, however, is brief and futile. In his closing sentences, Justice Jackson falls in line and makes obeisance to the Court's current fetish by saluting "the legal [sic] 'wall of separation between Church and State.'"

19 *Ibid.*, p. 4228.
20 *Ibid.*

The Frankfurter Opinion

Mr. Justice Frankfurter's opinion, in which Mr. Justice Jackson, Mr. Justice Rutledge, and Mr. Justice Burton join, is a startling document. It is, as a whole, essentially a perfect example of the classic fallacy of begging the question—*viz.*, *assuming* the one point in controversy and then talking about something else.

The opening sentences of this opinion read as follows:

> We dissented in *Everson* v. *Board of Education*, 330 U.S. 1, because in our view the Constitutional principle requiring separation of Church and State compelled invalidation of the ordinance sustained by the majority. Illinois has here authorized the commingling of religious with secular instruction in the public schools. The Constitution of the United States forbids this.
>
> This case, in the light of the *Everson* decision, demonstrates anew that the mere formulation of a relevant Constitutional principle is the beginning of the solution of a problem, not its answer. This is so because the meaning of a spacious conception like that of the separation of Church from State is unfolded as appeal is made to the principle from case to case. We are all agreed that the First and the Fourteenth Amendments have a secular reach far more penetrating in the conduct of Government than merely to forbid an "established church." But agreement, in the abstract, that the First Amendment was designed to erect a "wall of separation between Church and State," does not preclude a clash of views as to what the wall separates.

The first paragraph is a flat *assumption* that "separation of Church and State is a constitutional principle," and that, as such, it forbids the commingling of religious with secular instruction in the public schools. This settles by simple assumption everything involved in this case and a great deal more. The remainder of the quoted passage is the Supreme Court equivalent of what in less dignified but more realistic circles is called "double talk," or using language for the purpose of concealing thought. What Justice Frankfurter seems to me (and to some good lawyers who have tried to interpret this turgid prose) to be trying to say here is the following:

1. In the Everson case, the Supreme Court made a "beginning of the solution of a problem"—the problem of the relation of govern-

ment to religion. (This new beginning of course wiped out the work of Jefferson, Madison, the Congress, the Presidency and the Supreme Court up to date.)

2. The Court made the new beginning by formulating "a new constitutional principle." (Authority for thus putting new principles into the Constitution not specified.)

3. The new principle is the separation of church and state.

4. This is a "spacious conception"; that is, it is such a thoroughly ambiguous phrase that no literate and honest person can ever claim to know what it means except as its meaning can be derived from its particular context in each instance in which it is used. Since this phrase is not in the written Constitution, it has no constitutional context, and so has no constitutional meaning whatever.

5. This principle is *not* in the written Constitution, but floats somewhere in the (so far) uncharted depths of the Justices' private philosophy—their "zeal" and "prepossessions," in Justice Jackson's words.

6. The "meaning" of the principle will be "unfolded [or fished up] as appeal is made to the principle from case to case." Simple, isn't it? If any state court judge, lawyer, or school boy wishes to know what the Bill of Rights says about government and religion, the answer is "No one knows. The first clause of the Bill of Rights has been abolished, and the meaning of the secret principle which has been put in its place will be unfolded from time to time as the Justices of the Supreme Court feel the urge to issue new edicts."

Justice Frankfurter says in a footnote (p. 4) "The fathers put into the Constitution the principle of complete 'hands off,' for a people as religiously heterogeneous as ours." This is inexcusably bad history for a Justice of the Supreme Court. What the Fathers put into the Constitution was *Congressional, Federal, hands off, leaving exclusively in the hands of the people of the states* complete freedom to deal with "an establishment of religion" (however one defines or understands this phrase) as they saw fit. This precise freedom which the First Amendment was supposed to preserve to the people of Illinois is by this decision denied to them. The decision in this case with which Mr. Justice Frankfurter concurs, with a flourish of "spacious concept," antique fallacy, and bad history, precisely reverses the purpose and language of the First Amendment.

Justice Frankfurter's bizarre theory of the function of the Supreme Court is shown by the following statement:

> We cannot illuminatingly apply the "wall-of-separation" metaphor until we have considered the relevant history of religious education in America, the place of the "released time" movement in that history, and its precise manifestation in the case before us.[21]

Why four justices of the Supreme Court feel under obligation to "apply the 'wall-of-separation' metaphor" rather than the First Amendment is not divulged. Nor is it divulged just how the justices select the particular figure of speech from Jefferson (or anyone else) which they wish to "apply" instead of the passage from the Constitution of the United States which is before them for interpretation. Some time, when some other section of the Constitution of which the Court does not approve is embarrassingly before them, I should like to see what they could do with another figure of Jefferson's: "Religion is the Alpha and Omega of the moral law." Or some time when the Justices feel up to leaving the comfortable ambiguity of figures of speech and facing the rigors of literal language they might try "applying" Jefferson's statement in his discussion of religion at the University of Virginia:

> It was not, however, to be understood that *instruction in religious opinion and duties was meant to be precluded by the public authorities,* as indifferent to the interests of society. On the contrary, the relations which exist between Man and his Maker, and the duties resulting from those relations, *are the most interesting and important to every human being, and the most incumbent on his study and investigation.*[22] [Italics mine.]

Justice Frankfurter's attitude is particularly surprising in a Frankfurter opinion in 1948. He took a diametrically opposite position in Adamson v. California (decided June 24, 1947):

> It would be extraordinarily strange for a Constitution to convey such specific commands in such a roundabout and inexplicit way. After all, an

[21] *Law Week* (March 9, 1948), p. 4229.
[22] "Freedom of Religion at the University of Virginia," Padover, *The Complete Jefferson,* p. 957. (See also Appendix D.)

amendment to the Constitution should be read in a "sense most obvious to the common understanding at the time of its adoption". . . . For it was for public adoption that it was proposed. . . . Remarks of a particular proponent of the Amendment, no matter how influential, are not to be deemed part of the Amendment. What was submitted for ratification was his proposal, not his speech.[23]

This procedure, of avoiding the constitutional issue before them to indulge in fanciful "interpretation" and "application" of an irrelevant figure of speech, allows the Justices free play for their emotional and ideological "zeal" and "prepossessions" which the specific and literal language of the First Amendment would deny them. Only as the Justices of the Supreme Court can substitute for the language of the First Amendment, the metaphorical slogan of atheists and others united for the elimination of the First Amendment and the avoidance of the democratic process, can they save the people of America from the incompetence of their state legislatures and the Congress, from the misconceptions of Jefferson and Madison, from the inadequacies of democracy, and from the blunders embedded in the Constitution of the United States!

In pursuit of the above objectives Justice Frankfurter presents a long, irrelevant, and inaccurate history of the development of secular education in the United States. He omits the essential facts in the clash between Protestants and Catholics which was the principal cause of our having secularism as the only point of view in regard to religion to have full public support in American education. (See pp. 25-27.) He mentions Madison's *Remonstrance* as "a proposal which involved support to religious education." This is true, but is only a fragment of the truth. The *Remonstrance* was against the establishment of Christianity as the state religion of Virginia. Financial support was not the subject of even one of the fifteen numbered reasons which Madison gave for his opposition. He was fighting "an establishment of religion" in the exact meaning of the term in the First Amendment. He did not there, or elsewhere, ever oppose public money in support of religion *per se*, or ever advocate "complete separation of church and state."

[23] 332 U. S. 46.

Justice Frankfurter continues:

Separation in the field of education, then, was not imposed upon unwilling States by force of superior law. In this respect the Fourteenth
Amendment merely reflected a principle then dominant in our national
life. To the extent that the Constitution thus made it binding upon the
States, the basis of the restriction is the whole experience of our people.[24]

This passage is almost wholly inaccurate both as educational history and constitutional history. The only "separation" we have in
the field of education is the separation of positive religion from secularism and leaving the field of public education in the possession of
the latter. The kind of "separation between church and state" which
Justice Frankfurter is advocating in this opinion has never obtained
in any state at any time. (See pp. 145-6.) The "separation" we have
in public education was in no sense "imposed" on the States. The
Fourteenth Amendment had nothing to do with it. It was brought
about in every state by state action alone—and in none of the states
by reliance on the language which Justice Frankfurter here assumes
prescribes "separation." In many states this state action antedated the
Fourteenth Amendment, and so could not be credited to it. In *all
states* this action antedated the recognition by the Supreme Court
that the Fourteenth Amendment *might* have influence in state matters such as religion and education (see pp. 176, 266). This recognition
came substantially sixty years after the ratification of the Fourteenth
Amendment, and some three or four decades after the states had
adopted state constitutional provisions specifically prohibiting public
money for denominational religious teaching. The Fourteenth
Amendment had no more to do with this situation than the Eighteenth.

The decision which Justice Frankfurter is here helping to inflict on
the school systems of the States, is the *first decision* in our Supreme
Court history in which the first clause of the First Amendment has
been used to interfere with the freedom in religion or education of
the people of the states—a freedom which the First Amendment was
specifically written to preserve. The passage quoted above is not only

<hr/>

[24] *Law Week* (March 9, 1948), p. 4229.

bad history in a general way; it is definitely bad constitutional and Supreme Court history.

Justice Frankfurter mentions as a support for his position the law by Congress compelling every State admitted since 1876 "to write into its constitution a requirement that it maintain a school system 'free from sectarian control.'" This is no support at all for two reasons: *First*, it is a semantic absurdity to hold that the Champaign system, or any other system of equal treatment of all religions, constitutes "sectarian control" of the public school system. *Second*, if "an establishment of religion" in the First Amendment means "religion, religious establishment, or establishments having a religious foundation whatever their form or special religious function," as asserted in the Rutledge dissent in the Everson case (in which Justice Frankfurter concurred) then the law referred to was and always has been unconstitutional since (under the Frankfurter-Rutledge theory) the First Amendment forbade Congressional legislation respecting *religion*, and this is clearly a law respecting *religion*.

In addition to inaccurate history there is in this opinion considerable discussion of the *wisdom* of the Champaign system. This of course was not properly before the Court. The wisdom of *state legislation* in religion and education always has been up to March 8, 1948, a problem for the people and the legislatures of the several states. According to both our constitutions and our traditions in this country, democratic government in order to be allowed to function in this area has never before been required to meet whatever ideas of good government happen to be held by the Justices of the Supreme Court.

After his excursion into selected history, Justice Frankfurter returns finally to the question begging assumption with which he started: "The basic Constitutional principle of absolute separation." He reveals that Jefferson's metaphor "speaks of a 'wall of separation' not a fine line easily overstepped." How he found out just what kind of a wall Jefferson meant in his little note of courtesy in 1802 (see page 286), the Justice does not reveal. We do know, however, that he did not find it in the words or actions of Thomas Jefferson. The Baptists of Danbury, Connecticut, to whom Jefferson's remark was addressed, certainly knew all about walls of separation that could be easily overstepped. In Connecticut now there is a wall of separation between my meadow and the meadow of Mrs. Abbie Briggs that I am sure every Justice of the Supreme Court could easily overstep!

This opinion closes with a phrase from good old Robert Frost, "Good fences make good neighbors." True enough! But only fences that allow for cooperation, friendly intercourse. Fences so "high and impregnable" as not to permit the slightest breach *never* make good neighbors. They are called "spite fences" and are *never* built by good neighbors. They are only the instruments of extreme unneighborliness.

Justice Frankfurter repeats from the Rutledge dissent in the Everson case:

"We have staked the very existence of our country on the faith that complete separation between state and religion is best for the state and best for religion."

He does not say when, where, how, or by whom this act of faith (denying American history, both state and national, both legislative and judicial, from the beginning down to March 8, 1948) was indulged in. But it could not have been any action of the responsible representatives of the American people in the Congress of the United States (a necessary step in putting anything into the Constitution), because, as Justice Frankfurter says in a footnote [25] the Congress has six times [sic] voted down amendments to the Constitution expressing this doctrine in some form or other. He did not even get this matter straight. Congress repudiated *eleven* such proposals from 1870 to 1888. This doctrine—which the official and responsible representatives of the American people repudiated in all proposals ever submitted to Congress to deprive the states of the exact freedom which the First Amendment guaranteed to them in the matters of religion and education—this *always repudiated* doctrine, is now a "basic Constitutional principle!"

Does actual adoption and ratification of a proposed amendment to the Constitution make the matter covered by such a proposal *unconstitutional* in the thinking of Justice Frankfurter? If not, why not?

[25] No. 6, p. 4230.

He must have *some* theory of how we can amend or refuse to amend the Constitution. I wonder what it is, and if, as he sees it, accepting and rejecting proposed amendments have identical effects, *viz.*, no effects whatever, the control in all cases being only the "zeal" and "prepossessions" of the Justices of the Supreme Court.

Even this is not the climax of this bewildering document. I think the Justice is at his best in the field of semantics. Here he shows originality, unusual genius. Count Korzybski and Dr. Irving Lee should look to their laurels. Justice Frankfurter makes this unique contribution: "Separation means separation, not something less." What thoroughness! What lucidity! Not only does this settle all doubts as to what "separation" means, but it gives to the world a universal formula for defining words. Here we have the Frankfurter universal definer. It fits every word in every language. It eliminates entirely the use of dictionaries. When in doubt about a word just say it twice with the connective "means," add the clincher "not something less," and it is all made crystal clear! The only addition that might be suggested for those interested in Constitutional law is an appendix to this treatise on the meaning of the word "separation" phrased somewhat as follows:

"What difference does it make? The word does not appear in the Constitution anyway."

THE REED OPINION

Mr. Justice Reed's dissenting opinion correctly stated the issue in this case and he, in contrast to his colleagues on the Bench, seemed willing to discuss the question instead of begging it. He wrote:

As no issue of prohibition upon the free exercise of religion is before us, we need only examine the School Board's action to see if it constitutes "an establishment of religion." [26]

He observes that the opposing "opinions do not say in words that the condemned practice of religious education is a law respecting an establishment of religion contrary to the First Amendment." [27] This is clearly what any opinion on the majority side in this case has

[26] *Loc. cit.*, p. 4235.   [27] *Ibid.*

to mean even though the writer of the opinion hesitates to spell it out.

Justice Reed naturally finds it "difficult to extract from the opinions any conclusion as to what it is in the Champaign plan that is unconstitutional." [28] The opposing opinions make no attempt to explain why the Champaign plan is unconstitutional. They assume that it constitutes "an establishment of religion," and simply proclaim it. In addition to remarking on the absence of any reasoned defense of the majority position, probably Judge Reed's best point is this one:

> But as Illinois has held that it is within the discretion of the School Board to permit absence from school for religious instruction no legal [29] duty of school attendance is violated.

Unfortunately this opinion as a whole, in spite of its arrival at the only position consistent with the Constitution of the United States, is very weakly argued. In this respect, it closely resembles Judge Black's majority opinion in the Everson case.

Twice Justice Reed uses, like Judge Black (see p. 290), *the* establishment of religion, instead of *an* establishment of religion, as First Amendment language. He passes over too lightly the opposing position that the parents "consented" to the attendance of their children at the religious classes. The parents "requested" it. No child was admitted except on a formal, written request of the parent. These are slight blemishes perhaps, but others are serious indeed. He wrote:

> The phrase "an establishment of religion" *may have been intended* by Congress to be aimed only at a state church. When the First Amendment was pending in Congress in substantially its present form, "Mr. Madison said, he apprehended the meaning of the words to be, that Congress should not establish *a* religion, and enforce the legal observation of it by law, nor compel men to worship God in any manner contrary to their conscience." *Passing years, however, have brought about acceptance of a broader meaning,* although never until today, I believe, has this Court widened its interpretation to any such degree as holding that recognition of the interest of our nation in religion, through the granting, to qualified representatives of the principal faiths, of opportunity to present religion as an optional, extracurricular subject during

released school time in public school buildings, was equivalent to an establishment of religion.[30] [Italics mine.]

When Justice Reed says Congress *may have* been aiming at a state church, he is uncertain where there should be no uncertainty. The First Congress aimed to make it unconstitutional for any future Congress to set up *a national church*, by requiring that they keep off the subject altogether. This is what they wrote in the First Amendment. This is what Madison said the words meant in the passage quoted by Justice Reed. This is what Congress has always held the words to mean from the First Congress to the last, as shown in Chapter Seven. This is what the authorities on constitutional law say. This is what all Presidents, including Jefferson and Madison, have held the words to mean—if their actions and their writings are evidence of their understanding of the Constitution. No other interpretation has ever been accepted by the Supreme Court, or expressed by the Court, before February 10, 1947, in the *Everson* case. The contrary statements by Justice Rutledge are wholly without foundation in fact. (See pp. 129-130, 212.)

In the light of the above, Justice Reed should have furnished some explanation, evidence, or citation, for his idea that "passing years have brought about a broader meaning." What meaning? What years? How? Congress has emphatically refused many times to allow the "broader meaning" of the Justices in the Everson case, and, in this case, to have a place in the Constitution. The position that there is a *broad meaning* of this historic clause in the First Amendment (or of any other clause in the Constitution) which has never been anywhere phrased, adopted, or ratified, which cannot be identified and examined, and its authenticity discussed, means inevitably the beginning of the end of government under a written constitution. This is Justice Frankfurter's "spacious conception" which will be unfolded all in the Court's good time, as their subjects ask the favor of knowing what freedoms of the Bill of Rights are permitted this week!

When Justice Reed's broad meaning is expressed only in the thoroughly ambiguous words "the separation of church and state" or

[30] *Loc. cit.*, p. 4236.

the still worse figurative language of the "wall of separation between
Church and State," we have *no constitutional situation* left. Even
with wide, profound, and accurate knowledge, and the purest and
most exalted motives, no one can *possibly know* what such language
permits or prohibits. Such language can never, anywhere, to anyone,
have specific meaning except as that specificity is given by the particular context in each instance of its use. Justice Frankfurter's "spacious conception" and Justice Reed's "broad meaning" have *no
context* anywhere. They, therefore, have no negotiable meaning. They
mean only what the user wishes them to mean. In Government, such
language is useful only to a dictator. Such language does not and
cannot constitute *laws.* Such language is *never* found in constitutions or statutes drawn by competent statesmen. It is not in any of
the forty-nine American constitutions. It should never be found in
court opinions. Under such language, in constitutions or court decisions, there can be no form of government under which the citizen
knows his privileges and protections except as these are told him from
time to time. This means inevitably a government of men not of
laws. If we are to abandon a written constitution and have some
other form of government, the American people should make that
decision—not the Supreme Court.

Justice Reed is right in remarking (anent his colleague's attempt
to put Jefferson's wall of separation into the Constitution) that "a
rule of law should not be drawn from a figure of speech." He fails,
however, to go on to point out that it is a still further offense to use
the figure of speech to mean something that it could not possibly
have meant either to the man using it or to the men to whom it
was addressed. (See p. 83.) The same kind of a half-job is done on
Madison's *Memorial and Remonstrance.* Justice Reed properly points
out that the issues in the instant case were not discussed in the
Memorial, that it was written in opposition to an "establishment"
of Christianity in Virginia. Justice Rutledge's total missing of the
point of the *Memorial* is politely handled, and Justice Black's misrepresentation of it is not mentioned. (See p. 198.) But more important than these, is the fact that Judge Reed never says that the
Memorial dealt only with *state law* in Virginia, and that the assump-

tion that any man would *necessarily* mean in a constitutional provision dealing with the powers of Congress what he meant in a political argument opposing a specific law in Virginia, is an absurd assumption for any one to make about the work of any statesman. The paucity of words in the English language sufficiently expressive to characterize adequately such an assumption on the part of Supreme Court Justices when applied to Jefferson and Madison and sufficiently dignified to expect Harper's to print *about* Supreme Court Justices, makes it impossible for me to do justice to this point. I am sorry, however, that Justice Reed, from his favored position on the Bench, did not let himself go all out on this item, instead of skipping it.

Again, Jefferson's discussion of religious education in the University of Virginia shows not only a "clearer indication of his views on the constitutionality of religious education in the public schools," but is positive proof. Jefferson's total record is consistent proof. In fact he never did or said anything at any time to indicate that he thought the states could not do whatever they thought wise in regard to government provision for religion or religious education so long as they treated all religions alike and preserved religious freedom.

The most serious errors in the Reed opinion are contained in the following statements:

"I agree that they cannot 'aid' all or any religions"; [31] and

"Of course, no tax can be levied to support organizations intended 'to teach or practice religion.' " [32]

Why cannot the states aid all religions impartially? The clear purpose of the First Amendment was to keep any federal control out of the situation and *to protect the freedom of the states to do as they pleased in regard to such matters.* When and by whom was that arrangement changed? It does no good to say that the Fourteenth Amendment changed it because the Fourteenth Amendment in this respect is only a channel and contains no new doctrine of any kind in regard to religion. The idea that no tax can be levied to support organizations teaching or practicing religion is flatly contradicted by Justice Reed's own listing [33] of the various ways in which the Congress of the United States has provided tax funds to support or-

[31] *Loc cit.,* p. 4237.   [32] *Ibid.*   [33] *Loc. cit.,* p. 4239.

ganizations practicing or teaching religion from the very foundation of the Republic.

The idea that tax funds may not be so used by the United States government (which has been subject to the First Amendment from the day of its ratification) has never yet been accepted by any President or any Congress of the United States. It has never appeared in a majority opinion speaking for the Court until it was expressed in the flatly erroneous *dicta* of Justice Black in the Everson case. No Supreme Court *decision* has ever even approached the expression of this idea until the decision in the McCollum case to which Judge Reed was dissenting when he made this misstatement.

Even the McCollum case does not necessarily say in the decision that tax money cannot be so used. The decision says only that classes in religious education may not be taught in public school buildings during school hours. Since that decision was handed down, the United States has continued to use tax money to promote the teaching and practice of religion in West Point and Annapolis, in Congress, and in the Army and Navy.

Every state in the union is still using tax-supported property and tax-supported personnel in carrying out various education laws which assist and promote religious education. Today, even after the revolutionary McCollum decision, this statement of Judge Reed is still everywhere untrue in state and nation. In other words, we do not yet have, in the United States or in any individual state, a constitutional provision, a set of statutes, or a Supreme Court decision (as distinct from *dicta*) which prohibits "the use of public money for religion." [34]

Finally, Justice Reed remarks:

This Court cannot be too cautious in upsetting practices embedded in our society by many years of experience. A state is entitled to have great leeway in its legislation when dealing with the important social problems of its population.

This is good as far as it goes, but the clear historical and constitutional fact is that the State is entitled not only to great leeway in

[34] *Ibid.*

matters dealing with such domestic concerns as religion or with "an establishment of religion," regardless of how terms are defined. Under the First Amendment to the Constitution the State is entitled to absolute freedom in this matter. That was the clear purpose of the First Amendment, clearly expressed in its language, stated at the time to be Madison's understanding of the language and repeated by Madison many, many years later to be his understanding of the language. In other words, it is worth repeating that the McCollum decision denies to the people of the State of Illinois the exact freedom which the first clause of the First Amendment was deliberately designed to preserve to the people of each of the states.

Here is no government by the consent of the governed. This is government by a federal agency, dictated to the people of Illinois, contrary to the consent and decision of the people of Illinois as shown by the actions of their legislature, courts, and educational machinery. It is dictation from without, callously based on a perversion of the passage in the Constitution which was deliberately designed to preserve complete freedom from such dictation to the people of each of the states. The crowning effrontery of this dictation from afar, overturning state decisions about "domestic concerns," is that it is handed down in the name of Thomas Jefferson!

The absurdities and inaccuracies of the Supreme Court opinions in the McCollum case, and the paragraphs solemnly "interpreting" these fantastic "interpretations" of an imaginary amendment to the Constitution, unfortunately cannot be treated simply as occasions for hilarity. Those opinions are not comic compositions. They are, or well may be, tragic. It is heartening to notice that the danger is being increasingly recognized as the opinions are being read and discussed.

An article which recognizes the danger and discusses it with the insight of an experienced educator who has long been devoted to civil liberties has been published by Dean Christian Gauss of Princeton University.[35] He reminds us that

[35] *The Ladies' Home Journal* (September, 1948), p. 40.

There are zealots in education as there are in religion and in politics. Occasionally one of them feels that a certain text book or method of teaching is perfect and that there "ought to be a law" to impose it upon every school. To such zealots our former commissioner, genial John W. Studebaker, was in the habit of replying, "In this country we have only a commissioner, not a commissar of education."

As I have indicated elsewhere, it seems to me that the Supreme Court in the McCollum case tried as well as it could to make up for our failure to have a commissar of education.

In his closing paragraph Dean Gauss shows that he does not consider the situation completely hopeless.

One service the McCollum case has rendered. It has called attention in startling fashion to what is perhaps the most important single question which we now face in public education. All interested groups of citizens, particularly of teachers, are called upon to restudy and reassess the results of programs that have now been in operation for many years. The least; and perhaps the most, that they can do is to make their convictions and, above all, their findings known. In a matter of such importance to the training of our future citizens, we can be confident that our justices will not be indifferent to reasoned public opinion and what the majority of Americans regard as sound public policy.

If more leaders of public opinion will speak out as Dean Gauss has spoken, I believe that the American people will see to it that the determination and expression of "sound public policy" will not continue to be usurped by the Supreme Court, but will be returned to the Constitution, the Congress, and the legislatures of the several states.

The *American Bar Association Journal* [36] gives an excellent editorial warning of the threats to the freedom and competent functioning of the state contained in recent actions of the Supreme Court and particularly in the *McCollum* case. The editorial is headed *"No Law But Our Own Prepossessions?"*

In our May issue we commented on what appears to be a tendency in the Supreme Court to invalidate under the First and Fourteenth Amendments State laws and State law enforcement measures which have worked

[36] Vol. 34, No. 6 (June, 1948), pp. 482-484. Quoted by permission.

well in the States for many years and have long been upheld, as valid under the same constitutional provisions, by the highest Courts of law in the States ("Striking Down State Laws", 34 A.B.A.J. 390).

The editor quotes Justice Jackson in the McCollum case:

It is idle to pretend that this task is one for which we can find in the Constitution one word to help us as judges to decide where the secular ends and the sectarian begins in education. Nor can we find guidance in any other legal source. It is a matter on which we can find no law but our own prepossessions.

We should place some bounds on the demands for interference with local schools that we are empowered or willing to entertain.

The *Bar Association Journal* mentioned the fact that at least eleven states had the exact plan used in Champaign, Illinois, and at least thirty-six states had the plan, "also 'unconstitutional' under the ruling," of releasing pupils in school hours for religious education off school premises. In all, thirty-six states had one or both of these practices in operation in 1948. Virginia (the Supreme Court's favorite exhibit) had both!

Again I quote:

Under the 1944 legislation, a discharged veteran may be educated at public expense to be a clergyman, in a denominational school of his choice. A month after the decision in the *McCollum* case, the Congress passed an appropriation of $500,000 to erect a chapel for religions at the United States Merchant Marine Academy at King's Point, New York. On May 28 the United States Post Office placed on sale a postage stamp bearing the legend: "These Immortal Chaplains . . . Interfaith in Action." It bears portraits of four young ministers of religion—a Methodist, a Roman Catholic priest, a Jewish rabbi, and a Baptist—and also a painting of a torpedoed troop-ship which carried them to their graves off Greenland on February 3, 1943—the S. S. *Dorchester* of our Navy. They were on government property at taxpayers' expense, to hold religious services and give instruction and ministration in religion. And when they made their way to the deck of the stricken ship, they gave their life-jackets to four young men who had lost theirs in the confusion. Having given away their own chance to live, the four chaplains stood close together, holding hands, as the ship went under—an immortal demonstration of the unity of religious faiths and what religion does for people —now appropriately commemorated by our government. Was all this "constitutional"? Maybe there was something in the *Dorchester* incident which the majority in the Supreme Court missed—something to which the highest Courts of our States and countless local communities have held fast.

Of course, the decision has a far deeper significance, in the philosophy of law and government and the role of the Court, than the interdiction of the arrangement worked out by the religious faiths with the school board in Champaign, Illinois. As Mr. Justice Jackson and Mr. Justice Reed solemnly warned, new and far more vexatious aspects will arise, in litigation which will seek to carry the present ruling to further extremes.

The final warning of this editorial must be heeded if we are to preserve the democratic process, civil liberties, and any genuine form of constitutional government.

The *McCollum* case may be one of those fateful decisions which is ignored at the time and regretted in the future. It deserves thorough consideration now.

Chapter 13

ANTIDOTES FOR CHAOS

*B*EFORE taking up the problem of what the people of the United States can do to prevent the legal and educational chaos created by the Supreme Court opinions in the McCollum case, we should have in mind certain basic features of the constitutional situation before March 8, 1948.

The original Constitution as adopted September 17, 1787, and effective (by Congressional declaration that it had been ratified by a sufficient number of states) March 4, 1789, contained the following passages relative to the power of the Supreme Court:

ARTICLE III

Section 1. The judicial power of the United States shall be vested in one Supreme Court, and in such inferior courts as the Congress may from time to time ordain and establish. . . .

Section 2. 1. The judicial power shall extend to all cases, in law and equity, arising under this Constitution, the laws of the United States, . . .

2. [After a sentence dealing with "original jurisdiction"] In all the other cases before mentioned, the Supreme Court shall have appellate jurisdiction, both as to law and to fact, with such exceptions, and under such regulations as the Congress shall make.

ARTICLE VI

Section 2. This Constitution, and the laws of the United States which shall be made in pursuance thereof; and all treaties made, or which shall be made, under the authority of the United States, shall be the supreme law of the land; and the Judges in every State shall be bound thereby, any thing in the Constitution or laws of any State to the contrary notwithstanding.

The following passages from Amendments to the Constitution are specifically relevant to our problem.

From the BILL OF RIGHTS, 1791

The First Amendment:	Congress shall make no law respecting an establishment of religion, or prohibiting the free exercise thereof; or abridging the freedom of speech, or of the press; or the right of the people peaceably to assemble, and to petition the Government for a redress of grievances.
The Fifth Amendment:	No person shall be . . . deprived of life, liberty, or property, without due process of law; nor shall private property be taken for public use without just compensation.
The Tenth Amendment:	The powers not delegated to the United States by the Constitution, nor prohibited by it to the States, are reserved to the States respectively, or to the people.

Since the BILL OF RIGHTS (1868)

The Fourteenth Amendment:	Section 1. . . . No State shall make or enforce any law which shall abridge the privileges or immunities of citizens of the United States, nor shall any State deprive any person of life, liberty, or property, without due process of law; nor deny to any person within its jurisdiction the equal protection of the laws.

The passages just quoted contain all the actual language to be found in the Constitution of the United States which had a bearing on the issue in the McCollum case. However, there are certain acts of Congress which hold key positions in the development of the authority of the Supreme Court over state legislation, i.e., its right to declare *state laws* unconstitutional because they violate the Constitution of the United States.

Probably today no one seriously questions the power of the Supreme Court to declare "void" an act of Congress or a state statute on the ground that it violates the Constitution of the United States.

The bitter controversies over the power of the Court in this area are doubtless only interesting chapters in constitutional history and not rehearsals for controversies yet to come. But certain chapters in constitutional history are worth studying to learn the nature and the limitations of the Court's power. Such a study will reveal the revolutionary nature of the decision in the McCollum case. In this case the Supreme Court took action which had *no precedent in either the doctrine which the Court enunciated* or in *the theory of interpretation of the Fourteenth Amendment* which the Court had to assume in order to apply the new doctrine to the State of Illinois (see Chapter 10, pp. 161-2). What the Court did to the Constitution in the McCollum case violates any theory of interpretation of the First and Fourteenth Amendments in the great key cases in the development of our constitutional law.

The McCollum decision required the assumption of the transfer to the states of the *whole* of the First Amendment as written. In no other way could the "establishment of religion" clause be carried to the states. But the Court has consistently held since 1873 that "privileges and immunities" in the Fourteenth Amendment mean only the privileges and immunities of national citizenship (see p. 163), and that the "due process of law" clause carries only those personal *liberties* inherent in the concept of ordered liberty. Until one or both of these old positions of the Court are abandoned there is no "carrier clause" available to take the whole of the First Amendment to the states. No literate and informed person could contend that a prohibition of laws by Congress on any subject *in order to leave such law-making to the states* dealt with a fundamental *personal* freedom which is so clearly inherent in the concept of ordered liberty that its defense is to be assumed as an "implied power" (see p. 261) in the constitution of any free society. Only on such a contention would it be possible to interfere with state action on this subject *outside* of the Fourteenth Amendment. Further if any person, on any grounds whatever, holds that a "keep out" order to Congress *was* in defense of a fundamental *personal liberty* of the people of the states, then he must hold the McCollum decision invalid, since it denies to the people of the states this exact liberty of action.

In addition to all this there is one statement each from Justices Frankfurter and Reed in this case which indicate a belief in a vague, oracular, unidentifiable source of Court authority to make specific *changes in the Constitution,* which goes way beyond the doctrine of "implied powers" (see above) or the doctrine of Court protection of freedom "implicit in the concept of ordered liberty." Judge Frankfurter wrote: "The meaning of a spacious concept like that of separation of Church and State is unfolded as appeal is made to the principle from case to case" (see p. ˙237). Judge Reed: "The passing years have brought about a broader meaning" (see p. 245). The "spacious concept," the meaning of which is reserved for future revelation, and the "broader meaning," which though credited to the past rather than to the future, is still not explained to us, give no sound basis for a new theory for Constitutional changes.

These makeshifts for meaningful communication are dangerously echoed by those not on the Court who are emotionally in tune with the effect of the decision in the McCollum case. Here are some of the phrases which I have heard or read in recent months from those who are pleased (on some unspecified basis) by Mrs. McCollum's victory over the people of Champaign, Illinois.

"History has amended it (the First Amendment)."

"The new interpretation is what the people want."

"The developed meaning of the First Amendment."

"The temper of the people have amended it (the First Amendment)."

"The now [since March 8, 1948] traditional meaning of the First Amendment."

"The tide of democratic progress requires it."

"The popular determination to keep church and state separate."

"What has happened since 1791 to give clear purpose to this Amendment."

These remarks have been offered without any specification or citation which would make possible any checking or verification. Without backing of some kind these expressions are only different ways of saying "I like the decision." Out of such scattered puffs of fog is distilled the validity of the Justices' position that "an establishment of religion" means public financial support of religion, or public co-operation with religion in any guise, form, or degree; or the position that a provision that the states only, *and not the Congress,* should have authority to legislate concerning "an establishment of religion," means that there can be no commingling of religious and secular education in the public schools *of the states.*

The fact that some persons on and off the Supreme Court "like the decision" is as irrelevant as that some do not like it. The question for those who like constitutional democracy is: May the private preferences of the Justice be substituted for constitutional provisions? Corwin [1] mentions "the doctrine upon which Justice Holmes based so much of his constitutional jurisprudence, that all doubts must be resolved in favor of the legislature."

In one of his dissents [2] Justice Holmes remarked that the Fourteenth Amendment "does not condemn everything that we may think undesirable on economic or social grounds." In another of Holmes' most celebrated dissents, in which he was joined by Brandeis and Stone, he wrote: [3]

> I have not yet adequately expressed the more than anxiety that I feel at the ever increasing scope given to the Fourteenth Amendment in cutting down what I believe to be the constitutional rights of the states. As the decisions now stand, I see hardly any limit but the sky to the invalidating of those rights if they happen to strike a majority of this court as for any reason undesirable. I cannot believe that the amendment was intended to give us *carte blanche* to embody our economic or moral beliefs in its prohibitions. Yet I can think of no narrower reason that seems to me to justify the present and the earlier decisions to which I have referred. Of course the words "due process of law" if taken in their literal meaning, have no application to this case; and while it is too late to deny that they have been given a much more extended and artificial signification, still we ought to remember the great caution shown by the constitution in limiting the power of the states and should be slow to construe the clause in the Fourteenth Amendment as committing to the court with no guide but the Court's own discretion the validity of whatever laws the States may pass.

[1] Corwin, *Court over Constitution,* p. 123.
[2] *Farmers Loan and Trust Company* vs. *Minnesota,* 280 U.S. 204 (1930).
[3] *Baldwin* vs. *Missouri,* 281 U.S. 586.

At the close of this opinion Justice Holmes protests against "evoking a constitutional prohibition from the void of 'due process of law,' when logic, tradition, and authority have united to declare the right of the State to lay the now prohibited tax." On reading these sentences the believer in constitutional government naturally regrets the absence of an Oliver Wendell Holmes from the Supreme Bench in 1948.

A brief consideration of the Constitutional and legislative basis of the Supreme Court's general authority to invalidate laws which violate the Constitution, plus the key cases in which the doctrine has been developed and expressed, will show the lack of grounding for the action of the Court in the McCollum case. The Court's *specific* use of this authority in cases involving religion is covered in Chapter 10, pp. 175-184. In the present chapter the survey will have to be brief indeed. The details of old controversies must be omitted and there is room for only the most important law cases.

One part of the "Virginia Plan" submitted to the Constitutional Convention in 1787 provided that Congress should have the power to declare void any state law which Congress should hold to violate the Constitution. This had the ardent support of the advocates of a strong national government, and was opposed by the men who were devoted to rather extreme state power as against the federal government. In July, 1787, the latter group succeeded in defeating the plan of congressional review of state legislation.

Luther Martin of Maryland, a strong supporter of state sovereignty, then moved a plan which became Section 2 of Article VI of the Constitution.

This Constitution, and the Laws of the United States which shall be made in Pursuance thereof; and all Treaties made, or which shall be made, under the Authority of the United States, shall be the Supreme Law of the Land, and the Judges of every State shall be bound thereby, any thing in the Constitution or Laws of any State to the Contrary notwithstanding.

In this way the Constitution made the laws to be enacted by Congress the supreme law of the land and provided that the judges of the several states should be bound by these laws.

The first, and probably the most important federal law passed under the authority of Article VI was the Judiciary Act of 1789. Section 25 of the Act provided for appeals to the Supreme Court from the highest courts of the states in three types of cases. "In effect, this meant that appeals would be taken in all instances where the state judiciary assertedly failed to give full recognition to the supremacy of the Constitution, or to the treaties and laws of the United States, as provided by Article VI of the Constitution." [4] This allowed an appeal to the Supreme Court when a claim under a federal law was *denied* by a state court.

The Judiciary Act of 1914 greatly broadened the field of possible appeals from state courts to the Supreme Court by permitting such appeals in cases in which state courts had *granted* claims under federal law as well as cases in which such claims had been disallowed. This Act allowed appeals on a writ of *certiorari* ("a device for requesting review by a higher court, in cases where the higher court has a discretionary right to accept or reject the appeal" [5]).

Since the Constitution as ratified provided that the "Constitution, and the laws of the United States which shall be made in pursuance thereof . . . shall be the supreme law of the land," and since Congress has made laws of the United States granting the Supreme Court the right to hear appeals from state court decisions [6] in order to decide whether or not these decisions violate the Constitution or the laws of the United States, it follows that the Court has this right (through federal laws) from the Constitution itself clearly expressed in Articles III and VI.

That this effect was intended by the original author of Article VI of the Constitution (Luther Martin of Maryland) has been held, and may still be held, to be extremely doubtful, if not in fact clearly inaccurate. Here again we might remember with profit Justice Frankfurter's remark in *Adamson* v. *California* in reference to another

[4] Kelly, Alfred H., and Harbison, Winfred A., *The American Constitution, Its Origins and Development* (New York, W. W. Norton & Co., 1948), p. 173.
[5] *Ibid.*, p. 628.
[6] *See* Hughes, Charles Evans, *The Supreme Court of the United States* (New York, Columbia University Press, 1928), pp. 80-89; also Ch. IV, "The States and the Nation," pp. 118-156.

passage in the Constitution and a speech made about it: "It was his proposal not his speech that was submitted for ratification." [7]

The acceptance and endorsement by the Supreme Court of the provisions for review of state laws is shown clearly in two famous cases. In *Martin v. Hunter's Lessee* [8] Justice Story, speaking for the Supreme Court, said "that the Constitution, laws, and treaties of the United States could be maintained uniformly as the supreme law of the land only if the Supreme Court had the right to review and to harmonize the decisions of all inferior courts applying that supreme law." [9]

Five years later Chief Justice John Marshall said: "America has chosen to be, in many respects, and to many purposes, a nation; and for all these purposes, her government is complete; to all these objects, it is competent. The people have declared that in the exercise of all powers given for these objects it is supreme." [10] In such a nation, said Marshall, the supreme authority in the national judiciary must of necessity be able to determine whether or not the laws of a state violate the Constitution or laws of the United States.[11]

The United States Supreme Court exercises two different types of appellate jurisdiction—one over federal laws and the other over state laws. The Court's authority to void a law passed by Congress rests upon no specific grant of such power either in the Constitution or by congressional action. This authority comes to the Court essentially through the doctrine of "implied powers" as enunciated by Hamilton in 1791 [12] and developed and applied by Chief Justice John Marshall. Marshall's most noted expressions of this doctrine are found in the following cases.

In *Marbury v. Madison* [13] Marshall said: "Thus the particular

---

[7] *See* in Ch. 12 how completely Justice Frankfurter abandoned his own wisdom in "applying" Jefferson's metaphor from a letter of courtesy instead of the "proposal" that the First Congress (not Jefferson) had submitted for *ratification* —and which had been ratified as the First Amendment.

[8] 1 Wheaton 304 (1816).

[9] Kelly and Harbison, p. 285.

[10] *Cohen v. Virginia*, 6 Wheaton 264 (1821).

[11] *See* Kelly and Harbison, pp. 285-288.

[12] In a memorandum to President Washington concerning the constitutionality of an act to create a national bank. *See* Kelly and Harbison, pp. 177-180.

[13] 1 Cranch 137 (1803).

phraseology of the Constitution of the United States confirms and strengthens the principle, *supposed to be essential to all written constitutions,* that a law repugnant to the constitution is void, and that the courts, as well as all other departments, are bound by that instrument." (Italics mine. Note that Marshall said that the Constitution confirms and strengthens the principle—not states it.)

The Chief Justice concluded that when the Supreme Court found a conflict between a passage in the Constitution and an Act of Congress, the Court had no choice but to uphold the Constitution and declare the law unconstitutional. The Court then, under this doctrine, declared unconstitutional that part of the Judiciary Act of 1789 which extended (beyond the Constitution's specific statement of the Supreme Court's jurisdiction) the power of the Court to issue writs of mandamus to federal officials.

In *McCulloch* v. *Maryland* Marshall interpreted the "necessary and proper" clause of Section 8, Article I of the Constitution, following Hamilton's doctrine mentioned above: "Let the end be legitimate, let it be within the scope of the Constitution, and all means which are appropriate, which are plainly adapted to that end, which are not prohibited, but consist under the letter and spirit of the Constitution, are constitutional." [14]

The discussion of possible remedies for the situation created by the opinions of the Justices in the Everson and McCollum cases is made difficult by the lack of clarity, definiteness, accurate citation of precedent, and by the garbling of historical documents. It is somewhat like trying to deal with a fog instead of a stream of water. The opinions have no reachable source, no markable boundaries, nor wholly foreseeable consequences in the wrecks and disorders to which they may well make major contributions. In the generation of the fog the Justices did the following:

1. Abandoned the literal and specific language of the First Amendment.

2. Substituted for the above the figurative and ambiguous "wall

[14] 4 Wheaton 316 (1819). *See* also Hughes, pp. 97-101.

of separation between church and state," omitting to say what they meant by any of the superlatively ambiguous words, "church," "state," and "separation."

3. Took the position that "an establishment of religion" meant "religion, religious organization or institution, whatever its form or specific religious function."

4. Took the position that "an establishment of religion" meant "financial support of religion in any guise, form, or degree."

5. Took the position that a prohibition of a law by Congress dealing with "an establishment of religion" forbade the "commingling of religious and secular instruction in the public schools of the several states."

6. Took the over-all position that a constitutional provision forbidding *Congress* to make a law about "an establishment of religion," which was put into the Constitution in answer to the specific demands that laws on this subject (among others) should be *left exclusively in the hands of the several states*, became through the Fourteenth Amendment also *a prohibition of state laws on this subject*. (This is true regardless of how the Justices define "an establishment of religion.")

7. Necessarily, in order to have any constitutional authority for the decision, the Court had to assume (though probably without clearly realizing it) a theory of the transfer of the First Amendment to the states through the Fourteenth which has never been explained or defended, or even openly stated, by any Justice at any time, and which underlies no other decision in the entire history of the United States Supreme Court.

If and when any Supreme Court Justice, or anyone else, gets around to giving a factually accurate and reasoned defense or explanation of his idea that the establishment of a religion clause is applied to the states by the Fourteenth Amendment, he will have to rest his defense or explanation on the contention that New Jersey in the Everson case, or Illinois in the McCollum case, had a law which violated one or more of the following passages from the first section of the Fourteenth Amendment:

1. No State shall make or enforce any law which shall abridge the privileges or immunities of the citizens of the United States,

2. nor shall any State deprive any person of life, liberty, or property without due process of law;

3. nor deny to any person within its jurisdiction the equal protection of the laws.

The amorphous nature of the opinions in these two cases is indicated by the fact that not a single Justice in either case *defended* his position as grounded in the functioning of any *one of these passages* from the Fourteenth Amendment. However, it may be worthwhile to state briefly just what the burden of proof will be if ever one of the Justices, or other defender of new doctrine, offers the American people a reasoned argument upholding the Court's reversal of the language and purpose of the first clause of the First Amendment through one of the above clauses of the Fourteenth.

First, under number 1 above, the apologists for the new doctrine will have to demonstrate the validity of one or more of the following positions:

1. The Supreme Court has been wrong in the position it has taken without a single exception in every case that has ever been before it involving this passage from the Fourteenth Amendment that the "privileges and immunities" mentioned are exclusively the "privileges and immunities" inherent in *national* citizenship, not those belonging to citizenship *in a state*. (See p. 163.)

2. That (a) immunity from *state* taxation used to pay for transportation of school children to schools chartered and supervised (in a number of ways) by the *state* and which meet the requirements of the *state* laws compelling school attendance, is an immunity inherent in *national* citizenship, and not (if it exists at all) an immunity belonging simply to *state* citizenship (the Everson bus case), or (b) the privilege of being free from "the commingling of religious with secular education" in *state* public schools is inherent in *national* citizenship (the McCollum religious education case).

3. That legal scholars have been wrong in taking the position that under the unvarying interpretation of the Supreme Court, the privileges and immunities clause of the Fourteenth Amendment is devoid

of any effect whatever, because no state, has, or ever has had, *any authority to deprive a citizen of the United States* of the privileges of immunities of *national* citizenship. (See p. 165.)

If anyone with any respect for our political, judicial, and legislative history ever seriously attempts to argue that the privileges and immunities clause of the Fourteenth makes the establishment of a religion clause of the First a restriction on the states, he will easily understand why the Justices of the Supreme Court dodged this task by the simple expedient of assuming the transfer without trying to show how it came about.

If our future possible apologist for the new doctrine, in his "zeal" for his "own prepossessions" in regard to religion and education elects to rely only on the sacred utterances of the Supreme Court, he will find himself back on the frying-pan-to-the-fire circuit. The Supreme Court has said consistently from 1875 to 1947 inclusive (the Slaughterhouse cases to the Adamson case) that the privileges and immunities mentioned in the Fourteenth Amendment are only those inherent in national citizenship.

Second, under number 2 above, the apologist for the new doctrine will have to show that New Jersey or Illinois *had a law* which deprived someone of life, liberty, or property without *due process* of law. (It is true that in the Everson case the New Jersey law was upheld by the majority of the Court. But this was done in a very poorly argued opinion in which Justice Black seemed to be in agreement with the modern attack on the First Amendment. And the errors in historical fact and in the treatment of Supreme Court cases in both the majority and minority opinions constitute the basis (aside from sheer assumption) of the opinions in the McCollum case). "Due process" is the only possible "carrier" for use in these cases.

Third, there has been, and seemingly can be, no argument in support of the positions taken in either of these cases that any person has been denied "equal protection of the laws." The new provision in the Fourteenth Amendment that no state shall "deny any person within its jurisdiction the equal protection of the laws," clearly is not *a transfer* of any part of the Bill of Rights to the states as a restriction on state power to deal with *subjects* which were *implicitly* reserved to the states in the original Constitution and *explicitly* stated to be so reserved in the Bill of Rights. Obviously in dealing with *any matter* at all a state is forbidden to deny equal protection of the laws. The fact that such a matter may be mentioned in the Bill of Rights adds nothing to the requirement that all persons shall have equal protection. This clause is not, and has never been, said to be a "carrier clause."

"Due process" is, therefore, the only phrase upon which it is possible to base any pretence that the First Amendment, *as a whole*, has, through the Fourteenth, become a set of restrictions on state power. While this theory was not defended by any Justice in either of these cases, it *of necessity* has to be assumed in order to provide any constitutional validity to the opinions in these cases. A detailed discussion of due process is in Chapter 10. Few comments will suffice here.

The due process clause of the Fourteenth Amendment, as written and ratified, was not a sweeping transfer of the Bill of Rights (or other constitutional restrictions on Congress) to the several states as restrictions on state power. It was a direct and specific transfer to the states of a federal restriction in the Fifth Amendment, in the words of that amendment. It added nothing and referred to nothing other than the old restrictions binding on the federal government since 1791.

In the Gitlow case [15] the Court abandoned (without any explanation or argument) this position which had been held for fifty-seven years. They gave up the doctrine that "there are no superfluous words in the Constitution," and that identical language in both the Fifth and Fourteenth Amendments necessarily means the same in both places, and assumed the opposite doctrine (see pp. 174-5). The specific assumption was that the word "liberty" in the Fourteenth Amendment covered *some* of the freedoms mentioned in the First, *viz.*, freedom of speech and of the press. Since 1925 freedom of religion and assembly have been added (see pp. 173, 177). However, so far as I am aware, no responsible person has ever yet had sufficient contempt for history, language, and the intelligence of the Founding Fathers, to argue openly that a prohibition of action by Congress,

[15] 268 U.S. 652 (1925).

designed to protect *freedom of action by the states,* could be a defense of any kind of liberty except *state* liberty. It follows, therefore, since the word liberty can cover only some kind of liberty, that the "liberty without due process of law" clause of the Fourteenth Amendment can never carry the "establishment of religion" clause to the states as a denial of *state liberty* in regard to "an establishment of religion"— however defined.

There are theoretically a number of possible ways open to the American people for counteracting chaos, and perhaps for bringing the Supreme Court back within the confines of the Constitution, language, and logic.

The decision, it should be remembered, as distinct from the statements in the opinions, said that the plan used in Champaign was unconstitutional. This means that voluntary classes in religion in public school buildings during school hours are unlawful. No system which varies from this plan is banned. Since this decision was not explained, argued, or defended, but simply assumed and proclaimed (with some reference to an irrelevant figure of speech taken violently out of context, along with some reference to the bad history and bad logic in the Everson opinions), there is no guidance to be obtained from principles underlying this decision. It is impossible to make negotiable legal principles out of the "zeal" and "prepossessions" of Supreme Court Justices in the areas of religion and education.

There are at least four possible antidotes for the McCollum chaos.

First, there is the method of simply ignoring the decision. There are reliable reports both from persons interested in law and persons interested in religious education that this is one of the most unpopular decisions in our history. There are further reports that the indignation at such unwarranted interference in state control of education is resulting in clergymen representing a number of denominations agreeing with school boards wholly to disregard the McCollum decision. Such reports may of course come from communities in which the program differs in some way from the Champaign plan.

Ignoring the McCollum decision might be compared to the widespread defiance of the Eighteenth Amendment. There is, however, a real difference. The prohibition amendment was in the Constitution. This decision is not. It is itself an attempt to alter the Constitution. Here refusal to accept this edict would be more like the refusals to accept Taney's Dred Scott decision.[16] Hughes [17] lists the Dred Scott decision as one of "three notable instances [in which] the Court has suffered severely from self-inflicted wounds." The other two mentioned are the legal tender cases [18] and the income tax cases.[19]

The issue in the Dred Scott decision was decided by the Civil War; that in the income tax cases by the Sixteenth Amendment to the Constitution. Unless the Court quickly recovers the standing lost by the vagaries in the McCollum opinions, this case will doubtless be listed by some future Hughes as number four of the Court's great "self-inflicted wounds."

However, while ignoring bad laws and bad court pronouncements may be an effective demonstration of public opinion, it is not a method to be recommended except in desperate circumstances. There are some better ways.

Corwin [20] has an instructive passage on the finality and scope of application of Supreme Court decisions.

Thus in the Adkins Case, decided in 1923, we find Justice Sutherland [21] saying:

"From the authority to ascertain and determine the law in a given case, there necessarily results, in case of conflict, the duty to declare and enforce the rule of the supreme law and reject that of an inferior act of legislation which, transcending the Constitution, is of no effect and binding on no one. This is not the exercise of a substantive power to review or nullify acts of Congress, for no such substantive power exists. It is simply a necessary concomitant of the power to hear and dispose of a case or controversy properly before the Court, to the determination of which must be brought the test and measure of the law."

No talk here, it will be observed, about "the peculiar" or "exclusive"

[16] *Scott v. Sandford*, 19 Howard 393 (1857).
[17] *Op. cit.*, pp. 50-53.   [18] *Knox vs. Lee*, 12 Wallace 457 (1870).
[19] *Pollock vs. Farmers Loan and Trust Co.*, 157 U.S. 429 and 158 U.S. 601 and 696.
[20] *Court Over Constitution*, pp. 75-76.   [21] 261 U.S. 525 (1923).

power of judges in law interpretation—no talk about their occupying an "intermediate role" between the other departments and the people—no suggestion that the judicial version of the Constitution is *final* except for the case in which it is pronounced. And the view which is predominant among leading historians of the Court and the Constitution is substantially the same. The essence of learned opinion is condensed in Mr. Warren's epigram: [22] "However the Court may interpret the Constitution, it is still the Constitution which is the law and not the decision of the Court."

It should be understood that the Court has no specific power to obliterate laws or constitutional provisions either in state or nation. It has power only to settle "cases" and "controversies" between litigants properly before it. There is impressive legal opinion that in the McCollum case the United States Supreme Court should have refused to accept jurisdiction—in other words this controversy was not properly before the Court. This consideration, however, is not relevant to the subject of this volume.

Second, there is the possibility of a constitutional amendment spelling out in very simple and completely modern idiom the purpose of the first clause of the First Amendment as it was accepted from 1791 to 1948—or some other purpose if that is the will of the American people! However, this method probably would not be worth the effort it would require. The first clause of the First Amendment is literal and specific, and phrased in clear and careful language. A Court which can find in that simple prohibition of Congressional legislation all the things which the Justices said were the intent or purpose of that language, could say almost anything was the intent or purpose of almost any English phrase that could be written. The only language cure is a Court that is competent in language, informed in history, and that believes in the democratic procedures expressed in the Constitution of the United States.

Third, the technique that has worked in the past in a number of important Court reversals of position has been *public criticism and protest—the pressure of public opinion.* This is the method in which lies the greatest hope of checking quickly the present tendency to

[22] Warren, Charles, *The Supreme Court in United States History* (Boston, Little, Brown and Company, 1922), Vol. III, p. 470.

destroy the First Amendment in the interests of secularism, and ultimately of reversing the McCollum decision. Mr. Dooley in his frequently quoted phrase expressed the general idea when he said "The Supreme Court follows th' iliction returns." The Supreme Court of course follows other types of expression of public opinion and pressure than are contained in election returns. Professor Corwin, in discussing the McCollum opinion, recently expressed confidence in this method of relief. He reminded his audience that the Justices read newspapers as well as the Constitution. A sufficient expression of public opinion in defense of the integrity of the Bill of Rights, of the work of Jefferson and Madison, and of the democratic method of Constitutional amendment, will almost surely bring about a reversal of this decision. There are impressive precedents for such a course.

The differing philosophies of Chief Justice Marshall and of his successor, Chief Justice Taney, doubtless required the encouraging atmospheres of their respective times to bring out the strong nationalist position of Marshall and the States Rights position of Taney.

The "Big Business" decisions between the eighteen-seventies and the nineteen-twenties are clear examples of the Court responding to the temper of the times. So also the succeeding swing away from the almost exclusive defense of property regardless of public welfare, culminating in the New Deal decisions of recent years, is another instance of the Court going with the prevailing winds of political opinion. Furthermore, in none of these shifts of Court position was the Court surrendering such a completely untenable position as that which they took in the McCollum case. The Supreme Court has never in its whole history in any other case which has attracted public interest attempted to strike from the Constitution a deliberately written and legally ratified clause and to substitute for it a doctrine that had been many times formally refused a place in the Constitution. There seems to be ground for hope that exposure and protest will be sufficient to move the Supreme Court to put the First Amendment back into the Constitution.

Chief Justice Hughes' frequently quoted statement that the Constitution means what the Supreme Court says it means cannot be legitimately held to indicate that Hughes was endorsing the idea that the Supreme Court's power was that of an irresponsible dictator.

In the last eighty years the Constitution has become more and more, as Charles Evans Hughes put it in 1926, "What the Supreme Court says it is." . . . In spite of judicial supremacy, however, it is public opinion and not the Court that has the last word on constitutional matters.[23]

In his lectures at Columbia University in 1927 Hughes said: [24]

The Court is the final interpreter of the Acts of Congress. Statutes come to the judicial test, not simply of constitutional validity but with respect to their true import and a federal statute finally means what the Court says it means. . . . The Legislature, . . . often resorts to needless verbal complications which must be disentangled by the Courts to get at the Legislature's intent; *not, of course, an intent outside, but one which must be found inside, the words used.* [Italics mine.]

Fourth, if exposure and protest fail to persuade the Court to give back to the states and the local school boards of the country the constitutional freedom of action which was theirs up to March 8, 1948, we have left a clear, unquestionable, and effective method of preventing the Supreme Court from assuming the role of absolute dictator over American religion and education. That is through congressional legislation concerning the powers and methods of the Court. Article III, section 2, paragraph 2 of the Constitution reads in part "The Supreme Court shall have appellate jurisdiction both as to law and fact *with such exceptions, both as to law and fact as the Congress shall make.*" (Italics mine.) Article VI of the Constitution reads in part "This constitution and the laws of the United States which shall be made in pursuance thereof . . . shall be the supreme law of the land." The Constitution plus well over a century of laws and precedents give Congress authority to pass such laws as will make impossible any further "interpretations" which if accepted would destroy a century and a half of state and national legislation and practice.

In discussing the control of Congress over the Supreme Court Pritchett remarks: [25]

[23] Kelly and Harbison, *op cit.,* p. 4.
[24] Hughes, *op. cit.,* pp. 229-230.

[25] Pritchett, *op. cit.,* p. 21.

There is a tendency to forget the extent to which the Supreme Court's supremacy is grounded in psychological rather than legal foundations. Its function is extremely limited—to decide "cases" and "controversies" —and *even its jurisdiction to do that can be largely taken away by Congress*. It lacks power to execute its demands, and must rely on the executive for their enforcement. . . . Their salaries are constitutionally irreducible, but payment is contingent upon congressional appropriations. *Dependent as it is, the Supreme Court enjoys the privilege of becoming unrepresentative only at its peril,* for the methods of retaliation are readily available should the representative branches of the government have cause to resort to them. [Italics mine.]

In suggesting that Congress in the present crisis may wish to assert its authority to curb the absolute dictatorship of the Supreme Court I am not suggesting a return to the attempt in the 1820's to get Congress to curb the Court in defense of the ancient argument about the Court's invasion of the "sovereignty" of the states. The present issue is not the issue of states rights *versus* the federal government. It is the issue of the purpose and language of the Constitution, of the total record of Congress, of the whole history of the presidency, of the laws and practices of every state in the union, and of the relevant decisions of the Supreme Court down to March, 1948, *versus* the private ideology of the present Supreme Court Justices. Congress can, if it needs to and if it will, resolve that controversy in favor of the Constitution, the democratic process, and American history and tradition.

Appendix A

THE BILL OF RIGHTS IN THE
CONSTITUTION OF THE UNITED STATES

First Ten Amendments passed by Congress Sept. 25, 1789.
Ratified by three-fourths of the States December 15, 1791.

ARTICLE I

Congress shall make no law respecting an establishment of religion, or prohibiting the free exercise thereof; or abridging the freedom of speech, or of the press; or the right of the people peaceably to assemble, and to petition the government for a redress of grievances.

ARTICLE II

A well regulated militia, being necessary to the security of a free State, the right of the people to keep and bear arms, shall not be infringed.

ARTICLE III

No soldier shall, in time of peace be quartered in any house, without the consent of the owner, nor in time of war, but in a manner to be prescribed by law.

ARTICLE IV

The right of the people to be secure in their persons, houses, papers, and effects, against unreasonable searches and seizures, shall not be violated, and no warrants shall issue, but upon probable cause, supported by oath or affirmation, and particularly describing the place to be searched, and the persons or things to be seized.

ARTICLE V

No person shall be held to answer for a capital, or otherwise infamous crime, unless on a presentment or indictment of a grand jury, except in cases arising in the land or naval forces, or in the militia, when in actual service in time of war or public danger; nor shall any person be subject for the same offense to be twice put in jeopardy of life or limb; nor shall be compelled in any criminal case to be a witness against himself, nor be deprived of life, liberty, or property, without due process of law; nor shall private property be taken for public use without just compensation.

ARTICLE VI

In all criminal prosecutions, the accused shall enjoy the right to a speedy and public trial, by an impartial jury of the State and district wherein the crime shall have been committed, which district shall have been previously ascertained by law, and to be informed of the nature and cause of the accusation; to be confronted with the witnesses against him; to have compulsory process for obtaining witnesses in his favor, and to have the assistance of counsel for his defense.

ARTICLE VII

In suits at common law, where the value in controversy shall exceed twenty dollars, the right of trial by jury shall be preserved, and no fact tried by a jury shall be otherwise reëxamined in any court of the United States, than according to the rules of the common law.

ARTICLE VIII

Excessive bail shall not be required, nor excessive fines imposed, nor cruel and unusual punishments inflicted.

ARTICLE IX

The enumeration in the Constitution of certain rights shall not be construed to deny or disparage others retained by the people.

ARTICLE X

The powers not delegated to the United States by the Constitution, nor prohibited by it to the States, are reserved to the States respectively, or to the people.

Appendix B

JEFFERSON'S *BILL FOR ESTABLISHING RELIGIOUS FREEDOM IN VIRGINIA*

Introduced 1779——Passed 1786

SECTION I. Well aware

1. that the opinions and belief of men depend on their own will, but follow involuntarily the evidence proposed to their minds;
2. that Almighty God hath created the mind free, and manifested His supreme will that free it shall remain by making it altogether insusceptible of restraint;
3. that all attempts to influence it by temporal punishments, or burthens, or by civil incapacitations, tend only to beget habits of hypocrisy and meanness, and are a departure from the plan of the holy author of our religion, who being lord both of our body and mind, yet choose not to propagate it by coercions on either, as was in His Almighty power to do, but to exalt it by its influence on reason alone;
4. that the impious presumption of legislature and ruler, civil as well as ecclesiastical, who, being themselves but fallible and uninspired men, have assumed dominion over the faith of others, setting up their own opinions and modes of thinking as the only true and infallible, and as such endeavoring to impose them on others, hath established and maintained false religions over the greatest part of the world and through all time;
5. that to compel a man to furnish contributions of money for the propagation of opinions which he disbelieves and abhors, is sinful and tyrannical;
6. that even the forcing him to support this or that teacher of his own religious persuasion, is depriving him of the comfortable liberty of giving his contributions to the particular pastor whose morals he would make his pattern, and whose powers he feels most persuasive to righteousness; and is withdrawing from the ministry whose temporary rewards, which proceeding from an approbation of their per-

sonal conduct, are an additional incitement to earnest and unremitting labours for the instruction of mankind;

7. that our civil rights have no dependence on our religious opinions, any more than our opinions in physics or geometry; and therefore the proscribing any citizen as unworthy the public confidence by laying upon him an incapacity of being called to offices of trust or emolument, unless he profess or renounce this or that religious opinion, is depriving him injudiciously of those privileges and advantages to which, in common with his fellow-citizens, he has a natural right;

8. that it tends also to corrupt the principles of that very religion it is meant to encourage, by bribing with monopoly of worldly honours and emoluments, those who will externally profess and conform to it;

9. that though indeed these are criminals who do not withstand such temptation, yet neither are those innocent who lay the bait in their way;

10. that the opinions of men are not the object of civil government, nor under its jurisdiction;

11. that to suffer the civil magistrate to intrude his powers into the field of opinion and to restrain the profession or propagation of principles on supposition of their ill tendency is a dangerous fallacy, which at once destroys all religious liberty, because he being of course judge of that tendency will make his opinions the rule of judgment, and approve or condemn the sentiments of others only as they shall square with or suffer from his own;

12. that it is time enough for the rightful purposes of civil government for its officers to interfere when principles break out into overt acts against peace and good order; and finally,

13 that truth is great and will prevail if left to herself;

14. that she is the proper and sufficient antagonist to error, and has nothing to fear from the conflict unless by human interposition disarmed of her natural weapons, free argument and debate; errors ceasing to be dangerous when it is permitted freely to contradict them.

SECTION II. We the General Assembly of Virginia do enact

1. that no man shall be compelled to frequent or support any religious worship, place, or ministry whatsoever,

2. nor shall be enforced, restrained, molested, or burthened in his body or goods, or shall otherwise suffer, on account of his religious opinions or belief; but

3. that all men shall be free to profess, and by argument to maintain, their opinions in matters of religion, and

4. that the same shall in no wise diminish, enlarge, or affect their civil capacities.

SECTION III. And though we well know that this Assembly, elected by the people for their ordinary purposes of legislation only, have no power to restrain the acts of succeeding Assemblies, constituted with powers equal to our own, and that therefore to declare this act to be irrevocable would be of no effect in law; yet we are free to declare, and do declare, that the rights thereby asserted are of the natural rights of mankind, and that if any act shall be hereafter passed to repeal the present or to narrow its operations, such act will be an infringement of natural right.

Appendix C

MADISON'S MEMORIAL AND REMONSTRANCE

Against a Bill Establishing a Provision for Teachers
of the Christian Religion.

To the Honorable the General Assembly
of
The Commonwealth of Virginia.
A Memorial and Remonstrance.

We, the subscribers, citizens of the said Commonwealth, having taken
into serious consideration, a Bill printed by order of the last Session of
General Assembly, entitled "A Bill establishing a provision for Teachers
of the Christian Religion," and conceiving that the same, if finally armed
with the sanctions of a law, will be a dangerous abuse of power, are
bound as faithful members of a free State, to remonstrate against it, and
to declare the reasons by which we are determined. We remonstrate
against the said Bill,

1. Because we hold it for a fundamental and undeniable truth, "that
Religion or the duty which we owe to our Creator and the Manner of
discharging it, can be directed only by reason and conviction, not by
force or violence." [1] The Religion then of every man must be left to the
conviction and conscience of every man; and it is the right of every man
to exercise it as these may dictate. This right is in its nature an unalienable right. It is unalienable; because the opinions of men, depending only
on the evidence contemplated by their own minds, cannot follow the
dictates of other men: It is unalienable also; because what is here a right
towards men, is a duty towards the Creator. It is the duty of every man to
render to the Creator such homage, and such only, as he believes to be
acceptable to him. This duty is precedent both in order of time and
degree of obligation, to the claims of Civil Society. Before any man can
be considered as a member of Civil Society, he must be considered as a

[1] Decl. Rights, Art. 16. [Note in the original.]

subject of the Governor of the Universe: And if a member of Civil Society, who enters into any subordinate Association, must always do it
with a reservation of his duty to the general authority; much more must
every man who becomes a member of any particular Civil Society, do it
with a saving of his allegiance to the Universal Sovereign. We maintain
therefore that in matters of Religion, no man's right is abridged by the
institution of Civil Society, and that Religion is wholly exempt from its
cognizance. True it is, that no other rule exists, by which any question
which may divide a Society, can be ultimately determined, but the will
of the majority; but it is also true, that the majority may trespass on
the rights of the minority.

2. Because if religion be exempt from the authority of the Society at
large, still less can it be subject to that of the Legislative Body. The
latter are but the creatures and vicegerents of the former. Their jurisdiction is both derivative and limited: it is limited with regard to the co-
ordinate departments, more necessarily is it limited with regard to the
constituents. The preservation of a free government requires not merely,
that the metes and bounds which separate each department of power may
be invariably maintained; but more especially, that neither of them be
suffered to overleap the great Barrier which defends the rights of the people. The Rulers who are guilty of such an encroachment, exceed the commission from which they derive their authority, and are Tyrants. The
People who submit to it are governed by laws made neither by themselves, nor by an authority derived from them, and are slaves.

3. Because, it is proper to take alarm at the first experiment on our
liberties. We hold this prudent jealousy to be the first duty of citizens,
and one of [the] noblest characteristics of the late Revolution. The free-
men of America did not wait till usurped power had strengthened itself
by exercise, and entangled the question in precedents. They saw all the
consequences in the principle, and they avoided the consequences by
denying the principle. We revere this lesson too much, soon to forget it.
Who does not see that the same authority which can establish Christianity, in exclusion of all other Religions, may establish with the same
ease any particular sect of Christians, in exclusion of all other Sects?
That the same authority which can force a citizen to contribute three
pence only of his property for the support of any one establishment, may
force him to conform to any other establishment in all cases whatsoever?

4. Because, the bill violates that equality which ought to be the basis
of every law, and which is more indispensable, in proportion as the validity or expediency of any law is more liable to be impeached. If "all men
are by nature equally free and independent," [2] all men are to be con-

2 Decl. Rights, Art. 1. [Note in the original.]

sidered as entering into Society on equal conditions; as relinquishing no more, and therefore retaining no less, one than another, of their natural rights. Above all are they to be considered as retaining an *"equal* title to the free exercise of Religion according to the dictates of conscience." [3] Whilst we assert for ourselves a freedom to embrace, to profess and to observe the Religion which we believe to be of divine origin, we cannot deny an equal freedom to those whose minds have not yet yielded to the evidence which has convinced us. If this freedom be abused, it is an offense against God, not against man: To God, therefore, not to men, must an account of it be rendered. As the Bill violates equality by subjecting some to peculiar burdens; so it violates the same principle, by granting to others peculiar exemptions. Are the Quakers and Mennonists the only sects who think a compulsive support of their religions unnecessary and unwarrantable? Can their piety alone be intrusted with the care of public worship? Ought their Religions to be endowed above all others, with extraordinary privileges, by which proselytes may be enticed from all others? We think too favorably of the justice and good sense of these denominations, to believe that they either covet preeminences over their fellow citizens, or that they will be seduced by them, from the common opposition to the measure.

5. Because the bill implies either that the Civil Magistrate is a competent Judge of Religious truth; or that he may employ Religion as an engine of Civil policy. The first is an arrogant pretension falsified by the contradictory opinions of Rulers in all ages, and throughout the world: The second an unhallowed perversion of the means of salvation.

6. Because the establishment proposed by the Bill is not requisite for the support of the Christian Religion. To say that it is, is a contradiction to the Christian Religion itself; for every page of it disavows a dependence on the powers of this world: it is a contradiction to fact; for it is known that this Religion both existed and flourished, not only without the support of human laws, but in spite of every opposition from them; and not only during the period of miraculous aid, but long after it had been left to its own evidence, and the ordinary care of Providence: Nay, it is a contradiction in terms; for a Religion not invented by human policy, must have pre-existed and been supported, before it was established by human policy. It is moreover to weaken in those who profess this Religion a pious confidence in its innate excellence, and the patronage of its Author; and to foster in those who still reject it, a suspicion that its friends are too conscious of its fallacies, to trust it to its own merits.

7. Because experience witnesseth that ecclesiastical establishments, instead of maintaining the purity and efficacy of Religion, have had a contrary operation. During almost fifteen centuries, has the legal estab-

[3] Art. 16. [Note in the original.]

lishment of Christianity been on trial. What have been its fruits? More or less in all places, pride and indolence in the Clergy; ignorance and servility in the laity; in both, superstition, bigotry and persecution. Enquire of the Teachers of Christianity for the ages in which it appeared in its greatest lustre; those of every sect, point to the ages prior to its incorporation with Civil policy. Propose a restoration of this primitive state in which its Teachers depended on the voluntary rewards of their flocks; many of them predict its downfall. On which side ought their testimony to have greatest weight, when for or when against their interest?

8. Because the establishment in question is not necessary for the support of Civil Government. If it be urged as necessary for the support of Civil Government only as it is a means of supporting Religion, and it be not necessary for the latter purpose, it cannot be necessary for the former. If Religion be not within [the] cognizance of Civil Government, how can its legal establishment be said to be necessary to civil Government? What influence in fact have ecclesiastical establishments had on Civil Society? In some instances they have been seen to erect a spiritual tyranny on the ruins of Civil authority; in many instances they have been seen upholding the thrones of political tyranny; in no instance have they been seen the guardians of the liberties of the people. Rulers who wished to subvert the public liberties, may have found an established clergy convenient auxiliaries. A just government, instituted to secure & perpetuate it, needs them not. Such a government will be best supported by protecting every citizen in the enjoyment of his Religion with the same equal hand which protects his person and his property; by neither invading the equal rights by any Sect, nor suffering any Sect to invade those of another.

9. Because the proposed establishment is a departure from that generous policy, which, offering an asylum to the persecuted and oppressed of every Nation and Religion, promised a lustre to our country, and an accession to the number of its citizens. What a melancholy mark is the Bill of sudden degeneracy! Instead of holding forth an asylum to the persecuted, it is itself a signal of persecution. It degrades from the equal rank of Citizens all those whose opinions in Religion do not bend to those of the Legislative authority. Distant as it may be, in its present form, from the Inquisition it differs from it only in degree. The one is the first step, the other the last in the career of intolerance. The magnanimous sufferer under this cruel scourge in foreign Regions, must view the Bill as a Beacon on our Coast, warning him to seek some other haven, where liberty and philanthropy in their due extent may offer a more certain repose from his troubles.

10. Because it will have a like tendency to banish our Citizens. The

allurements presented by other situations are every day thinning their number. To superadd a fresh motive to emigration, by revoking the liberty which they now enjoy, would be the same species of folly which has dishonoured and depopulated flourishing kingdoms.

11. Because it will destroy that moderation and harmony which the forbearance of our laws to intermeddle with Religion, has produced amongst its several sects. Torrents of blood have been spilt in the old world, by vain attempts of the secular arm to extinguish Religious discord, by proscribing all difference in Religious opinions. Time has at length revealed the true remedy. Every relaxation of narrow and rigorous policy, wherever it has been tried, has been found to assuage the disease. The American Theatre has exhibited proofs, that equal and compleat liberty, if it does not wholly eradicate it, sufficiently destroys its malignant influence on the health and prosperity of the State. If with the salutary effects of this system under our own eyes, we begin to contract the bonds of Religious freedom, we know no name that will too severely reproach our folly. At least let warning be taken at the first fruit of the threatened innovation. The very appearance of the Bill has transformed that "Christian forbearance,[4] love and charity," which of late mutually prevailed, into animosities and jealousies, which may not soon be appeased. What mischiefs may not be dreaded should this enemy to the public quiet be armed with the force of a law?

12. Because the policy of the bill is adverse to the diffusion of the light of Christianity. The first wish of those who enjoy this precious gift, ought to be that it may be imparted to the whole race of mankind. Compare the number of those who have as yet received it with the number still remaining under the dominion of false Religions; and how small is the former! Does the policy of the Bill tend to lessen the disproportion? No; it at once discourages those who are strangers to the light of [revelation] from coming into the Region of it; and countenances, by example the nations who continue in darkness, in shutting out those who might convey it to them. Instead of levelling as far as possible, every obstacle to the victorious progress of truth, the Bill with an ignoble and unchristian timidity would circumscribe it, with a wall of defence, against the encroachments of error.

13. Because attempts to enforce by legal sanctions, acts obnoxious to so great a proportion of Citizens, tend to enervate the laws in general, and to slacken the bands of Society. If it be difficult to execute any law which is not generally deemed necessary or salutary, what must be the case where it is deemed invalid and dangerous? and what may be the effect of so striking an example of impotency in the Government, on its general authority?

4 Art. 16. [Note in the original.]

14. Because a measure of such singular magnitude and delicacy ought not to be imposed, without the clearest evidence that it is called for by a majority of citizens: and no satisfactory method is yet proposed by which the voice of the majority in this case may be determined, or its influence secured. "The people of the respective counties are indeed requested to signify their opinion respecting the adoption of the Bill to the next Session of Assembly." But the representation must be made equal, before the voice either of the Representatives or of the Counties, will be that of the people. Our hope is that neither of the former will, after due consideration, espouse the dangerous principle of the Bill. Should the event disappoint us, it will still leave us in full confidence, that a fair appeal to the latter will reverse the sentence against our liberties.

15. Because, finally, "the equal right of every citizen to the free exercise of his Religion according to the dictates of conscience" is held by the same tenure with all our other rights. If we recur to its origin, it is equally the gift of nature; if we weigh its importance, it cannot be less dear to us; if we consult the Declaration of those rights which pertain to the good people of Virginia, as the "basis and foundation of Government," [5] it is enumerated with equal solemnity, or rather studied emphasis. Either then, we must say, that the will of the Legislature is the only measure of their authority; and that in the plentitude of this authority, they may sweep away all our fundamental rights; or, that they are bound to leave this particular right untouched and sacred: Either we must say, that they may control the freedom of the press, may abolish the trial by jury, may swallow up the Executive and Judiciary Powers of the State; nay that they may despoil us of our very right of suffrage, and erect themselves into an independent and hereditary assembly: or we must say, that they have no authority to enact into law the Bill under consideration. We the subscribers say, that the General Assembly of this Commonwealth have no such authority: And that no effort may be omitted on our part against so dangerous an usurpation, we oppose to it, this remonstrance; earnestly praying, as we are in duty bound, that the Supreme Lawgiver of the Universe, by illuminating those to whom it is addressed, may on the one hand, turn their councils from every act which would affront his holy prerogative, or violate the trust committed to them: and on the other, guide them into every measure which may be worthy of his [blessing, may re]dound to their own praise, and may establish more firmly the liberties, the prosperity, and the Happiness of the Commonwealth.

II Madison, 183–191.

[5] Decl. Rights-title. [Note in the original.]

Appendix D

JEFFERSON'S FREEDOM OF RELIGION
AT THE UNIVERSITY OF VIRGINIA

1822

In the same report of the commissioners of 1818 it was stated by them that "in conformity with the principles of constitution, which place all sects of religion on an equal footing, with the jealousies of the different sects in guarding that equality from encroachment or surprise, and with the sentiments of the legislature in freedom of religion, manifested on former occasions, they had not proposed that any professorship of divinity should be established in the University; that provision, however, was made for giving instruction in the Hebrew, Greek and Latin languages, the depositories of the originals, and of the earliest and most respected authorities of the faith of every sect, and for courses of ethical lectures, developing those moral obligations in which all sects agree. That, proceeding thus far, without offence to the constitution, they had left, at this point, to every sect to take into their own hands the office of further instruction in the peculiar tenet of each."

It was not, however, to be understood that instruction in religious opinion and duties was meant to be precluded by the public authorities, as indifferent to the interests of society. On the contrary, the relations which exist between man and his Maker, and the duties resulting from those relations, are the most interesting and important to every human being, and the most incumbent on his study and investigation. The want of instruction in the various creeds of religious faith existing among our citizens presents, therefore, a chasm in a general institution of the useful sciences. But it was thought that this want, and the entrustment to each society of instruction in its own doctrine, were evils of less danger than a permission to the public authorities to dictate modes or principles of religious instruction, or than opportunities furnished them by giving countenance or ascendancy to any one sect over another. A remedy, however, has been suggested of promising aspect, which, while it excludes the public authorities from the domain of religious freedom, will give to the sectarian schools of divinity the full benefit of the public provisions made for instruction in the other branches of science. These branches are equally necessary to the divine as to the other professional or civil characters, to enable them to fulfill the duties of their calling with understanding and usefulness. It has, therefore, been in contemplation, and suggested by some pious individuals, who perceive the advantages of associating other studies with those of religion, to establish their religious schools on the confines of the University, so as to give to their students ready and convenient access and attendance on the scientific lectures of the University; and to maintain, by that means, those destined for the religious professions on as high a standing of science, and of personal weight and respectability, as may be obtained by others from the benefits of the University. Such establishments would offer the further and greater advantage of enabling the students of the University to attend religious exercises with the professor of their particular sect, either in the rooms of the building still to be erected, and destined to that purpose under impartial regulations, as proposed in the same report of the commissioners, or in the lecturing room of such professor. To such propositions the Visitors are disposed to lend a willing ear, and would think it their duty to give every encouragement, by assuring to those who might choose such a location for their schools, that the regulations of the University should be so modified and accommodated as to give every facility of access and attendance to their students, with such regulated use also as may be permitted to the other students, of the library which may hereafter be acquired, either by public or private munificence. But always understanding that these schools shall be independent of the University and of each other. Such an arrangement would complete the circle of the useful sciences embraced by this institution, and would fill the chasm now existing, on principles which would leave inviolate the constitutional freedom of religion, the most inalienable and sacred of all human rights, over which the people and authorities of this state, individually and publicly, have ever manifested the most watchful jealousy: and could this jealousy be now alarmed, in the opinion of the legislature, by what is here suggested, the idea will be relinquished on any surmise of disapprobation which they might think proper to express.

Appendix E

JEFFERSON'S REPLY TO THE BAPTISTS
OF DANBURY

January 1, 1802

GENTLEMEN: The affectionate sentiments of esteem and approbation which you are so good as to express towards me, on behalf of the Danbury Baptist Association, give me the highest satisfaction. My duties dictate a faithful and zealous pursuit of the interests of my constituents, and in proportion as they are persuaded of my fidelity to those duties, the discharge of them becomes more and more pleasing.

Believing with you that religion is a matter which lies solely between man and his God, that he owes account to none other for his faith or his worship, that the legislative powers of government reach actions only, and not opinions, I contemplate with sovereign reverence that act of the whole American people which declared that their legislature should "make no law respecting an establishment of religion, or prohibiting the free exercise thereof," thus building a wall of separation between church and State. Adhering to this expression of the supreme will of the nation in behalf of the rights of conscience, I shall see with sincere satisfaction the progress of those sentiments which tend to restore to man all his natural rights, convinced he has no natural right in opposition to his social duties.

I reciprocate your kind prayers for the protection and blessing of the common Father and Creator of man, and tender you for yourselves and your religious association, assurances of my high respect and esteem.

Appendix F

EXCERPTS FROM SUPREME COURT OPINIONS IN THE *EVERSON* AND *MCCOLLUM* CASES

The Everson Case

Justice Black, speaking for the Court:

Insofar as the second phase of the due process argument may differ from the first, it is by suggesting that taxation for transportation of children to church schools constitutes support of a religion by the State. But if the law is invalid for this reason, it is because it violates the First Amendment's prohibition against the establishment of religion by law. This is the exact question raised by appellant's second contention, to consideration of which we now turn.

Second. The New Jersey statute is challenged as a "law respecting the establishment of religion." The First Amendment, as made applicable to the states by the Fourteenth, *Murdock* v. *Pennsylvania*, 319 U. S. 105, commands that a state "shall make no law respecting an establishment of religion, or prohibiting the free exercise thereof." These words of the First Amendment reflected in the minds of early Americans a vivid mental picture of conditions and practices which they fervently wished to stamp out in order to preserve liberty for themselves and for their posterity. Doubtless their goal has not been entirely reached; but so far has the Nation moved toward it that the expression "law respecting the establishment of religion," probably does not so vividly remind present-day Americans of the evils, fears, and political problems that caused that expression to be written into our Bill of Rights. Whether this New Jersey law is one respecting the "establishment of religion" requires an understanding of the meaning of that language, particularly with respect to the imposition of taxes.

    .   .   .   .   .   .

But Virginia, where the established church had achieved a dominant influence in political affairs and where many excesses attracted wide public attention, provided a great stimulus and able leadership for the movement. The people there, as elsewhere, reached the conviction that individual religious liberty could be achieved best under a government which was stripped of all power to tax, to support, or otherwise to assist any or all religions, or to interfere with the beliefs of any religious individual or group.

The movement toward this end reached its dramatic climax in Virginia in 1785–86 when the Virginia legislative body was about to renew Virginia's tax levy for the support of the established church. Thomas Jefferson and James Madison led the fight against this tax. Madison wrote his great *Memorial and Remonstrance* against the law. In it, he eloquently argued that a true religion did not need the support of law; that no person, either believer or non-believer, should be taxed to support a religious institution of any kind; that the best interest of a society required that the minds of men always be wholly free; and that cruel persecutions were the inevitable result of government-established religions.

The meaning and scope of the First Amendment, preventing establishment of religion or prohibiting the free exercise thereof, in the light of its history and the evils it was designed forever to suppress, have been several times elaborated by the decisions of this Court prior to the application of the First Amendment to the states by the Fourteenth. The broad meaning given the Amendment by these earlier cases has been accepted by this Court in its decisions concerning an individual's religious freedom rendered since the Fourteenth Amendment was interpreted to make the prohibitions of the First applicable to state action abridging religious freedom. There is every reason to give the same application and broad interpretation to the "establishment of religion" clause. The interrelation of these complementary clauses was well summarized in a statement of the Court of Appeals of South Carolina, quoted with approval by this Court in *Watson* v. *Jones*, 13 Wall. 679, 730: "The structure of our government has, for the preservation of civil liberty, rescued the temporal institutions from religious interference. On the other hand, it has secured religious liberty from the invasions of the civil authority."

The "establishment of religion" clause of the First Amendment means at least this: Neither a state nor the Federal Government can set up a church. Neither can pass laws which aid one religion, aid all religions, or prefer one religion over another. Neither can force nor influence a person to go to or to remain away from church against his will or force him to profess a belief or disbelief in any religion. No person can be punished for entertaining or professing religious beliefs or disbeliefs, for church attendance or non-attendance. No tax in any amount, large or small, can be levied to support any religious activities or institutions, whatever they may be called, or whatever form they may adopt to teach or practice religion. Neither a state nor the Federal Government can, openly or secretly, participate in the affairs of any religious organizations or groups and *vice versa*. In the words of Jefferson, the clause against establishment of religion by law was intended to erect "a wall of separation between Church and State." *Reynolds* v. *United States*, 98 U. S. 145.

The First Amendment has erected a wall between church and state. That wall must be kept high and impregnable. We could not approve the slightest breach. New Jersey has not breached it here.

Affirmed.

Justice Jackson, dissenting:

Our public school, if not a product of Protestantism, at least is more consistent with it than with the Catholic culture and scheme of values. It is a relatively recent development dating from about 1840. It is organized on the premise that secular education can be isolated from all religious teaching so that the school can inculcate all needed temporal knowledge and also maintain a strict and lofty neutrality as to religion. The assumption is that after the individual has been instructed in worldly wisdom he will be better fitted to choose his religion. Whether such a disjunction is possible, and if possible whether it is wise, are questions I need not try to answer.

The Court's holding is that this taxpayer has no grievance because the state has decided to make the reimbursement a public purpose and therefore we are bound to regard it as such. I agree that this Court has left, and always should leave to each state, great latitude in deciding for itself, in the light of its own conditions, what shall be public purposes in its scheme of things. It may socialize utilities and economic enterprises and make taxpayers' business out of what conventionally had been private business. It may make public business of individual welfare, health, education, entertainment or security. But it cannot make public business of religious worship or instruction, or of attendance at religious institutions of any character. There is no answer to the proposition more fully expounded by MR. JUSTICE RUTLEDGE that the effect of the religious freedom Amendment to our Constitution was to take every form of propagation of religion out of the realm of things which could directly or indirectly be made public business and thereby be supported in whole or in part at taxpayers' expense. That is a difference which the Constitution sets up between religion and almost every other subject matter of legislation, a difference which goes to the very root of religious freedom and which the Court is overlooking today. This freedom was first in the Bill of Rights because it was first in the forefathers' minds; it was set forth in absolute terms, and its strength is its rigidity. It was intended not only to keep the states' hands out of religion, but to keep religion's hands off the state, and above all, to keep bitter religious controversy out of public life by denying to every denomination any advantage from getting control of public policy or the public purse. Those great ends I cannot but think are immeasurably compromised by today's decision.

．　　．　　．　　．　　．　　．　　．

Justice Rutledge, dissenting:

"Well aware that Almighty God hath created the mind free; . . . that to compel a man to furnish contributions of money for the propagation of opinions which he disbelieves, is sinful and tyrannical; . . .

"*We, the General Assembly, do enact,* That no man shall be compelled to frequent or support any religious worship, place, or ministry whatsoever, nor shall be enforced, restrained, molested, or burthened in his body or goods, nor shall otherwise suffer on account of his religious opinions or belief. . . ."

I cannot believe that the great author of those words, or the men who made them law, could have joined in this decision. Neither so high nor so impregnable today as yesterday is the wall raised between church and state by Virginia's great statute of religious freedom and the First Amendment, now made applicable to all the states by the Fourteenth. New Jersey's statute sustained is the first, if indeed it is not the second breach to be made by this Court's action. That a third, and a fourth, and still others will be attempted, we may be sure. For just as *Cochran* v. *Board of Education,* 281 U. S. 370, has opened the way by oblique ruling for this decision, so will the two make wider the breach for a third. Thus with time the most solid freedom steadily gives way before continuing corrosive decision.

This case forces us to determine squarely for the first time what was "an establishment of religion" in the First Amendment's conception; and by that measure to decide whether New Jersey's action violates its command．　　．　　．　　．　　．　　．　　．

Not simply an established church, but any law respecting an establishment of religion is forbidden. The Amendment was broadly but not loosely phrased. It is the compact and exact summation of its author's views formed during his long struggle for religious freedom. In Madison's own words characterizing Jefferson's Bill for Establishing Religious Freedom, the guaranty he put in our national charter, like the bill he piloted through the Virginia Assembly, was "a Model of technical precision, and perspicuous brevity." Madison could not have confused "church" and "religion," or "an established church" and "an establishment of religion."

The Amendment's purpose was not to strike merely at the official establishment of a single sect, creed or religion, outlawing only a formal relation such as had prevailed in England and some of the colonies. Necessarily it was to uproot all such relationships. But the object was broader than separating church and state in this narrow sense. It was to create a complete and permanent separation of the spheres of religious activity and civil authority by comprehensively forbidding every form of public aid or support for religion. In proof the Amendment's wording and history unite with this Court's consistent utterances whenever attention has been fixed directly upon the question.

"Religion" appears only once in the Amendment. But the word governs two prohibitions and governs them alike. It does not have two meanings, one narrow to forbid "an establishment" and another, much broader, for securing "the free exercise thereof." "Thereof" brings down "religion" with its entire and exact content, no more and no less, from the first into the second guaranty, so that Congress and now the states are as broadly restricted concerning the one as they are regarding the other.   .   .   .   .

"Religion" has the same broad significance in the twin prohibition concerning "an establishment." The Amendment was not duplicitous. "Religion" and "establishment" were not used in any formal or technical sense. The prohibition broadly forbids state support, financial or other, of religion in any guise, form or degree. It outlaws all use of public funds for religious purposes.

II.

No provision of the Constitution is more closely tied to or given content by its generating history than the religious clause of the First Amendment. It is at once the refined product and the terse summation of that history. The history includes not only Madison's authorship and the proceedings before the First Congress, but also the long and intensive struggle for religious freedom in America, more especially in Virginia, of which the Amendment was the direct culmination. In the documents of the times, particularly of Madison, who was leader in the Virginia struggle before he became the Amendment's sponsor, but also in the writings of Jefferson and others and in the issues which engendered them is to be found irrefutable confirmation of the Amendment's sweeping content.   .   .   .   .

. . . in the fall he issued his historic *Memorial and Remonstrance*. This is Madison's complete, though not his only, interpretation of religious liberty. It is a broadside attack upon all forms of "establishment" of religion, both general and particular, nondiscriminatory or selective. Reflecting not only the many legislative conflicts over the Assessment Bill and the Bill for Establishing Religious Freedom but also, for example, the struggles for religious incorporations and the continued maintenance of the glebes, the *Remonstrance* is at once the most concise and the most accurate statement of the views of the First Amendment's author concerning what is "an establishment of religion."

·   ·   ·   ·   ·   ·   ·

All the great instruments of the Virginia struggle for religious liberty thus became warp and woof of our constitutional tradition, not simply by the course of history, but by the common unifying force of Madison's life, thought and sponsorship. He epitomized the whole of that tradition in the Amendment's compact, but nonetheless comprehensive, phrasing.

As the *Remonstrance* discloses throughout, Madison opposed every form and degree of official relation between religion and civil authority. For him religion was a wholly private matter beyond the scope of civil power either to restrain or to support. Denial or abridgment of religious freedom was a violation of rights both of conscience and of natural equality. State aid was no less obnoxious or destructive to freedom and to religion itself than other forms of state interference. "Establishment" and "free exercise" were correlative and coextensive ideas, representing only different facets of the single great and fundamental freedom. The *Remonstrance*, following the Virginia statute's example, referred to the history of religious conflicts and the effects of all sorts of establishments, current and historical, to suppress religion's free exercise. With Jefferson, Madison believed that to tolerate any fragment of establishment would be by so much to perpetuate restraint upon that freedom. Hence he sought to tear out the institution not partially but root and branch, and to bar its return forever.

In no phase was he more unrelentingly absolute than in opposing state support or aid by taxation. Not even "three pence" contribution was thus to be exacted from any citizen for such a purpose. *Remonstrance*, Par. 3. Tithes had been the life blood of establishment before and after other compulsions disappeared. Madison and his coworkers made no exceptions or abridgments to the complete separation they created. Their objection was not to small tithes. It was to any tithes whatsoever. "If it were lawful to impose a small tax for religion the admission would pave the way for oppressive levies." Not the amount but "the principle of assessment was wrong."

·   ·   ·   ·   ·   ·   ·

In view of this history no further proof is needed that the Amendment forbids any appropriation, large or small, from public funds to aid or support any and all religious exercises. But if more were called for, the debates in the First Congress and this Court's consistent expressions, whenever it has touched on the matter directly, supply it.

.   .   .   .

Hence today, apart from efforts to inject religious training or exercises and sectarian issues into the public schools, the only serious surviving threat to maintaining that complete and permanent separation of religion and civil power which the First Amendment commands is through use of the taxing power to support religion, religious establishments, or establishments having a religious foundation whatever their form or special religious function.

Does New Jersey's action furnish support for religion by use of the taxing power? Certainly it does, if the test remains undiluted as Jefferson and Madison made it, that money taken by taxation from one is not to be used or given to support another's religious training or belief, or indeed one's own. Today as then the furnishing of "contributions of money for the propagation of opinions which he disbelieves" is the forbidden exaction; and the prohibition is absolute for whatever measure brings that consequence and whatever amount may be sought or given to that end.

The funds used here were raised by taxation. The Court does not dispute, nor could it, that their use does in fact give aid and encouragement to religious instruction. It only concludes that this aid is not "support" in law. But Madison and Jefferson were concerned with aid and support in fact, not as a legal conclusion "entangled in precedents."

.   .   .   .

But whatever may be the philosophy or its justification, there is undeniably an admixture of religious with secular teaching in all such institutions. That is the very reason for their being. Certainly for purposes of constitutionality we cannot contradict the whole basis of the ethical and educational convictions of people who believe in religious schooling.

Yet this very admixture is what was disestablished when the First Amendment forbade "an establishment of religion." Commingling the religious with the secular teaching does not divest the whole of its religious permeation and emphasis or make them of minor part, if proportion were material. Indeed, on any other view, the constitutional prohibition always could be brought to naught by adding a modicum of the secular.

.   .   .   .

To say that New Jersey's appropriation and her use of the power of taxation for raising the funds appropriated are not for public purposes but are for private ends, is to say that they are for the support of religion and religious teaching. Conversely, to say that they are for public purposes is to say that they are not for religious ones.

This is precisely for the reason that education which includes religious training and teaching, and its support, have been made matters of private right and function, not public, by the very terms of the First Amendment. That is the effect not only in its guaranty of religion's free exercise, but also in the prohibition of establishments.

. . . .

Our constitutional policy is exactly the opposite. It does not deny the value or the necessity for religious training, teaching or observance. Rather it secures their free exercise. But to that end it does deny that the state can undertake or sustain them in any form or degree. For this reason the sphere of religious activity, as distinguished from the secular intellectual liberties, has been given the twofold protection and, as the state cannot forbid, neither can it perform or aid in performing the religious function. The dual prohibition makes that function altogether private. It cannot be made a public one by legislative act. This was the very heart of Madison's *Remonstrance*, as it is of the Amendment itself.

It is not because religious teaching does not promote the public or the individual's welfare, but because neither is furthered when the state promotes religious education, that the Constitution forbids it to do so. Both legislatures and courts are bound by that distinction.

. . . .

By no declaration that a gift of public money to religious uses will promote the general or individual welfare, or the cause of education generally, can legislative bodies overcome the Amendment's bar.

. . . .

Legislatures are free to make, and courts to sustain, appropriations only when it can be found that in fact they do not aid, promote, encourage or sustain religious teaching or observances, be the amount large or small. No such finding has been or could be made in this case. The Amendment has removed this form of promoting the public welfare from legislative and judicial competence to make a public function.

. . . .

This is not therefore just a little case over bus fares. In paraphrase of Madison, distant as it may be in its present form from a complete establishment of religion, it differs from it only in degree; and is the first step in that direction. *Id.*, Par. 9. Today as in his time "the same authority which can force a citizen to contribute three pence only . . . for the support of any one religious establishment, may force him" to pay more; or "to conform to any other establishment in all cases whatsoever."

. . . .

The problem then cannot be cast in terms of legal discrimination or its absence. This would be true, even though the state in giving aid should treat all religious instruction alike. Thus, if the present statute and its application were shown to apply equally to all religious schools of whatever faith, yet in the light of our tradition it could not stand. For then the adherent of one creed still would pay for the support of another, the childless taxpayer with others more fortunate. Then too there would seem to be no bar to making appropriations for transportation and other expenses of children attending public or other secular schools, after hours in separate places and classes for their exclusively religious instruction. The person who embraces no creed also would be forced to pay for teaching what he does not believe. Again, it was the furnishing of "contributions of money for the propagation of opinions which he disbelieves" that the fathers outlawed. That consequence and effect are not removed by multiplying to all-inclusiveness the sects for which support is exacted. The Constitution requires, not comprehensive identification of state with religion, but complete separation.

The McCollum Case

Mr. Justice Black for the Court:

The petitioner charged that this joint public-school religious-group program violated the First and Fourteenth Amendments to the United States Constitution. The prayer of her petition was that the Board of Education be ordered to "adopt and enforce rules and regulations prohibiting all instruction in and teaching of all religious education in all public schools in Champaign District Number 71, . . . and in all public school houses and buildings in said district when occupied by public schools."

. . . .

The foregoing facts, without reference to others that appear in the record, show the use of tax-supported property for religious instruction and the close cooperation between the school authorities and the religious council in promoting religious education. The operation of the state's compulsory education system thus assists and is integrated with the program of religious instruction carried on by separate religious sects.

Pupils compelled by law to go to school for secular education are released in part from their legal duty upon the condition that they attend the religious classes. This is beyond all question a utilization of the tax-established and tax-supported public school system to aid religious groups to spread their faith. And it falls squarely under the ban of the First Amendment (made applicable to the States by the Fourteenth) as we interpreted it in *Everson* v. *Board of Education*, 330 U. S. 1. There we said: "Neither a state nor the Federal Government can set up a church. Neither can pass laws which aid one religion, aid all religions, or prefer one religion over another. Neither can force or influence a person to go to or to remain away from church against his will or force him to profess a belief or disbelief in any religion. No person can be punished for entertaining or for professing religious beliefs or disbeliefs, for church attendance or nonattendance. No tax in any amount, large or small, can be levied to support any religious activities or institutions, whatever they may be called, or whatever form they may adopt to teach or practice religion. Neither a state nor the Federal Government can, openly or secretly, participate in the affairs of any religious organizations or groups, and *vice versa*. In the words of Jefferson, the clause against establishment of religion by law was intended to erect 'a wall of separation between church and State.' " The majority in the *Everson* case, and the minority as shown by quotations from the dissenting views in our notes 6 and 7, agreed that the First Amendment's language, properly interpreted, had erected a wall of separation between Church and State. They disagreed as to the facts shown by the record and as to the proper application of the First Amendment's language to those facts.

Recognizing that the Illinois program is barred by the First and Fourteenth Amendments if we adhere to the views expressed both by the majority and the minority in the *Everson* case, counsel for the respondents challenge those views as dicta and urge that we reconsider and repudiate them. They argue that historically the First Amendment was intended to forbid only government preference of one religion over another, not an impartial governmental assistance of all religions. In addition they ask that we distinguish or overrule our holding in the *Everson* case that the Fourteenth Amendment made the "establishment of religion" clause of the First Amendment applicable as a prohibition against the States. After giving full consideration to the arguments presented we are unable to accept either of these contentions.

• • • • • • •

For the First Amendment rests upon the premise that both religion and government can best work to achieve their lofty aims if each is left free from the other within its respective sphere. Or, as we said in the

Everson case, the First Amendment has erected a wall between Church and State which must be kept high and impregnable.

Here not only are the state's tax-supported public school buildings used for the dissemination of religious doctrines. The State also affords sectarian groups an invaluable aid in that it helps to provide pupils for their religious classes through use of the state's compulsory public school machinery. This is not separation of Church and State.

The cause is reversed and remanded to the State Supreme Court for proceedings not inconsistent with this opinion.

Reversed and remanded.

Mr. Justice Jackson, concurring (Passages quoted at length in Chapter 12 are not repeated here):

I think it remains to be demonstrated whether it is possible, even if desirable, to comply with such demands as plaintiff's completely to isolate and cast out of secular education all that some people may reasonably regard as religious instruction. Perhaps subjects such as mathematics, physics or chemistry are, or can be, completely secularized. But it would not seem practical to teach either practice or appreciation of the arts if we are to forbid exposure of youth to any religious influences. Music without sacred music, architecture minus the cathedral, or painting without the scriptural themes would be eccentric and incomplete, even from a secular point of view. Yet the inspirational appeal of religion in these guises is often stronger than in forthright sermon. Even such a "science" as biology raises the issue between evolution and creation as an explanation of our presence on this planet. Certainly a course in English literature that omitted the Bible and other powerful uses of our mother tongue for religious ends would be pretty barren. And I should suppose it is a proper, if not an indispensable, part of preparation for a worldly life to know the roles that religion and religions have played in the tragic story of mankind. The fact is that, for good or for ill, nearly everything in our culture worth transmitting, everything which gives meaning to life, is saturated with religious influences, derived from paganism, Judaism, Christianity— both Catholic and Protestant—and other faiths accepted by a large part of the world's peoples. One can hardly respect a system of education that would leave the student wholly ignorant of the currents of religious thought that move the world society for a part in which he is being prepared.

But how one can teach, with satisfaction or even with justice to all faiths, such subjects as the story of the Reformation, the Inquisition, or even the New England effort to found "a Church without a Bishop and a State without a King," is more than I know. It is too much to expect that mortals will teach subjects about which their contemporaries have passionate controversies with the detachment they may summon to teaching about remote subjects such as Confucius or Mohamet. When instruction turns to proselyting and imparting knowledge becomes evangelism is, except in the crudest cases, a subtle inquiry.

The opinions in this case show that public educational authorities have evolved a considerable variety of practices in dealing with the religious problem. Neighborhoods differ in racial, religious and cultural compositions. It must be expected that they will adopt different customs which will give emphasis to different values and will induce different experiments. And it must be expected that, no matter what practice prevails, there will be many discontented and possibly belligerent minorities. We must leave some flexibility to meet local conditions, some chance to progress by trial and error. While I agree that the religious classes involved here go beyond permissible limits, I also think the complaint demands more than plaintiff is entitled to have granted. So far as I can see this Court does not tell the State court where it may stop, nor does it set up any standards by which the State court may determine that question for itself.

The task of separating the secular from the religious in education is one of magnitude, intricacy and delicacy. To lay down a sweeping constitutional doctrine as demanded by complainant and apparently approved by the Court, applicable alike to all school boards of the nation, "to immediately adopt and enforce rules and regulations prohibiting all instruction in and teaching of religious education in all public schools," is to decree a uniform, rigid and, if we are consistent, an unchanging standard for countless school boards representing and serving highly localized groups which not only differ from each other but which themselves from time to time change attitudes. It seems to me that to do so is to allow zeal for our own ideas of what is good in public instruction to induce us to accept the role of a super board of education for every school district in the nation.

It is idle to pretend that this task is one for which we can find in the Constitution one word to help us as judges to decide where the secular ends and the sectarian begins in education. Nor can we find guidance in any other legal source. It is a matter on which we can find no law but our own prepossessions. If with no surer legal guidance we are to take up and decide every variation of this controversy, raised by persons not subject to penalty or tax but who are dissatisfied with the way schools are dealing with the problem, we are likely to have much business of the sort. And, more importantly, we are likely to make the legal "wall of separation between church and state" as winding as the famous serpentine wall designed by Mr. Jefferson for the University he founded.

Mr. Justice Frankfurter (joined by Justices Jackson, Rutledge, and Burton. In addition to the passages which referred to the Constitutional question before the Court, quoted in the text of Chapter 12, the following may be enlightening):

To understand the particular program now before us as a conscientious attempt to accommodate the allowable functions of Government and the special concerns of the Church within the framework of our Constitution and with due regard to the kind of society for which it was designed, we must put this Champaign program of 1940 in its historic setting. Traditionally, organized education in the Western world was Church education. It could hardly be otherwise when the education of children was primarily study of the World and the ways of God. Even in the Protestant countries, where there was a less close identification of Church and State, the basis of education was largely the Bible, and its chief purpose inculcation of piety. To the extent that the State intervened, it used its authority to further aims of the Church.

· · · · · · ·

This development of the public school as a symbol of our secular unity was not a sudden achievement nor attained without violent conflict. While in small communities of comparatively homogeneous religious beliefs, the need for absolute separation presented no urgencies, elsewhere the growth of the secular school encountered the resistance of feeling strongly engaged against it. But the inevitability of such attempts is the very reason for Constitutional provisions primarily concerned with the protection of minority groups. And such sects are shifting groups, varying from time to time, and place to place, thus representing in their totality the common interest of the nation.

Enough has been said to indicate that we are dealing not with a full-blown principle, nor one having the definiteness of a surveyor's metes and bounds. But by 1875 the separation of public education from Church entanglements, of the State from the teaching of religion, was firmly established in the consciousness of the nation.

· · · · · · ·

According to responsible figures almost 2,000,000 in some 2,200 communities participated in "released time" programs during 1947. A movement of such scope indicates the importance of the problem to which the "released time" programs are directed. But to the extent that aspects of these programs are open to Constitutional objection, the more extensively the movement operates, the more ominous the breaches in the wall of separation.

Of course, "released time" as a generalized conception, undefined by differentiating particularities, is not an issue for Constitutional adjudication. Local programs differ from each other in many and crucial respects. Some "released time" classes are under separate denominational auspices, others are conducted jointly by several denominations, often embracing all the religious affiliations of a community. Some classes in religion teach a limited sectarianism; others emphasize democracy, unity and spiritual values not anchored in a particular creed. Insofar as these are manifestations merely of the free exercise of religion, they are quite outside the scope of judicial concern, except insofar as the Court may be called upon to protect the right of religious freedom. It is only when challenge is made to the share that the public schools have in the execution of a particular "released time" program that close judicial scrutiny is demanded of the exact relation between the religious instruction and the public educational system in the specific situation before the Court.

The substantial differences among arrangements lumped together as "released time" emphasize the importance of detailed analysis of the facts to which the Constitutional test of Separation is to be applied.

Mr. Justice Reed, dissenting:

The decisions reversing the judgment of the Supreme Court of Illinois interpret the prohibition of the First Amendment against the establishment of religion, made effective as to the states by the Fourteenth Amendment, to forbid pupils of the public schools electing, with the approval of their parents, courses in religious education. The courses are given, under the school laws of Illinois as approved by the Supreme Court of that state, by lay or clerical teachers supplied and directed by an interdenominational, local council of religious education. The classes are held in the respective school buildings of the pupils at study or released time periods so as to avoid conflict with recitations. The teachers and supplies are paid for by the interdenominational group. As I am convinced that this interpretation of the First Amendment is erroneous, I feel impelled to express the reasons for my disagreement. By directing attention to the many instances of close association of church and state in American society and by recalling that many of these relations are so much a part ᵣᵣdition and culture that they are accepted without more, this dissent may help in an appraisal of the meaning of the clause of the First Amendment concerning the establishment of religion and of the reasons which lead to the approval or disapproval of the judgment below.

. . . .

The opinions do not say in words that the condemned practice of religious education is a law respecting an establishment of religion contrary to the First Amendment. The practice is accepted as a state law by all. I take it that when the first opinion says that "The operation of the state's compulsory education system thus assists and is integrated with the program of religious instruction carried on by separate religious sects" and concludes "This is beyond all question a utilization of the tax-established and tax-supported public school system to aid religious groups to spread their faith," the intention of its author is to rule that this practice is a law "respecting an establishment of religion." That was the basis of *Everson* v. *Board of Education,* 330 U. S. 1. It seems obvious that the action of the School Board in permitting religious education in certain grades of the schools by all faiths did not prohibit the free exercise of religion. Even assuming that certain children who did not elect to take instruction are embarrassed to remain outside of the classes, one can hardly speak of that embarrassment as a prohibition against the free exercise of religion. As no issue of prohibition upon the free exercise of religion is before us, we need only examine the School Board's action to see if it constitutes an establishment of religion.

Mr. Jefferson, as one of the founders of the University of Virginia, a school which from its establishment in 1819 has been wholly governed, managed and controlled by the State of Virginia, was faced with the same problem that is before this Court today: the question of the constitutional limitation upon religious education in public schools. In his annual report as Rector, to the President and Directors of the Literary Fund, dated October 7, 1822, approved by the Visitors of the University of whom Mr. Madison was one, Mr. Jefferson set forth his views at some length. These suggestions of Mr. Jefferson were adopted and ch. II § 1, of the Regulations of the University of October 4, 1824, provided that: "Should the religious sects of this State, or any of them, according to the invitation held out to them, establish within, or adjacent to, the precincts of the University, schools for instruction in the religion of their sect, the students of the University will be free, and expected to attend religious worship at the establishment of their respective sects, in the morning, and in time to meet their school in the University at its stated hour."

Thus, the "wall of separation between church and State" that Mr. Jefferson built at the University which he founded did not exclude religious education from that school. The difference between the generality of his statements on the separation of church and state and the specificity of his conclusions on education are considerable. A rule of law should not be drawn from a figure of speech.

Mr. Madison's *Memorial and Remonstrance against Religious Assessments* relied upon by the dissenting Justices in *Everson* is not applicable here. Mr. Madison was one of the principal opponents in the Virginia General Assembly of *A Bill Establishing a Provision for Teachers of the Christian Religion.* The monies raised by the taxing section of that bill were to be appropriated "by the Vestries, Elders, or Directors of each religious society, . . . to a provision for a Minister or Teacher of the Gospel of their denomination, or the providing places of divine worship, and to none other use whatsoever. . . ." The conclusive legislative struggle over this act took place in the fall of 1785 before the adoption of the Bill of Rights. The *Remonstrance* had been issued before the General Assembly convened and was instrumental in the final defeat of the act which died in committee. Throughout the *Remonstrance,* Mr. Madison speaks of the "establishment" sought to be effected by the act. It is clear from its historical setting and its language that the *Remonstrance* was a protest against an effort by Virginia to support Christian sects by taxation. Issues similar to those raised by the instant case were not discussed. Thus, Mr. Madison's approval of Mr. Jefferson's report as Rector gives, in my opinion, a clearer indication of his views on the constitutionality of religious education in public schools than his general statements on a different subject.

. . . .

The practices of the federal government offer many examples of this kind of "aid" by the state to religion. The Congress of the United States has a chaplain for each House who daily invokes divine blessings and guidance for the proceedings. The armed forces have commissioned chaplains from early days. They conduct the public services in accordance with the liturgical requirements of their respective faiths, ashore and afloat, employing for the purpose property belonging to the United States and dedicated to the services of religion. Under the Servicemen's Readjustment Act of 1944, eligible veterans may receive training at government expense for the ministry in denominational schools. The schools of the District of Columbia have opening exercises which "include a reading from the Bible without note or comment, and the Lord's prayer."

In the United States Naval Academy and the United States Military Academy, schools wholly supported and completely controlled by the federal government, there are a number of religious activities. Chaplains are attached to both schools. Attendance at church services on Sunday is compulsory at both the Military and Naval Academies. At West Point the Protestant services are held in the Cadet Chapel, the Catholic in the Catholic Chapel, and the Jewish in the Old Cadet Chapel; at Annapolis only Protestant services are held on the reservation, midshipmen of other religious persuasions attend the churches of the city of Annapolis. These facts indicate that both schools since their earliest beginnings have maintained and enforced a pattern of participation in formal worship.

Appendix G

EXCERPTS FROM OPINIONS OF UNITED STATES
SUPREME COURT

Adamson v. *California*, 332 U. S. 46, June 23, 1947

Mr. Justice Reed, for the Court:

The reasoning that leads to those conclusions starts with the unquestioned premise that the Bill of Rights, when adopted, was for the protection of the individual against the federal government and its provisions were inapplicable to similar actions done by the states. *Barron* v. *Baltimore*, 7 Pet. 243; *Feldman* v. *United States*, 322 U. S. 487, 490. With the adoption of the Fourteenth Amendment, it was suggested that the dual citizenship recognized by its first sentence, secured for citizens federal protection for their elemental privileges and immunities of state citizenship. The *Slaughterhouse Cases* decided, contrary to the suggestion, that these rights, as privileges and immunities of state citizenship, remained under the sole protection of the state governments. This Court, without the expression of a contrary view upon that phase of the issues before the Court, has approved this determination. The power to free defendants in state trials from self-incrimination was specifically determined to be beyond the scope of the privileges and immunities clause of the Fourteenth Amendment in *Twining* v. *New Jersey*, 211 U. S. 78, 91-98. "The privilege against self-incrimination may be withdrawn and the accused put upon the stand as a witness for the state." The *Twining* case likewise disposed of the contention that freedom from testimonial compulsion, being specifically granted by the Bill of Rights, is a federal privilege or immunity that is protected by the Fourteenth Amendment against state invasion. This Court held that the inclusion in the Bill of Rights of this protection against the power of the national government did not make the privilege a federal privilege or immunity secured to citizens by the Constitution against state action. *Twining* v. *New Jersey, supra*, at 98-99; *Palko* v. *Connecticut, supra*, at 328. After declaring that state and national citizenship co-exist in the same person, the Fourteenth Amendment forbids a state from abridging the privileges and immunities of citizens of the United States. As a matter of words, this leaves a state free to abridge, within the limits of the due process clause, the privileges and immunities flowing from state citizenship. This reading of the Federal Constitution has heretofore found favor with the majority of this Court as a natural and logical interpretation. It accords with the constitutional doctrine of federalism by leaving to the states the responsibility of dealing with the privileges and immunities of their citizens except those inherent in national citizenship. It is the construction placed upon the amendment by justices whose own experience had given them contemporaneous knowledge of the purposes that led to the adoption of the Fourteenth Amendment. This construction has become embedded in our federal system as a functioning element in preserving the balance between national and state power. We reaffirm the conclusion of the *Twining* and *Palko* cases that protection against self-incrimination is not a privilege or immunity of national citizenship.

The due process clause of the Fourteenth Amendment, however, does not draw all the rights of the federal Bill of Rights under its protection. That contention was made and rejected in *Palko* v. *Connecticut*, 302 U. S. 319, 323. It was rejected with citation of the cases excluding several of the rights, protected by the Bill of Rights, against infringement by the National Government. Nothing has been called to our attention that either the framers of the Fourteenth Amendment or the states that adopted intended its due process clause to draw within its scope the earlier amendments to the Constitution. *Palko held that such provisions of the Bill of Rights as were "implicit in the concept of ordered liberty,"* p. 325, *became secure from state interference by the clause. But it held nothing more.* [Italics mine.]

Mr. Justice Frankfurter concurring:

Decisions of this Court do not have equal intrinsic authority. The *Twining* case shows the judicial process at its best—comprehensive briefs and powerful arguments on both sides, followed by long deliberation, resulting in an opinion by Mr. Justice Moody which at once gained and has ever since retained recognition as one of the outstanding opinions in the history of the Court. After enjoying unquestioned prestige for forty years, the *Twining* case should not now be diluted, even unwittingly, either in its judicial philosophy or in its particulars. As the surest way of keeping the *Twining* case intact, I would affirm this case on its authority.

I put to one side the Privileges or Immunities Clause of that Amendment. For the mischievous uses to which that clause would lend itself if its scope were not confined to that given it by all but one of the decisions beginning with the *Slaughterhouse Cases*, 16 Wall. 36, see the deviation in *Colgate* v. *Harvey*, 296 U. S. 404, overruled by *Madden* v. *Kentucky*, 309 U. S. 83.

Between the incorporation of the Fourteenth Amendment into the Constitution and the beginning of the present membership of the Court —a period of seventy years—the scope of that Amendment was passed upon by forty-three judges. Of all these judges, only one, who may respectfully be called an eccentric exception, ever indicated the belief that the Fourteenth Amendment was a shorthand summary of the first eight Amendments theretofore limiting only the Federal Government, and that due process incorporated those eight Amendments as restrictions upon the powers of the States. Among these judges were not only those who would have to be included among the greatest in the history of the Court, but—it is especially relevant to note—they included those whose services in the cause of human rights and the spirit of freedom are the most conspicuous in our history. It is not invidious to single out Miller, Davis, Bradley, Waite, Matthews, Gray, Fuller, Holmes, Brandeis, Stone and Cardozo (to speak only of the dead) as judges who were alert in safeguarding and promoting the interests of liberty and human dignity through law. But they were also judges mindful of the relation of our federal system to a progressively democratic society and therefore duly regardful of the scope of authority that was left to the States even after the Civil War.

The short answer to the suggestion that the provision of the Fourteenth Amendment, which ordains "nor shall any State deprive any person of life, liberty, or property, without due process of law," was a way of saying that every State must thereafter initiate prosecutions through indictment by a grand jury, must have a trial by a jury of twelve in criminal cases, and must have trial by such a jury in common law suits where the amount in controversy exceeds twenty dollars, is that it is a strange way of saying it. It would be extraordinarily strange for a Constitution to convey such specific commands in such a roundabout and inexplicit way. After all, an amendment to the Constitution should be read in a " 'sense most obvious to the common understanding at the time of its adoption.' . . . For it was for public adoption that it was proposed."

The notion that the Fourteenth Amendment was a covert way of imposing upon the States all the rules which it seemed important to Eighteenth Century statesmen to write into the Federal Amendments, was rejected by judges who were themselves witnesses of the process by which the Fourteenth Amendment became part of the Constitution. Arguments that may now be adduced to prove that the first eight Amendments were concealed within the historic phrasing of the Fourteenth Amendment were probably known at the time of its adoption. Insofar as they were known, a surer estimate of their bearing was possible for judges at the time than may be vouchsafed when considered through distorting distance. Any evidence of design or purpose not contemporaneously known could hardly have influenced those who ratified the Amendment. Remarks of a particular proponent of the Amendment, no matter how influential, are not to be deemed part of the Amendment. What was submitted for ratification was his proposal, not his speech.

Mr. Justice Black dissenting:

I agree that if *Twining* be reaffirmed, the result reached might appropriately follow. But I would not reaffirm the *Twining* decision. I think that decision and the "natural law" theory of the Constitution upon which it relies, degrade the constitutional safeguards of the Bill of Rights and simultaneously appropriate for this Court a broad power which we are not authorized by the Constitution to exercise.

My study of the historical events that culminated in the Fourteenth Amendment, and the expressions of those who sponsored and favored, as well as those who opposed its submission and passage, persuades me that one of the chief objects that the provisions of the Amendment's first section, separately, and as a whole, were intended to accomplish was to make the Bill of Rights, applicable to the states.

In construing other constitutional provisions, this Court has almost uniformly followed the precept of *Ex parte Bain*, 121 U. S. 1, 12, that "It is never to be forgotten that, in the construction of the language of the Constitution . . . , as indeed in all other instances where construction becomes necessary, we are to place ourselves as nearly as possible in the condition of the men who framed that instrument."

In the *Twining* opinion the Court explicitly declined to give weight to the historical demonstration that the first section of the Amendment was intended to apply to the states the several protections of the Bill of Rights. It held that that question was "no longer open" because of previous decisions of this Court which, however, had not appraised the historical evidence on that subject.

In my judgment that history [of the Fourteenth Amendment] conclusively demonstrates that the language of the first section of the Fourteenth Amendment, taken as a whole, was thought by those responsible for its submission to the people, and by those who opposed its submission, sufficiently explicit to guarantee that thereafter no state could deprive its citizens of the privileges and protections of the Bill of Rights. And I further contend that the "natural law" formula which the Court uses to reach its conclusion in this case should be abandoned as an incongruous excrescence on our Constitution. I believe that formula to be itself a violation of our Constitution, in that it subtly conveys to courts, at the expense of legislatures, ultimate power over public policies in fields where no specific provision of the Constitution limits legislative power. For the *Twining* decision, giving separate consideration to "due process" and "privileges or immunities" clause of the Fourteenth Amendment "did not forbid the States to abridge the personal rights enumerated in the first eight Amendments. . . ." And in order to be certain, so far as possible, to leave this Court wholly free to reject all the Bill of Rights as specific restraints upon state action, the decision declared that even if this Court should decide that the due process clause forbids the states to infringe personal liberties guaranteed by the Bill of Rights, it would do so, not "because those rights are incorporated in the first eight Amendments, but because they are of such a nature that they are included in the conception of due process of law."

At the same time that the *Twining* decision held that the states need not conform to the specific provisions of the Bill of Rights, it consolidated the power that the Court had assumed under the due process clause by laying even broader foundations for the Court to invalidate state and even federal regulatory legislation.

Thus the power of legislatures became what this Court would declare it to be at a particular time independently of the specific guarantees of the Bill of Rights such as the right to freedom of speech, religion and assembly, the right to just compensation for property taken for a public purpose, the right to jury trial or the right to be secure against unreasonable searches and seizures. Neither the contraction of the Bill of Rights safeguards nor the invalidation of regulatory laws by this Court's appraisal of "circumstances" would readily be classified as the most satisfactory contribution of this Court to the nation. In 1912, four years after the *Twining* case was decided, a book written by Mr. Charles Wallace Collins gave the history of this Court's interpretation and application of the Fourteenth Amendment up to that time. It is not necessary for one fully to agree with all he said in order to appreciate the sentiment of the following comment concerning the disappointments caused by this Court's interpretation of the Amendment.

". . . It was aimed at restraining and checking the powers of wealth and privilege. It was to be a charter of liberty for human rights against property rights. The transformation has been rapid and complete. It operates today to protect the rights of property to the detriment of the rights of man. It has become the Magna Charta of accumulated and organized capital." Collins, The Fourteenth Amendment and the States (1912), 137-8.

In *Twining* the Court had declared that none of the rights enumerated in the first eight amendments were protected against state invasion because they were incorporated in the Bill of Rights. But the Court in *Palko*, answered a contention that all eight applied with the more guarded statement, similar to that the Court had used in *Maxwell* v. *Dow,* that "there is no such general rule." Implicit in this statement, and in the cases decided in the interim between *Twining* and *Palko* and since, is the understanding that some of the eight amendments do apply by their very terms. Thus the Court said in the *Palko* case that the Fourteenth Amendment may make it unlawful for a state to abridge by its statutes the "freedom of speech which the First Amendment safeguards against encroachment by the Congress . . . or the like freedom of the press . . . or the free exercise of religion . . . , or the right of peaceable assembly . . . or the right of one accused of crime to the benefit of counsel. . . . In these and other situations immunities that are valid as against the federal government by force of the specific pledges of particular amendments have been found to be implicit in the concept of ordered liberty, and thus, through the Fourteenth Amendment, become valid as against the states."

The Court went on to describe the Amendments made applicable to the States as "the privileges and immunities that have been taken over from the earlier articles of the Federal Bill of Rights and brought within the Fourteenth Amendment by a process of absorption." In the *Twining* case fundamental liberties were things apart from the Bill of Rights. Now it appears that at least some of the provisions of the Bill of Rights in their very terms satisfy the Court as sound and meaningful expressions of fundamental liberty. If the Fifth Amendment's protection against self-incrimination be such an expression of fundamental liberty, I ask, and have not found a satisfactory answer, why the Court today should consider that it should be "absorbed" in part but not in full? Nothing in the *Palko* opinion requires that when the Court decides that a Bill of Rights' provision is to be applied to the States, it is to be applied piecemeal. Nothing in the *Palko* opinion recommends that the Court apply part of an amendment's established meaning and discard that part which does not suit the current style of fundamentals.

In my judgment the people of no nation can lose their liberty so long as a Bill of Rights like ours survives and its basic purposes are conscientiously interpreted, enforced and respected so as to afford continuous protection against old, as well as new, devices and practices which might thwart those purposes. I fear to see the consequences of the Court's practice of substituting its own concepts of decency and fundamental justice for the language of the Bill of Rights as its point of departure in interpreting and enforcing that Bill of Rights. If the choice must be between the selective process of the *Palko* decision applying some of the Bill of Rights to the States, or the *Twining* rule applying none of them, I would choose the *Palko* selective process. But rather than accept either of these choices, I would follow what I believe was the original purpose of the Fourteenth Amendment—to extend to all the people of the nation the complete protection of the Bill of Rights. To hold that this Court can determine what, if any, provisions of the Bill of Rights will be enforced, and if so to what degree, is to frustrate the great design of a written Constitution.

Appendix H

ON MODERN INTOLERANCE [A]

By James N. Vaughan

A generation ago Monsignor Ryan stated his views on religious toleration.[1] Now he has restated them and they prove to be unchanged.[2]

He starts with the idea that it is obligatory upon the state publicly
to profess religion in some degree. In its highest development this obligation is fulfilled by profession of the true religion. Since the true religion is the Catholic religion, the conclusion is reached that every
state in a soundly organized world ought to profess the Catholic
religion. The world, however, is not soundly organized, for it is not
formed of Catholic states. In truth there does not exist today any specifically Catholic state. Consequently the obligation to profess the Catholic religion stands in abeyance in respect of all modern states. Specifically in 1941 it is inoperative in respect of the United States of America.

Existing facts are perishing facts. Catholic states have existed in the
past. They may exist again. If this should come to pass, the state would
be morally bound to profess Catholicism. The outcome of such profession
would not be a theocracy. Also ruled out would be the relationship between church and state in which the church would exist as a subordinate
agency of the state on the English or pre-revolutionary Russian model.
In an ideal union occurring in a Catholic state the Church would stand
to the state somewhat as the United States stands with reference to the
several states of the Union: each would be autonomous in its own sphere.
The jurisdiction of each would be restricted, but within their respective

---

[A] Reprinted by permission of *The Commonweal* and the author from *The Commonweal*, May 9, 1941.

[1] The State and the Church. John A. Ryan and Moorehouse I. X. Millar, S.J.
Macmillan. Out of print.

[2] Catholic Principles of Politics. John A. Ryan and Francis J. Boland. Macmillan. $3.00. This article deals with one special point covered in Monsignor Ryan's
and Father Boland's book. By and large this volume is the best discussion of its
subject in English. [Notes 1 and 2 are Mr. Vaughan's.]

limits each would be sovereign. Delicate problems of adjustment would no doubt arise, but in principle they would furnish no obstacle to a workable union.

Suppose a church-state union of the ideal type consummated in the United States. Of the many questions arising from such a change one stands out as supremely important. If the state recognizes and professes the Catholic religion, can the existence of non-believers be tolerated? Monsignor Ryan says that the unbaptized and those born into a non-Catholic sect can never be coerced into the Catholic Church. Existence in their errors is to be permitted. They are also to be allowed to practice their several forms of worship if they do this "within the family, or in such an inconspicuous manner as to be an occasion neither of scandal nor of perversion to the faithful." And what of propaganda in favor of their several species of untruths? "This," says Monsignor Ryan, "could become a source of injury, a positive menace, to the religious welfare of true believers. Against such an evil they have a right of protection by the Catholic state. On the one hand, this propaganda is harmful to the citizens and contrary to public welfare; on the other hand, it is not among the natural rights of propagandists. Rights are merely means to rational ends. Since no rational end is promoted by the dissemination of false doctrine, there exists no right to indulge in this practice."

It comes to this: Catholics today are a minority in this country; this country also has a Constitution which Catholics as well as non-Catholics are bound in conscience to uphold; this Constitution bars profession of Catholicism as the state religion. While these three conditions obtain Catholics cannot pretend to prohibit free circulation of non-Catholic religious doctrine. But make Catholics into an overwhelming majority, remove the Constitutional barrier and get state recognition of Catholicism, and doctrinal intolerance in the degree indicated above may follow without violence being done to anybody's legitimate rights. The reason why Catholics can promise intolerance when they shall have become a majority while demanding tolerance for themselves so long as they remain a minority is that "error has not the same rights as truth." Whoever defends "the principle of toleration for all varieties of religious opinion [must] assume either that all religions are equally true or that the true cannot be distinguished from the false." In these words Monsignor Ryan answers him who is disposed to murmur against his conclusions as harsh and illiberal.

The object of intolerance, Monsignor Ryan has said, is to prevent perversion of the faithful. We may add that the best of men—and the worst—have defended this notion. Intolerance is a kind of policeman for authority. Like blinders on a horse, it acts to keep eyes on the road untroubled by the pleasures or terrors of the wayside. It makes for unity, order and monotony. The principle of intolerance goes far beyond the question of religious orthodoxy. It weeds gardens, tames wild animals, corrects unruly children, rationalizes industries and suppresses crime. It beats down or tears up, it eliminates or sterilizes, it burns or mutilates whatever tends to mar unity, whether it be the unity, for example, of a garden, a family, a business, a nation or a religion. Intolerance considered with reference to human society and belief proceeds on the basis that there exists a definite plan, a definite belief or a definite policy. Its function is to forbid the proposal of any amendment to the plan, any doubt to the belief or any discussion in respect of the policy. Manifestly it is non-creative. In a benign mood it takes doubters, critics, dissenters, debaters and agitators into protective custody. When irritated it is more at home with whip, rack, gallows, guillotine and the stake. Intolerance accompanies success and efficiency in the world of action. It is the producer and conservator of likemindedness, which in turn is the source of all effective social action.

If man's vocation were to be merely a sheep, the case for intolerance would be perfectly unassailable. If man were designed to sacrifice individual existence in favor of the social whole, again the case for intolerance would be convincing. If ends could justify means, the case for intolerance would look good. If actions prompted by fears of disaster were necessarily holy actions, intolerance would carry the day. If dissent were always immorality, intolerance once more would sweep the board. It is the unhappy and historical fact that of the billions of men who have lived and died on this starved and blood-drenched earth only a trifling minority has constantly known the delights of a rich, secure and free existence. Men have in fact been handled as sheep, sacrificed to the social organism, employed as slaves in the service of the powerful and governed by gnawing anxieties as to the dangers inherent in dissent and social change. Intolerance has accordingly ruled the world, save for rare brief intervals. It is the subjective equivalent of war and it is no less widely distributed in time and space.

He would be a foolish, ridiculous man, wholly lacking in common sense, who would come forward with the idea that everywhere and at all times and in all situations intolerance is bad. No one in authority could long rule unless he could bend the human will to the ends to be served by authority. The problem of tolerance is a study in reconciliation of the permanent opposition between liberty and authority. A late example of how the issue arises in a concrete way is supplied by the opinion of the Supreme Court of the United States delivered on June 3, 1940, in the case of Minersville School Dist. v. Gobitis (84 L. Ed. 993). The Commonwealth of Pennsylvania exacts participation of school children in the ceremony of saluting our flag as a condition of attendance at Pennsylvania public schools. Parents are also by law of Pennsylvania required to see to it that their children attend school. For those lacking substantial means, obedience to the latter law involves attendance by their children at public schools. In practice this means the children of the majority are obliged to participate in the flag ceremony. Children reared in the Sect of Jehovah's Witnesses are taught to believe that the flag ceremony is forbidden by scripture. To them to salute is to worship a false God. The question became this: Could Pennsylvania properly force these children to participate in an exercise they regarded as irreligious or could the children, claiming the protection of the constitutional guaranty of freedom of religion, insist on toleration by the school authorities of their non-participation in the flag ceremony? This is plainly a problem in toleration, formed by categories of constitutional law. Deciding against the children the majority of the Supreme Court, speaking by Mr. Justice Frankfurter, said: "The ultimate foundation of a free society is the binding tie of cohesive sentiment." Saluting the flag, he said, is one agency for giving rise to that cohesive sentiment. To the objection that the ceremony should be exacted only of those who are not opposed to it on religious grounds, Justice Frankfurter said, ". . . an exemption might introduce elements of difficulty into the school discipline, *might cast doubts in the minds of the other children* which would themselves weaken the effect of the exercise. . . . A society which is dedicated to the preservation of these ultimate values [i.e., 'enjoyment of all freedom'] *may in self-protection utilize the educational process for inculcating those almost unconscious feelings which bind men together in a comprehending loyalty* . . . [italics supplied]."

With a little transposition these words of Mr. Justice Frankfurter could be easily used by Monsignor Ryan. They are words which remind one of Lunacharsky's program for soviet education. "Instruction is not enough," he said. "Taken by itself it cannot form communists. Many men know Marx perfectly and nevertheless remain our worst enemies. It is necessary to educate *sentiment and will* in the communist direction [italics supplied]." Is the nazi or fascist theory of education any different?

The case for intolerance is implicit in these remarks. We must have a care that nothing shall be done or said which will occasion "perversion to the faithful." The people have a right to compel dissidents to conformity in action so that "doubts in the minds" of others shall not arise. The important thing is to educate "sentiment and will." What is this thing which perverts the faithful, produces doubts and alienates sentiment and will? Isn't man a *rational* animal? Aquinas said so. Is he not exclusively attracted to that which he deems *good*? Such was the opinion of Augustine. Does he not aspire to be *happy*? This, said Aristotle, is indeed his aim. This rational animal aspiring to be happy and drawn on solely by apparent good—can it be that there is also something painfully criminal in his composition? Why is it that all these rational, happiness-seeking animals do not agree on doctrine, on ritual and on valuations, in matters political, economic and, particularly, religious? Why do critics, heretics, dissenters and agitators exist? We all agree in ruling out the Manichean principle of diabolism in the explanation of the facts. (We agree on this, I mean, while discussing the matter in cold blood.) If diabolism is rejected, we must look for some other source not inconsistent with the essential traits of rationality, aspiration toward happiness and the ubiquitous incidence of the good with relation to every human action. I fear we are come to this: in partial explanation of dissent it must be conceded that those who disagree with us have *some* reason, *some* motivation which is not impure, *some* just grievance which leads them to dissent, drives them on to search for converts and supporters, and moves them toward organization of followers and institutionalization of their beliefs.

Dissenters and orthodox, moreover, do not always do their thinking with that pure and dispassionate intelligence which we may suppose is characteristic of the angels. Men have feelings, passions, interests, diseases, traditions and habits which fuse to form prisms by which the objective truth is refracted in ways corresponding to the peculiarities of the prisms. That which is received is received according to the nature of the recipient, as Aquinas said over and over and over again. I add: according, also, to his *second* nature, that is according to his momentary composition as a totality of capacities and experiences. Dissent is a permanent *datum* of human life, because the same thing is not seen by different men in the same way.

Dissent is being produced every minute of the day in some soul which has taken up a new perspective with respect to some body of orthodox doctrine or aspiration. It may also arise if not from a new perspective then from a new configuration of objective truth which has exhibited itself. Often dissent merely restates something asserted by others many times in the past. It may consist of an old error repeatedly refuted. (Nothing new under the sun; Acton said history was the struggle for mastery of about 30 ideas.) However that may be, the definitive suppression of dissent is impossible. It can be choked off for a time, but those charged to suffocate it will in the end relax their vigilance and dissent will be heard.

Monsignor Ryan, himself a brave, free and distinguished man, would be the last who would wish this to be otherwise. But for the indomitable man who can say *no* to prevailing beliefs and practices what ground would there be for optimistic expectations in respect to the numberless people who live today, exemplifying a faith and practice which all civilized men agree are in turn detestable lies or debased activities? The power of dissent is the power to purge corrupt society and to unmask lies; at the same time it is, of course, the power to sap the foundation of a good society and the power to create and propagate lies. But whether it is employed for good or bad objectives it cannot be uprooted from human nature.

Since the power is there to stay, it follows that like every other human power it is certain of exercise. If it is certain of exercise, the real question is, indeed, whether it is to be met, in principle, with force (intolerance) or patience (tolerance). This question, owing to its generality, admits of no complete answer. It is indispensable that the general question should be particularized if it is to be a satisfactory question. In respect of religion, for example, it would be useful to ask a question like this: In a Catholic state should a person having an official position equivalent to that now occupied by Bishop Manning be permitted to have a handsome church from the pulpit of which each Sunday he might deliver a sermon on what he deemed to be the errors in the doctrine of Petrine supremacy? That question makes sense. The answer to it should be *yes, by all means.* Let the Bishop Manning, Bishop Cannon, Dr. Searles or Rabbi de Sola Pool—even the Father Divine and Judge Rutherford—of the future Catholic state, wherever it shall be, preach when and where he can find a group to listen. And let the Catholics of that future day and state study what these preachers have to say. Catholicism will not lose its integrity and truth if it is removed from an *ex parte* basis. Suppose some Catholics are thereby lost? It is man's privilege, a privilege marking him off from all other animals, to be absurd, to be insane and to choose to be damned.

Examine carefully the thesis Monsignor Ryan feels obliged to uphold. The faithful are entitled, when strong enough, to be protected from the errors of their weaker contemporaries—the irreducible dissidents. The dissenters are to be driven underground. True, they are not to be coerced to come into the Church. But the authorities are to quarantine them as they do the carriers of a noxious disease. Why? Because those who are weak may be fatally attacked by the disease of untruth. Should life then be had without risk and without courage? Should the spiritual life of man know neither doubts nor temptations? Should man be shamefully born, hurriedly shrived, and brought half blind through this world accompanied by armed guards as if at the slightest jar his spirit, like fragile china, would shiver into worthless fragments? To save so poor a thing it would be impossible to justify the utterance of even a harsh word to the unbeliever.

Intolerance, the scabbard of war, ever demonstrates the bankruptcy of living, vibrant faith. It coincides inevitably with the withdrawal of men from relationships naturally generated by love, understanding and mutual respect. Its presence says that priests as such have ceased to talk and that the time has come to hear the voice of the politicians. Each group must close its frontiers. Inside the group, members whisper, shout or storm, each according to his genius telling himself and all other insiders what fine fellows they are. The outlander is pronounced barbaric, ignorant, vicious. As "everyone" knows he is a mere liar and cheat. When these things happen, where is the principle of divine love and pity? Where is the voice of reason? Where are patience, charity and justice? The principle of intolerance of erroneous religious propaganda in the life of the true religion is, in my judgment, a dangerous, unwarranted usurper of the authentic religious spirit which is tolerant on this subject.

Historical reason should be one of the main sources of any theory of tolerance. Looking to history, we readily see that intolerance has a legitimate function, since by its means effect is given to community law. But intolerance readily expands its claims until it seeks to compel the human mind to conform to one rigid type, or, hypocritically, to profess a conformity it does not in fact experience. Some limits, if only in the interests of common safety, must be imposed on intolerance. History is the source of these limits. It is no longer legitimate to approach the matter of intolerance solely on terms of formal logic. And it is the teaching of historical experience that, however perfect the *logical* case for intolerance, especially intolerance of religious propaganda, intolerance has been a principal author of the most deep seated hatreds which have divided man from man and nation from nation. Only in very late times have forms of intolerance, closely related to politics, arisen capable of matching in fervor the hatred generated in the past by religious intolerance. The guaranty of religious freedom which finally gained place in the Constitution of this country was no child of logic. It was derived from historical understanding. But the gains made by historical understanding should be no less permanent than those achieved in the natural sciences. It is just as important to civilized life that men should believe in the doctrine of religious freedom as it is that they should believe that the earth is round. As the modern geographic idea on the shape of the earth adjusts itself to real fact, so also religious freedom, including the right to worship as one chooses and to propagate what one believes to be religious truth, adjusts itself to the historical facts of human life, thought and experience. History is strewn with the social shipwrecks of societies based on the principle of religious intolerance. Where such societies have not been destroyed they have tended to assume petrified forms and in the end to perish by way of desiccation.

God made man to be free; else men are only animals. Freedom is manhood. The area of human freedom should never be so narrowed as to make the fear of man's force and ostracism the substitute for self-responsibility and the fear of God which are alone the beginnings of all wisdom.

Bibliography

PUBLICATIONS CITED IN THIS BOOK

I. Books

American State Papers, class II Indian Affairs. Washington: Gales and Seaton, 1832.

Ames, Herman V., *Proposed Amendments to the Constitution, 1789-1889* (Vol. II House Document no. 353. 54th Congress, 2nd Session). Washington: Government Printing Office, 1897.

Attwater, Donald, ed., *A Catholic Dictionary.* New York: Macmillan Company, 1943.

Beale, Howard K., *A History of Freedom of Teaching in American Schools.* Report of the Commission on Social Studies of the American Historical Association. New York: Charles Scribner's Sons, 1941.

Beard, Charles A., *The Republic.* New York: Viking Press, 1943.

Benton, Thomas H., ed. (abridged by J. C. Rives). *Annals of Congress,* Vol. I. New York: D. Appleton Company, 1858.

Billington, Ray Allen, *The Protestant Crusade.* New York: Macmillan Company, 1938.

Brown, Samuel Windsor, *The Secularization of American Education,* Contributions to American Education, no. 49. New York: Teachers College, Columbia University, 1912.

Coffin, Charles Carlton, *Life of James A. Garfield.* Boston: J. H. Earle Company, 1880.

Collins, Charles Wallace, *The Fourteenth Amendment and the States.* Boston: Little Brown and Company, 1912.

Confrey, Burton, *Secularism in American Education.* Washington: Catholic University of America, 1931.

Congressional Globe, *Thirty-ninth Congress,* Part 2. Washington: Congressional Globe Office, 1866.

Cooley, Thomas M., *Constitutional Limitations* (4th ed.). Boston: Little, Brown and Company, 1878.

Cornelison, Isaac Amada, *The Relation of Religion to Civil Government.* New York: G. P. Putnam's Sons, 1895.

Corwin, Edward S., *The Constitution—What It Means Today* (9th ed.). Princeton: Princeton University Press, 1947.

Corwin, Edward S., *Court Over Constitution*. Princeton: Princeton University Press, 1938.

Eckenrode, Hamilton J., *Separation of Church and State in Virginia*. Virginia State Library Report 1910. Richmond: Davis Bottom, Supt. of Public Printing, 1911.

Elliot, Jonathan, ed., *Debates on the Adoption of the Constitution*. Washington: J. Elliot, 1836-1845.

Encyclopedia Britannica, 14th ed., Vol. VIII.

Flack, Horace Edgar, *The Adoption of the Fourteenth Amendment*. Baltimore: Johns Hopkins Press, 1908.

Fraenkel, Esmond K., *Our Civil Liberties*. New York: Viking Press, 1944.

Frankfurter, Felix, *Mr. Justice Holmes and the Supreme Court*. Cambridge: Harvard University Press, 1939.

Gay, Sidney Howard, *James Madison*. New York: Houghton Mifflin Company, 1899.

Gibbons, James Cardinal, *A Retrospect of Fifty Years*. Baltimore: J. Murphy Company, 1916.

Gobbel, Luther L., *Church-State Relationships in North Carolina*. Durham, N. C.: Duke University Press, 1938.

Guthrie, William D., *The Fourteenth Amendment*. Boston: Little, Brown and Company, 1898.

Hughes, Charles Evans, *The Supreme Court of the United States*. New York: Columbia University Press, 1928.

Humphrey, E. F., *Nationalism and Religion in America*. Boston: Chipman Law Publishing Company, 1924.

Hunt, Gaillard, ed., *The Writings of James Madison*, Vol. V. New York: G. P. Putnam's Sons, 1904.

Johnson, Alvin W., *The Legal Status of Church-State Relationships in the United States*. Minneapolis: University of Minnesota Press, 1934.

Kelly, Alfred H. and Harbison, Winfred A., *The American Constitution*. New York: W. W. Norton Company, 1948.

Konvitz, Milton R., *The Constitution and Civil Rights*. New York: Columbia University Press, 1947.

Maritain, Jacques, *The Rights of Man and Natural Law*. New York: Charles Scribner's Sons, 1943.

Moehlman, Conrad H., *School and Church*. New York: Harper & Brothers, 1944.

Morison, Samuel Eliot, and Commager, Henry Steele, *The Growth of the American Republic*. New York: Oxford University Press, 1942.

Myers, Gustavus, *History of Bigotry in the United States*. New York: Random House, 1943.

Nevins, Allan, and Commager, Henry Steele, *A Short History of the United States*. New York: The Modern Library, Random House, 1945.

Padover, Saul K., ed., *The Complete Jefferson*. New York: Duell, Sloan and Pearce, 1943.

Padover, Saul K., ed., *Democracy by Thomas Jefferson*. New York: Appleton-Century Company, 1939.

Padover, Saul K., *Jefferson*. New York: Harcourt Brace and Company, 1942.

Parsons, Wilfrid, *The First Freedom*. New York: Declan X. McMullen, 1948.

Pritchett, C. Herman, *The Roosevelt Court*. New York: Macmillan Company, 1948.

Reports of Committees of The House of Representatives. First Session, 33rd Congress, Vol. II, no. 124. Washington: Nicholson Printer, 1854.

Reports of Committees of the Senate of the United States. Second Session, 32nd. Congress. 1852-1853. No. 376. Washington: Robert Armstrong, 1853.

Richardson, J. D., *Messages of the Presidents*, Vol. VIII. New York: Bureau of National Literature, 1897.

Ryan, John A. and Boland, Francis J., *Catholic Principles of Politics*. New York: Macmillan Company, 1943.

———*Safeguarding Civil Liberty Today*. Ithaca: Cornell University Press, 1945.

Selected Essays on Constitutional Law. Compiled and Edited by a Committee of the Association of American Law Schools. Chicago: Foundation Press, 1938.

Smith, Theodore Clark, *Life of James Abram Garfield*. New Haven: Yale University Press, 1925.

Story, Joseph, *Commentaries on the Constitution* (5th. ed.). Boston: Hilliard, Gray and Company, 1833.

Sweet, William Warren, *The Story of Religions in America*. New York: Harper and Brothers, 1930.

Thayer, V. T., *Religion in Public Education*. New York: Viking Press, 1947.

Thorpe, F. N., *American Charters, Constitutions and Organic Laws*, Vol. VI. Washington: Government Printing Office, 1909.

Warren, Charles, *The Supreme Court in United States History*. Boston: Little, Brown and Company, 1922, 1926.

Washington, H. A., *The Writings of Thomas Jefferson* (9 Vols.). New York: John C. Riker, 1857.

Whipple, Leon, *The Story of Civil Liberty in the United States*. New York: Vanguard Press, 1927.

II. NEWSPAPERS AND PERIODICALS

America, editorial. New York: July 10, 1948.
American Bar Association Journal, editorials. Chicago: May through November 1948.
Billington, Ray Allen, "American Catholicism and the Church-State Issue." *Christendom*. New York: Vol. V, No. 3 (Summer), 1940.
The Chicago Tribune, editorial. Chicago: April 16, 1947.
The Christian Century, editorials. Chicago: November 26, 1947, May 12, 1948, June 30, 1948.
Fleet, Elizabeth, "Madison's Detached Memoranda." *William and Mary Quarterly*. Williamsburg: 3rd Series III, October 1946.
Franklin, John L., "Education and Religion." *Phi Delta Kappan*. Fulton, Missouri: May 1948.
Gauss, Christian, "Should Religion be Taught in Our Schools?" *The Ladies' Home Journal*. Philadelphia: September 1948.
Graham, H. J., "The 'Conspiracy Theory' of the Fourteenth Amendment." Reprinted in *Selected Essays*, Vol. I. 47 *Yale Law Journal* 271. New Haven: 1938.
Haines, Charles G., "The History of Due Process After the Civil War." Reprinted in *Selected Essays*, Vol. I. 3 *Texas Law Review* 1. Austin: 1924.
Heffron, Edward J., "Supreme Court Oversight." *The Commonweal*. New York: April 18, 1947.
Johnson, F. Ernest, "Some Crucial Contemporary Issues." *Social Action*. New York: Vol. XIII, No. 9, November 15, 1947.
Johnson, Williard, "Whose Country is This?" *Christendom*. New York: Vol. XII, No. 4 (Autumn), 1947.
Kales, A. M., "New Methods in Due Process." Reprinted in *Selected Essays*, Vol. I 12. Madison, Wis.: *American Political Science Review* 241. 1918.
Law Week, Vol. 15, No. 31, February 11, 1947; Vol. 15, No. 50, June 24, 1947; Vol. 16, No. 35, March 9, 1947; Washington.
New York Times. New York: May 15, 1947. March 13, 1948.
O'Brien, John A., "Equal Rights for All Children." *The Christian Century*. Chicago: May 19, 1948.
O'Neill, J. M., "Church, Schools and the Constitution." *Commentary*. New York: June 1947.
Vaughan, James H., "On Modern Intolerance." *The Commonweal*. New York: May 9, 1941.

Warren, Charles, "The New Liberty Under the Fourteenth Amendment." Reprinted in *Selected Essays*, Vol. II. Cambridge: 39 *Harvard Law Review* 431, 1926.

III. PAMPHLETS

Civil Liberty. New York: American Civil Liberties Union, 1945.
Cushman, Robert E., *New Threats to American Freedom*. Pamphlet No. 143. New York: Public Affairs Committee, 1948.
Garrison, W. E., *Religion and Civil Liberty in the Roman Catholic Tradition*. Chicago: Willett, Clark and Company, 1946.
Morrison, Charles C., *The Separation of Church and State in America*. Indianapolis: International Convention of Disciples of Christ, 1947.
Oral Arguments. McCollum v. Board of Education. Supreme Court. December 8, 1947. Althea Arceneaux, Reporter. Washington: 1948.
President's Committee on Civil Rights, *To Secure These Rights*. Reprinted in *PM*, November 2, 1947.
Protestants and Other Americans United for Separation of Church and State. A Manifesto. Washington: Protestants and Other Americans United, 1948.
The State and Sectarian Education. Research Bulletin XXIV, No. 1. Washington: National Education Association, February 1946.
Transcript of Record. McCollum v. Board of Education. United States Supreme Court 333 U.S. 203.

IV. LEGAL BRIEFS

Brief for Appellant. *McCollum v. Board of Education*. 333 U.S. 203.
Brief for Appellees. *McCollum v. Board of Education*. 333 U.S. 203.
Brief, Amicus Curiae. American Civil Liberties Union. *Everson v. Board of Education*. 330 U.S. 1.
Brief, Amicus Curiae. American Civil Liberties Union. *McCollum v. Board of Education*. 333 U.S. 203.
Brief, Amicus Curiae. General Conference of Seventh Day Adventists. *McCollum v. Board of Education*. 333 U.S. 203.
Brief, Amicus Curiae. Joint Conference Committee on Public Relations of Southern, Northern, and National Baptist Conventions. *McCollum v. Board of Education*. 333 U.S. 203.
Brief, Amicus Curiae. Synagogue Council for America. *McCollum v. Board of Education*. 333 U.S. 203.

V. LAW CASES (Numbers in right hand column indicate page references in this book)

Marbury v. *Madison*, 1 Cranch 137 (1803) — 261

Martin v. *Hunter's Lessee*, 1 Wheaton 304 (1816) — 261

Maxwell v. *Dow*, 176 U.S. 581 (1900) — 173

McCollum v. *Board of Education*, 333 U.S. 203 (1948) — 82, 100, 108, 145, 219, 223

McCulloch v. *Maryland*, 4 Wheaton 316 (1819) — 262

Minersville School District v. *Gobitis*, 310 U.S. 586 (1940) — 41, 179, Appendix H

Mitchell v. *Interstate Commerce Commission*, 313 U.S. 80 (1941) — 33

Murdock v. *Pennsylvania*, 319 U.S. 105 (1943) — 154, 181, 185, 287

Near v. *Minnesota*, 283 U.S. 697 (1931) — 173, 177

Palko v. *Connecticut*, 302 U.S. 319 (1937) — 173, 180, Appendix G, 303

Pierce v. *Society of Sisters*, 268 U.S. 510 (1925) — 186, 217, 230

Pollock v. *Farmers Loan and Trust Company*, 157 U.S. 429 (1895), 158 U.S. 601 (1895) — 268

Quick Bear v. *Leupp*, 210 U.S. 50 (1908) — 119, 130, 134

Reynolds v. *United States*, 98 U.S. 145 (1879) — 7, 136, Appendix F, 289

Santa Clara County v. *Southern Railroad*, 118 U.S. 394 (1886) — 170

Slaughter House Cases, 16 Wallace 36 (1873) — 156, Appendix G, 304

Stewart v. *School District No. 1*, Kalamazoo, 30 Michigan 69 (1878) — 78

Terret v. *Taylor*, 9 Cranch — 43, 135

Twining v. *New Jersey*, 211 U.S. 78 (1908) — 173, 180, Appendix G, 303

United States v. *Cruikshank*, 92 U.S. 542 (1875) — 157

Watson v. *Jones*, 13 Wallace 769 (1872) — 133, 138, Appendix F, 288

West Virginia State Board of Education v. *Barnette*, 319 U.S. 624 (1943) — 183

Winters v. *The People of New York*, March 29, 1948 — 157

Index

Maryland, Episcopalians dominant in, 22
  proposed Constitutional amendment on establishment, 112
Massachusetts Bill of Rights, 63
Meaning of First Amendment not a religious problem, 5-6
Medieval Christian tradition contained democratic values, 30
Memorial and Remonstrance, James Madison, *Appendix C*, 278-283
Menonists, *Appendix C*, 280
Methodist church, 28
  in Virginia, 58
Military training, compulsory, 177
Miller, Justice, on adjudication of a property dispute, 138
Misrepresentations of Jefferson and Madison, 189
  (*See also* United States Supreme Court)
Missionaries and missionary organizations, Congressional support, 117
Missions, Protestant, 27
"Mob Era," 20, 43
Modern Intolerance, On, James N. Vaughan, *Appendix H*, 310-317
Moehlman, Conrad, opinion on First Amendment, 213
Mohammedan, religious freedom of, 90
Morrison, Charles Clayton, on Constitutional Amendment, 53
Murray, John Courtney, S. J., on church and state, 39-40
Murray-Morse-Pepper Bill, 51

National Conference of Christians and Jews, 41
National Education Association tables on aid to schools, 145-146
Navy, tax support of, 78, 126
Negroes, citizenship, protection of, by Fourteenth Amendment, 187
  rights of not effectively protected, 155
New Deal decisions, 270
New Hampshire proposed constitutional amendment on establishment, 112
New Jersey statute challenged, *Appendix F*, 287, 289
New York, proposed constitutional amendment on establishment, 113
  religious status of, 59

Newspapers, *Bibliography II*, 321-322
"No established church principle", 23
North Carolina, Constitution, 28-29
  proposed amendment on establishment, 113-114
Norway, established churches in, 23

Obligations of scholarship, 2
Opinions and beliefs, influences affecting, 76
Opinions of justices lack clarity, 262
Opportunity, equality of, 17

Pamphlets, *see Bibliography III*, 323
Peacetime conscription, 3-4
Peckham, Justice, comment on First Amendment, 132
Pennsylvania, proposed amendment on establishment, 112
  religious status of, 59
Periodicals (*see Bibliography II*, 321-322)
Persecution by religious bodies, 191-192
Petition, rights of, 15
Political democracy, beginning of, 30
Political development (*see* United States Supreme Court)
Polygamy, Congressional prohibition of, 136
Powers, of Congress, 64-65
  of government and states compared, 67-68
Prepossessions of Supreme Court, 251-252
Presbyterian church, 28
  in Virginia, 58
Presbyterian Synod, Professors to report to, 29
President's Committee on Civil Rights, 16-17
Privileges, exclusive, in religious establishments, 87
Privileges and immunities, Constitutional meaning, 18, 180-181
  national, 164
  protected by Fourteenth Amendment, 163
Prohibition amendment in Constitution, 208
Property, defense of, 270
  freedom of private from confiscation, 15

Rutledge doctrine, defined, 62
refuted, 52
Rutledge, Justice, attack on *Memorial and Remonstrance*, 90, 99
Comment on First Amendment, 11, 97
described attack on First Amendment, 127-132
dissenting opinion in *Everson Case*, 91, *Appendix F*, 289-295
doctrine of not accepted by Congress, 125
interpretation of establishment, 203-206, 209, 216
of First Clause of First Amendment, 212
misinterprets position of Madison, 88
misrepresents opinion of Jefferson and Madison, 105
Ryan, Monsignor John A., on religious toleration, *Appendix H*, 310-315
on separation of church and state, 36-39

Sabine, George H., on civil liberties, 14-15
Salute to the Flag, 154
Sanford, Judge, interpretation of Fourteenth Amendment, 172
School laws, 217
for states, 216
School Lunch Bill, 120
Scotland, established churches, 23
Scott v. Sanford, 268
Search and seizure, 15
Sectarian religious instruction, in school hours, 221
Virginia, 146-147
Sects, equality, indicated by First Amendment, 63
Jefferson on, 85-86
Secular education in the United States, 241
Secularism, propagandists for, 166
Senate of Eighteenth Congress voted down amendment on schools, 121
of First Congress defeated "Lost Amendment", 110
Separation, ambiguous use of word, 263
Separation of church and state, 3-4, 23-24
Catholic viewpoint, 34-37, 39-42

Separation, *Continued*
defined by F. Ernest Johnson, 41-42
used in valid sense, 214
Shaver, Erwin, on Protestantism, 26
Shintoism, 9
Solemn Declaration and Protest of December, 1825, by Jefferson, 67
Spaulding, Archbishop, on separation of church and state, 36
Speech, freedom of, 15
State, action on public funds for schools, 141-143
ambiguous use of word, 263
cannot deprive citizens of immunities, 265
cannot make religious matters public business, *Appendix F*, 289
forbidding sectarian instruction in schools, 141-143
State church in Massachusetts, 65
State compulsory education system, 226
State constitutions, all prohibit establishment, 143-144
new, 193
State Conventions anxious about law-making, 96
State and Federal government, separation of powers, 80
State and government cooperation for schools, 199-200
State governments, support of, 69
State law, 73
State laws affecting religion, 165
State support of religion, 217
States, Federal encroachment on, 69
freedom of in domestic concerns, 91, 249-250
interpretation of First Amendment, 61-62
lack authority on establishment, *Appendix F*, 288
petitioned for a *Bill of Rights*, 111-112
powers of, 68
religious authority, 63
responsible for laws affecting own concerns, 81
rights, 208-209
united in foreign affairs, 68
Statutes, Virginia, 135
Stone, Chief Justice, on Amendments, 181-182